LESSONS FOR LIFE 4

LESSONS FOR LIFE 4

JILL MASTERS

THE WAKEMAN TRUST * LONDON

THE WAKEMAN TRUST
(UK Registered Charity)
5 Templar Street
London SE5 9JB

LESSONS FOR LIFE 4

ISBN 1 870855 20 5

Cover design by Andrew Sides

Visual aid drawings by Alan MacGregor
with graphics and presentation by Andrew Owen

Printed in Great Britain by Galliard (Printers) Ltd, Great Yarmouth

CONTENTS
Book 4

USING THIS BOOK

This is the fourth of a series of lesson books providing a four-year scheme (set out on pages 254-255). Take-home leaflets (in 'master' form for local photocopying), to accompany the lessons in this book, are also published. The address for enquiries is shown on page 253.

These lesson notes have an evangelistic aim, using Bible portions which clearly include an evangelistic application. Each lesson seeks to confront children with those truths and arguments which, by the Holy Spirit, could lead to conversion. Alongside this, the lessons are designed to give a good outline knowledge of all the Scriptures.

The syllabus has been arranged to present biblical events in an orderly manner, worthy of the Word of God. The Old Testament is mainly dealt with chronologically, so that God's dealings with mankind before Christ are known and appreciated. Series of Old Testament lessons are interleaved with series based on the Gospels and the *Book of Acts*. Both children and teachers prefer this method of following a basic historical plan, to an approach which jumps from one part of the Bible to another with such frequency that perspective is lost. Parents (unbelievers as well as believers) will appreciate that their children are receiving a biblical education.

Experience has shown that teachers are the best people to adapt the lessons to an individual class. These notes therefore contain material which can be adapted to the needs of all age groups, from Beginners (pre-school age) to the teenage Bible Class. A range of suggested applications and guidelines is provided so that teachers may utilise the particular points most suited to their age group. Teachers of older classes often use the complete lesson outline, while those teaching younger classes select fewer points. In the many years this scheme has been in use in Sunday Schools, no teacher has ever complained that this has presented a problem.

This lesson system is tailored to fit around the Sunday School year. Most Sunday Schools, like day-schools, divide their pro- gramme into three terms a year. Most suspend programmed lessons at such times as Christmas, New Year, Easter and other holidays and special occasions. Speakers usually choose and prepare their own subject on these Sundays, and it is assumed, therefore, that a maximum of 46 lessons per year is required. The lessons are grouped into series, and individual Sunday Schools may use these in any order to suit their Sunday School year. However, the Old Testament series should be kept in chronological order, whereas New Testament series may be fitted into the year according to choice.

In these volumes the aim is to offer the children a great and varied Gospel challenge as they set out on life's journey. Prayerfully, our concern is that it will lead them to the Saviour in early years, but if not, that it will plant in their minds and hearts a knowledge of the Lord which can be used by His Spirit in later years to prick their consciences and lead them to seek the Saviour.

The promise of the Lord that His Word will not return to Him void *(Isaiah 55.11)* provides a great incentive to continue through weeks of patient toil. In days of irreligion and apathy amongst the adult population, it is extremely touching to witness large numbers of children gathering together, and to see the Lord still preparing His praise out of the mouths of even the youngest *(Matthew 21.16)*.

He that goeth forth and weepeth, bearing precious seed, shall doubtless come again with rejoicing, bringing his sheaves with him (Psalm 126.6).

Series 17
The Division of the Kingdom to the Exile
A SERIES ON THE WORD
OF GOD

139 – The Word of God – The Holy Bible
Is it possible to believe that the Bible is God's divinely inspired Word and therefore absolutely credible and reliable? Why do we learn from it week by week at Sunday School? This lesson gives an opportunity to answer these and other questions.

140 – The Word of Help
– to the faithful kings of Judah, Asa and Jehoshaphat. Each wins battles he did not fight! If only we would trust and obey God, we too would have His help and blessing.

141 – The Word to Me
A warning from King Joash who relies on his guardian-uncle until the old man dies, but fails to love God for himself. How can we test our own standing before God?

142 – The Word of Warning
– to the sinful nation of Israel, is sounded out by Amos and Hosea. God's Word has many warnings for us too. Once people or nations become too proud to respect and obey His Word, danger lies ahead, as Amos and Hosea predicted. In 722 BC Israel was taken captive by the Assyrians. How long will it be before the Lord judges our foolish unbelief?

143 – The Word of Defence

The mighty king of Assyria cannot carry out his threats when King Hezekiah puts his trust in the Lord. This remarkable event (confirmed by archaeological discovery) shows how children can be protected from such enemies as sin, death, suffering and hell.

144 – The Word Authenticated

A plaque, inscribed by King Hezekiah's workmen in an underground tunnel they had built, is discovered 2,581 years later! The Siloam tablet and other archaeological treasures confirm the accuracy of the Word of God.

145 – The Word of Promise

Isaiah looks into the future and promises that the Saviour will come. How does he know these details 700 years before the birth of Christ? Only God's Word contains such detailed prophecies, and many of these have already been accurately fulfilled. Ought we not, therefore, to consider carefully all that Isaiah taught about the Saviour Who would come?

146 – The Word for Sinners

One of the most wicked men who ever lived, King Manasseh, is saved by God's grace and power. How? Does this offer hope to us? Have we ever been humbled, as Manasseh was in his prison cell hundreds of miles from home?

147 – The Word Rediscovered

– by King Josiah, who begins to reign when he is only eight years old. As God's Word is rediscovered and obeyed, amazing events take place. Do we know anything of this?

148 – The Word Under Attack

– by King Jehoiakim and King Zedekiah. God's servant, Jeremiah, is cruelly persecuted, but, in spite of opposition, God's Word is fulfilled. Civilisations have come and gone since then, but still the Word of God abides, and will do so for ever.

149 – The Word Fulfilled – Revision

Judah was taken captive exactly as the prophets had warned. The Saviour was born as they had predicted in detail. How much have these lessons convinced us that the Bible is truly the inspired Word of God, sufficient for our every need?

Teachers' Introduction to the Series

Homework for teachers. If teachers are to make a success of this series of lessons, they need to familiarise themselves with these events of the Old Testament. Many Christians know far less about Asa, Jehoshaphat, Joash, Hezekiah and Jeremiah than they do about Abraham, Isaac, Jacob, Joseph, David, etc. Those in this category should begin reading these chapters well in advance. They will find the exercise very rewarding. The society of *Kings* and *Chronicles* bears striking resemblances to our own, and God's messages to those people will be particularly apt for our classes.

Plan of campaign. We have always found it helpful and stimulating to place a series of lessons under a common heading. This series covers a long period of history towards the end of the Old Testament. The theme which shines throughout is *The Word of God.* As we follow this panorama of history across the centuries we are shown the enormous influence of God's Word in so many ways. It should not be difficult to so impress our children with its relevance that in future they will not be deceived by its critics.

This series covers a remarkably broad spectrum of issues. We hear the Word of God delivered by the prophets, sometimes in tones of warning and anguish, and at other times in hope and comfort. We watch the practical effects of God's Word both on the life of a nation and on individuals. In a day and age when the Bible's integrity and infallibility is questioned, we can examine the excellent historical, 'scientific' and archaeological reasons for accepting its testimony. We shall see how hostility towards it is no new thing. Above all we shall witness its power to convict people of their sin and convert them to God.

This series is a long one consisting of eleven lessons. It could be split into two series to fit the calendar of a local Sunday School. For example, lessons 139-145 could form Part A, and lessons 146-149 Part B. However, the entire series fits the average school term well, and makes a consolidated series on this vital subject.

Visual Aids

Psalm 119 describes the Word of God as *a lamp unto my feet,* *and a light unto my path.* The theme of light has been taken up as a common illustration running through the entire series. Suggestions are made for department leaders or teachers[*] to open each lesson demonstrating, or providing a picture of, a particular kind of light which illustrates the theme of that lesson. This should not only add an element of interest and surprise to each week's activities but provide a common visual theme which will act as an aid to the memory.

A large time-chart will be of particular value in this series. Teachers and children will benefit from seeing the kings and prophets placed in chronological order in brightly coloured, diagrammatic form. (See VA 1 on page 19.)

Dr Whitcomb's *Solomon to the Exile* (Baker Book House) provides a chart giving reliable datings which can be enlarged and embellished for the children. Details not relevant for these lessons can be omitted. (The same author's large 'Winona Lake' series chart is ideal for tracing off a simplified colour-chart.)

Draw a map of the area covered in this series. (Such maps are readily available at the back of Bibles and in Bible atlases.) Mark on the map:

Towns: Jerusalem, Lachish, Nineveh, Babylon, Susa

Countries: Israel, Judah, Assyria, Babylonia, Egypt

Round the edge of the map, place the weekly *Bible Learning Course* pictures (and other illustrations) and connect them to the place on the map where the events of the lesson took place.

---

[*]We recommend that teachers with classes of very young children omit the light illustration from the beginning of each lesson, and start with the Bible narrative. The suggested illustration of some aspect of Bible light could be used for a separate item in the Sunday School hour.

The Word of God – The Holy Bible (139)
A Remarkable Book

Psalm 119.105; Luke 24.44-48; 2 Peter 1.20-21

Aim: To present clearly and convincingly our reasons for believing the Bible to be the Word of God, tested, reliable and true. To encourage the children to turn to it without doubt or hesitation, so that in its pages they may hear the Lord Himself speaking to them.

Teachers' Introduction

As we embark upon this series from the latter part of the Old Testament, we pause for one lesson to explain to the children the grounds on which we have complete confidence in the Bible. Many of these arguments will be illustrated and enlarged upon as this series proceeds.

Most children are taught in school today that the Bible, especially the Old Testament, is largely a collection of religious myths and primitive thought – interesting, but not to be taken seriously in our scientific day and age. They imagine that we must be quaint and naive to accept it as literally true. They must wonder why we study it week after week with such care and trust.

Lesson Outline

According to the age of the class, make some introductory remarks. Show younger classes a Bible and ask if they know Who wrote it. Discuss with older classes, or summarise, some of the views of the Bible they will have heard at school. Suggest that they remove their prejudice and join you in making a factual survey.

Why is the Bible so special? Give the children a taste of some of the more remarkable features of God's Word by telling them that it is:

(1) An unusual book. (a) How many books are there in the Bible? Sixty-six. (b) When were they written? Over the course of about 1,600 years. (c) Who wrote them? Around forty different men, including all kinds of people; eg: Luke – the doctor, David – the king, Hosea – a herdsman, Peter – a fisherman, Moses – the lawgiver.

Suggest to the children that they try to imagine the strange hotchpotch which would come together if they gathered such a collection of writings beginning from AD 400 down to the present day. How would the superstitious ideas of the middle ages look between the same covers as a modern scientific journal? How contradictory the views would be, representing those who held that the world was flat and including pictures of the Earth taken from the moon! Teachers should employ arguments of this kind (appropriate for the age of the class) to drive home the point.

(2) A unified book. Yet as we read the Bible from cover to cover it strikes us very clearly that it is far from being a strange assortment of writings. Unless we knew the facts, we could well imagine that it had been written down by one person. The message, the atmosphere all the way through is the same. (Older classes may have been taught at day-school of the evolution of thought in the Bible, yet, on examination, the earliest books, like *Job*, have just the same teaching as the last – *Revelation*. Compare *Job 19.25* – *Job* is believed to be the earliest book – with *1 Corinthians 15.52*, etc.)

In every book of the Bible we read that men and women, created by God, have rebelled against Him. Throughout its pages we read the same message – God is holy and hates sin, but is willing to forgive any who show true repentance and trust in the Saviour He has sent. (Compare *Joel 2.12-13* with *2 Peter 3.9*.) From *Genesis* to *Revelation* its one great theme is the

Saviour of the world. All the books of the Bible agree perfectly. However minutely we examine them, the detailed teaching is the same! They all teach that there is one God; they say the same about His character, His standards and His plans. They all teach the same about His plan of salvation. This is quite amazing – for no human movement has books or literature which so perfectly agree. There is no other book in the world anything like the Bible. How do we explain this? How did its writers account for this remarkable unity? Quite simply, they claimed it was –

(3) A God-inspired book. They asserted that what they wrote was given them by God. He used their minds and their hands to write the text, but He was the Originator and Author of every word. Over 2,600 times the authors of the Old Testament claimed that God inspired them. They said, *Thus saith the Lord*, or words to that effect.

It is not only the Old Testament authors who insisted that God had inspired them to write. When God's own Son, the Lord Jesus Christ, came to Earth, He showed His disciples that He loved the Old Testament Scriptures and viewed them as God's actual Word which could not be broken *(John 10.35; Luke 24.44)*. There is no doubt that God's Son believed that every detail of the Old Testament was of importance and would be fulfilled *(Matthew 5.17)*. In the Gospels alone there are around 400 references to the Old Testament.

Explain that the New Testament writers were similarly inspired by God. The early churches were careful only to recognise as Scripture those books and epistles which came from the apostles who had been instructed by the Lord Jesus Himself *(Luke 24.45-48; 1 Corinthians 15.3)*. In case anyone doubted their right to pen Scripture they were given special powers by the Lord to perform amazing miracles and signs – so that there could be no doubt that they were God's penmen. Others were forbidden to add to or take away from the sacred writings *(Revelation 22.18-19)*.

What confirms the Bible as a unique book?

(a) Its effect on our world. Right down the course of history men and women have turned to God's Word to find out about the things which really matter – life, death, sin, forgiveness, guidance, etc. It is the only book which really deals with these matters. In every century they have found God through its message, and their lives and views have changed dramatically. Gradually the Gospel has passed round the world. The Bible – or parts of it – is now available in over 2,000 languages. In one year 10 million Bibles are sold. Between 1815 and 1975 2,500 million copies were distributed! In 1992, 618 million Bibles and Bible portions were distributed by one society alone.

As the teaching of the Bible has spread, and the lives of millions have been changed, an influence on society has inevitably been at work. Much of our modern system of education, medicine and care for the under-privileged has its roots in the loving work of those who were fired to help others by the Gospel of the grace of God.

(b) Its survival despite persecution. Very often the Bible's influence has been so great that people who oppose God have tried to prevent others from seeing or reading it. They have frequently threatened death on those who read and believed it. They have banned it and burned it. They have forbidden its translation into the language of the people. The fact that it has been preserved for so many hundreds of years – despite all this opposition – just goes to prove that it is of God.

(c) Its remarkable accuracy. As we proceed with this series of lessons we shall discover how well proven the historical records of the Bible are. Modern archaeology has repeatedly vindicated the dating and details of Bible history. Children will be surprised to hear the amazing discoveries and solid evidence which we will be able to produce to verify some of the smallest details. We will show that the Bible, far from being mythical, is the world's greatest history book. We shall examine some of its prophecies and their detailed fulfilment hundreds of years later. A few decades ago the theory of evolution was regarded as a fact by nearly all scientists, but now this theory has been shown to be fatally flawed. Many scientists have acknowledged that living things seem to have appeared on the Earth in a sudden way, just as the Bible says.

(d) Its great purpose. By way of application turn the class to *Psalm 119.105 – Thy word is a lamp unto my feet, and a light* *unto my path.* Explain that over and above all the other wonders and amazing characteristics of the Bible is this: that it is a book addressed to individual men, women and children to show them the way to God and to Heaven. Unlike any other book, it speaks God's own words to us.

It is like a light which reveals to us the very heart of God, our Maker. As it sets out His commandments for our lives it beams into our hearts and shows how full of rottenness and sin we are. It searches our hidden motives and desires and faces us with our need of forgiveness. Then it points us to the Saviour and His death for all who see their need and turn to Him. It searches our hearts like a great lamp and leads us to the Lord. It is full of warnings, encouragements and pleadings. The more we read it the more we see. It is like a great chandelier – the closer we survey it, the more surprised and enraptured we are. And when we listen to its message and obey its instruction and turn to the Lord for ourselves and discover Him, then we learn to treasure it above everything else in this world.

During the coming weeks we are going to explore the Bible and view it from many angles. Do not miss coming. Prepare yourself to see the great things which the Lord has provided for us here.

Visual Aid

Teachers could highlight the information presented in this lesson by producing a scrapbook entitled 'The Bible – God's Word'. Each page can be headed by one of the seven chief points of this lesson, with illustrations to strengthen each point.

The Word of Help (140)
To the Kings Asa and Jehoshaphat

2 Chronicles 14 – 20, particularly 14 and 20; see also 1 Kings 15.9-24

Aim: To encourage the children to believe God's Word and put their trust in it. To give examples of times when men have trusted the Lord and proved His power to bless in a remarkable way.

Teachers' Introduction

It is a great pity that the two kings Asa and Jehoshaphat are so little known. The accounts of their reigns rate highly for excitement, humour and teaching. The way in which the Lord rewarded these kings for their trust should shame away our unbelief.

Teachers' choice. Some teachers will probably want to confine the lesson to Jehoshaphat's battle, particularly those with young classes. Those with older classes should not spend too long on the first section so as to leave sufficient time for the section on King Jehoshaphat. Concentrate on following the Bible account closely. Then the children will grasp the lesson of faith contained in it with very little extra comment from teachers. This lesson should quickly become a favourite.

Object Lesson – Runway Lights

Arouse the children's curiosity by announcing that during this series we shall compare the Bible with the many kinds of lights in use today (lighthouses, searchlights, security lights, infra-red lamps, etc). Remind the class that God's Word has often been described as a light. This week we shall compare it with the strips of powerful lights to be found alongside airport runways. If a pilot were to try to land his aircraft at night without any lights to guide him, a terrible tragedy might result. But he can bring his aircraft down in complete confidence, knowing that the runway lights mark a path which is purpose-built, tried and tested. All over the world thousands of aircraft land safely every day because they are guided by runway beacon lights.

Hundreds of Bible chapters show us the way we should take if we want to know God, and have His blessing in our lives. They also recount the experiences of many people who have proved what God can do when they put their trust in His Word. We are going to examine the experience of two such men today.

Lesson Outline

A small country. Remind the class that following the reign of King Solomon the nation of Israel was divided into two (see VA 1, page 19). Tell them that the kingdom of Judah, to the south of Israel, was smaller (consisting of only two tribes

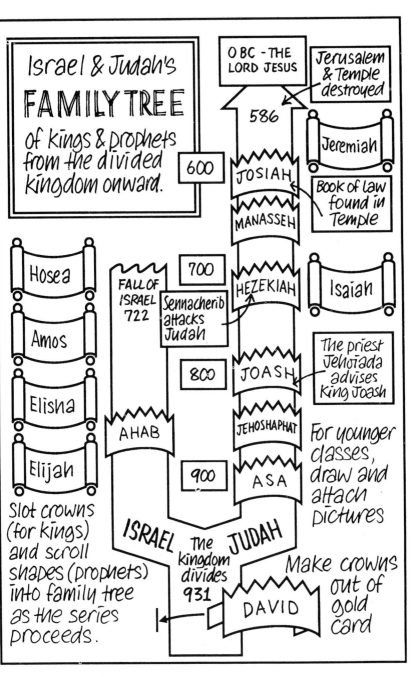

Israel & Judah's **FAMILY TREE** of kings & prophets from the divided kingdom onward.

0 BC – THE LORD JESUS

Jerusalem & Temple destroyed

586

Jeremiah

600

JOSIAH

Book of Law found in Temple

MANASSEH

Hosea

700

HEZEKIAH

Isaiah

Amos

FALL OF ISRAEL 722

Sennacherib attacks Judah

Elisha

800

JOASH

The priest Jehoiada advises King Joash

Elijah

AHAB

JEHOSHAPHAT

For younger classes, draw and attach pictures

900

ASA

Slot crowns (for kings) and scroll shapes (prophets) into family tree as the series proceeds.

ISRAEL

The kingdom divides 931

JUDAH

Make crowns out of gold card

DAVID

VA 1 – Visual Aid for use with lessons on 'The Word of God'.

compared with Israel's ten). Humanly speaking, it was much weaker. But we shall see how two of its kings put their trust in the Lord and received His help in most remarkable ways.

King Asa *(2 Chronicles 14)*. Describe how King Asa mounted an aggressive campaign against Baal and other idols in his kingdom (vv 2-5). Explain that he excused no one, and even his mother was condemned because she worshipped false gods *(1 Kings 15.13)*. Consider the uproar which would result from any such measures today! Imagine the outcry if pornography and bad language were to be banned, and people were urged to seek the God of the Bible! However, through Asa's campaign the nation gained strength *(2 Chronicles 14.6-7)*, and a period of peace and prosperity began.

Application 1 – Repentance. Remind the class that this is the Lord's top priority for us. If we want His help and guidance, we must first part company with any 'idols' which come before Him in our lives. We must decisively throw them out. Make practical suggestions to your own class.

God's help in trouble. King Asa enjoyed God's blessing in many ways in times of peace, but how could the Lord help in times of trouble and war? He was soon to discover, when attacked by the Ethiopians (the Cushites) under their military commander Zerah.

Describe the enormous army (twice as large as theirs) which threatened the people of Judah. Even today an army of a million men and three hundred tanks (chariots in Asa's day) would be frightening enough. But Asa believed in God and he turned to the Lord for help, praying: *Lord, it is nothing with thee to help, whether with many, or with them that have no power: help us, O Lord our God; for we rest on thee, and in thy name we go against this multitude. O Lord, thou art our God* (v 11). He knew there was no other help available to him, but he was confident that, if he relied on the Lord, the outcome would be a victory for Judah. And it was. In a remarkable way God struck down the Cushite army and they turned and fled, and could not rally or recover themselves. Asa and his men gave chase, and returned with riches, cattle, sheep and camels plundered from the enemy tents, and from the cities which were in league with them.

Application 2 – Faith. Show the class that a person who has faith is one who genuinely trusts in God. Asa did not pray, and then rush for help elsewhere, as if he did not really believe the answer would come. He firmly believed that God would settle the outcome of the battle.

Encourage young believers in your class by reminding them that the God of the universe is ready to help and bless any child who belongs to Him. Urge them to be like Asa and stand firm for Him, assuring them that the more they do so, the more they will be surprised to see God's power working for them *(2 Chronicles 16.8-9)*. Tell them how God directs and guides in events which seem threatening (such as exams and employment decisions, to name only two).

When, later, Asa sought help from Syria and then from his doctors, he was far less successful than when he sought it from the Lord.

King Jehoshaphat. As always, the Bible records the failings of its heroes as well as their virtues. Jehoshaphat (Asa's son) wrongly made an alliance with King Ahab who hated the Lord. But our lesson today emphasises the blessings which he experienced when he put his trust in the Lord.

(1) Outline the steps he took to ensure that his kingdom returned to the Lord *(2 Chronicles 17.1-9),* and the benefits of this (vv 10-19).

(2) After a foolish period of offending the Lord, he repented by introducing further practical measures to please God, particularly by establishing a right and fair system of justice throughout his land *(19.1-11).*

(3) Enthusiastically relate to the class the unusual and amazing account of the battle in chapter 20. Describe the army which relied not on armaments, but on singing! The following points should be highlighted:

(a) The strength of the enemy (vv 1-2).

(b) Jehoshaphat's reaction. Instead of going into a wild frenzy and seeking military aid from his neighbours, he, in the presence of his people, went to the house of the Lord and prayed, closing his prayer with these words: *O our God, wilt thou not judge them? for we have no might against this great company that cometh against us; neither know we what to do: but our eyes are upon thee* (vv 5-12). Tell the class that all true believers can speak to the Lord in this way. Their prayers are real and urgent and full of concern.

(c) The touching scene as not only the men, but also their wives and *little ones* stood before the Lord (v 13).

(d) The priest's assurance that their prayers had been heard, that the battle was not theirs but the Lord's (v 15). All they had to do was take up their positions on the field and they would see the salvation (victory) of the Lord with their own eyes.

(e) The extraordinary service of thanksgiving before the battle had begun! What a demonstration that they wholly trusted the Lord's Word (vv 18-19).

(f) Jehoshaphat's own certainty that they need have no fears (v 20).

(g) The amazing procedure that followed. (Teachers may like to provide a model battlefield displaying movements of the troops.) The choir marched before the soldiers in Judah's army, singing the great chorus of God's people (v 21).

(h) It was not until they began to consider the necessity of taking up arms that they looked to see the position of the enemy, only to discover this vast army lying dead on the ground (v 24)! The explanation for this amazing state of affairs is given in verses 22 and 23.

(i) Instead of losing from this war, they gained much (v 25).

(j) They did not forget to thank and praise the Lord (vv 27-28).

Application 3 – Finding the Saviour. Ask the class why this incident is recorded in God's Word. Help them to see that it is not just an historical account – like the Battle of Waterloo. It is written so that we can learn. It is a light to light up the path of life for us. It teaches us clearly that if we really believe in God and ask His help, there is nothing He cannot do for us. Why do we so often seek happiness and success from everyone and everything but the Lord? Do these other helpers do us any good? Why not put our trust in the Lord and prove that no one else can help us in the way He can?

The Bible alone tells us the truth about the enemies of our souls. It does not hide away the realities of sin and death and hell. Instead it points us to the Lord Jesus Who conquered each one of these foes. It gives us plain and simple instructions telling how we too can be saved. If we believe and obey the Scriptures which lead us to the Saviour, then, like Jehoshaphat of old, we shall rejoice to watch enemies, against whom we stood no chance of survival, lying at our feet, defeated by the Lord. Urge your class to cut their ties with this world and its broken promises and say to the Lord with all sincerity, *Lord, I believe; help thou mine unbelief.*

Visual Aid

Draw three silhouette outlines on card of soldiers of those days, dressed in heavy armour. One should be large, the next not so large, and the third quite small.

In the course of the lesson show how Asa, then Jehoshaphat, both represented by the smallest outline soldier, faced a larger enemy (the middle-sized soldier) and, humanly speaking, stood no chance. Then remind the children that these two kings had an unseen ally, the Lord (represented by the largest outline), Who stood on their side, thus altering the balance of the battle and ensuring their victory. Apply this to young believers as they face the battle of life.

The Word to Me (141)
King Joash

2 Chronicles 22.10 – 24.27, particularly chapter 24; see also 2 Kings 11.8-12

Aim: To show that it is vital to know the Lord for ourselves. Also, to give practical tests which will enable children to know whether or not they are converted Christians.

Object Lesson – My Own Light

To use another form of light, ask the class if it would be wise to go cycling at night without any lamps, even if going with a friend whose cycle was properly equipped. Discuss what could happen – the friend might take a different route, leaving you alone, etc.

Tell the class that there have always been those who rely on other people for all kinds of important things. Many will remember the parable of the ten virgins, five of whom relied on their friends for oil to light their lamps. Ask the class for up-to-date examples, such as the cheat who relies on other people's hard work to see him through his school work. Such a person usually comes unstuck sooner or later.

Apply the same thought to Christian conversion. Show that some people depend on others for their hope of going to Heaven. Mention how children sometimes put their trust in parents who are Christians, as though this gives *them* a right to Heaven. Others think that because they attend Bible Class or Sunday School, this will get them to Heaven. Introduce the subject of King Joash, himself a young child when he began to reign. Here is a case-history of such a person.

Lesson Outline

King Joash. (1) Describe how the wicked Queen Athaliah killed her family in order to secure the throne of Judah for herself. Tell how she had already influenced her son Ahaziah *to do wickedly*, continuing the Baal worship of Ahab and Omri. When he died, she was determined to hold on to power and to prevent any return to the Lord.

(2) Show how the baby Joash was rescued from Athaliah's murderers, and secretly cared for in the Temple by his aunt and her husband, Jehoiada, the priest *(2 Chronicles 22.10-12)*. Mention how this godly couple would have taught the young child the ways of the Lord.

(3) Describe the surprise coronation and Athaliah's horror and death *(23.11-15)*. The drama of this scene should hold the class spellbound. Joash became king when he was only seven years old.

(4) The young king always turned to Jehoiada for guidance. Soon the Temple worship was restored, the images of Baal broken down, and the burnt offerings again offered regularly. There was great rejoicing in the land as the people promised to be the Lord's people *(24.10)*. But still Joash did not turn to the Lord for himself. Perhaps he imagined he was a believer, like Jehoiada, because he helped with the work *(24.4-5)*. We read that he did what was *right in the sight of the Lord all the days of Jehoiada (24.2)*, and it appeared that he was behind the great reforms of that period.

(5) But then the old priest died (24.15), and others came to influence the king. Joash had no spiritual life or understanding of his own, so he saw nothing wrong in their wicked suggestions. Because he did not love the Lord with all his heart, he had no real zeal for God, and no hatred of those other, evil gods. Before long the princes deserted the Temple and set about rebuilding altars to Baal (v 18). When the Lord sent His prophets to condemn their idolatry, they refused to listen.

(6) Finally Joash received a rebuke from the Lord through Jehoiada's son Zechariah, but he refused to turn back. He who had once relied on Jehoiada was too weak to face criticism, and he commanded the murder of Zechariah, who was stoned to death in the Temple courtyard (vv 20-22).

(7) As time went on, even the servants of Joash were disgusted with him, and, following his defeat by the king of Syria (a judgement of God), they murdered him on his bed (vv 23-25). What a fall! The king who made such a promising start, judged a failure and a sinner by men and by God! What a tragedy that the one who owed so much to Jehoiada never had his own link with the Lord!

Putting ourselves to the test. How can we tell if *we* are really Christians? Can we be sure that we are not like Joash, following the Lord while it suits us, but having no real sympathy for His cause, and deserting Him as soon as other suggestions are made to us? If we were to move from our present neighbourhood, would we continue to attend God's house, or would we drop the practice? If our parents or Sunday School teachers no longer brought us to Sunday School would we make any effort to come ourselves?

The Bible assures us that once we belong to the Lord, the difference in our lives will be unmistakable, and the change will be permanent. There are certain great signs which mark out real Christians. Explain that it is possible to apply certain tests to people (ourselves and others) to establish whether or not they have been truly converted. These tests apply to believers of all ages. Being a Christian always includes:

Test 1 – Knowing the Lord personally. King Joash knew a lot about the Lord and His ways. He had spent his first six years hidden in the house of God. But his knowledge of religion was no substitute for knowing the Lord Himself. We see no evidence of his ever coming to the critical moment when he saw himself as a sinner needing personally to be forgiven by God. No wonder that on the death of Jehoiada all kinds of evil erupted from him, and the state of his heart was exposed for what it was.

Ask the children if they have ever seen the ugliness of their hearts and asked the Lord, very genuinely, to forgive them. Conversion implies a change. Can they remember a time when they began to know God for themselves, looked to the Saviour and experienced the joy of forgiven sin; when they deliberately turned their backs on this world and set out to follow the Lord?

Test 2 – Understanding His Word. Joash often heard the Scriptures read *(22.12)* and was very familiar with them, but obviously they meant little to him personally. He respected Jehoiada and fell in line with his measures, but soon after the old man died, Joash felt as though he had been set free, and he kicked over God's laws.

Real Christians see the Bible in a completely new light. They make the wonderful discovery that it is God's Word to them – like a long letter from the King of Heaven. The passages which once seemed long and dreary develop a fascination and interest they never had before, and believers want to learn and obey all God's commands. They long to know more about their Saviour, and experience great exhilaration as they read about Him in the Old Testament as well as the New.

Has anything like this happened to our children, or are they like Joash, appearing to be Christians because it suits them to please their parents and teachers? Do they think that acquiring Bible facts and learning Bible verses is enough to satisfy God? Real Christians love and fear the Lord and the Bible becomes their treasured guidebook.

Test 3 – Loving other believers. How surprising it is to read that Joash murdered his 'step-brother', after their 'father's' death. His action proved that he had been a 'false pretender'.

Hatred for believers is a symptom of a person still being in darkness *(1 John 2.9)*. In fact, when children or adults become

Christians we can usually tell because they suddenly develop a great attachment to the Lord's people. A small child will rather attend Sunday School than join a family outing, however exciting. They want to attend mid-week meetings and linger as long as possible afterwards. Christians belong to a family of the Lord's people and the ties are very close. Young believers away from home for the first time find themselves searching for other Christians. Their common love of the Saviour provides a much closer tie than any natural friendship.

Test 4 – Praying real prayers. Have you seen people who claim to be Christians chanting prayers without any concern or reverence? Joash probably did this many times. Often he would attend grand services in the Temple and as king he would lead the prayers. But probably he asked Jehoiada to write the prayers for him and he read them through mechanically.

How different from a real Christian whose prayers may be short and stumbling, but are sincere and spoken to God from the heart. When children come to the Lord, they no longer want to play about in Sunday School prayer-time. They begin to sense God's presence, stop gazing at their shoes and follow the prayers carefully because they love to speak to Him. Do you know what it is to pray? Have you ever tried to speak to God yourself?

Test 5 – Feeling the attacks of Satan. Soon after Jehoiada's death, Joash surrendered to the advice of the princes, and gave up the battle against idolatry. He took the easy way.

Satan leaves us alone if he can count on our loyalty. He allows us to enjoy life. But if we desert him and turn to the Lord, he begins to attack us with all kinds of doubts, fears and difficulties. It is so with all God's people. But there is some encouragement, because it is clear that God's Spirit is at work in the heart, and Satan is worried.

Test 6 – A permanent change. God promises that if we come to Him in real repentance and faith, trusting in His Son's death on Calvary as the only way sins can be forgiven, He will not send us away. He will receive us into His family and change our lives completely and for ever. Real Christians know joy and peace never experienced by the worldling. Everything is changed and even the trials of life cannot separate us from the Saviour. Had Joash known the Lord for Himself, he would never have turned aside so quickly to Baal.

Explain to the class that it is vital that they come to know and experience the Lord for themselves. It is no good pretending to be a Christian – not even to please their parents or their Sunday School teacher. Encourage them to examine their hearts to see whether or not they are His. If not, urge them to pray to the Lord – that His Spirit may perform His transforming work in their lives.

Visual Aid

Cut out of card a giant thermometer and mark it with a scale of six 'degrees spiritual'. As you describe the six tests of faith label the scale with the following six questions: (1) Do you know the Lord in a personal way? (Has He forgiven and converted you?) (2) Do you read and love His Word? (3) Do you like to be with other Christians? (4) Do you really pray? (5) Have you felt Satan's attacks? (6) Are you certain you belong to the Lord and will be His for ever?

Suggest that each 'degree' marked up is a sign of good spiritual health. The lesson shows how Joash failed all these tests.

The Word of Warning (142)
From the Prophets Amos and Hosea

Amos, particularly chapters 6, 7.14-17 and 8; Hosea, particularly chapters 1, 2, 4, 11; 2 Kings 17.6-23; see also texts quoted in lesson

Aim: To show that the Bible is a very practical book full of messages from God to us, and that to ignore its Author and His warnings leads swiftly to disaster for nations and individuals. To warn children that, although this world tolerates much wrong-doing, our holy God judges sin. Yet, in love, He gives us the opportunity to seek His forgiveness and pardon, and pleads with us not to refuse it.

Object Lesson – A Lighthouse

In this lesson we shall compare the Bible with a lighthouse. Provide a photograph or picture. Ask the class the main function of this light, ie: that it not only indicates the way, but *warns of danger*. Seamen are warned of huge rocks hidden beneath the waterline which would gash enormous holes in the ship's sides. Or they are warned of sandbanks on which their ship could be stranded for days. Tell how grateful the seamen are for these warning lights, and how disastrous it would be if the lights ceased to shine.

Then explain that the Bible is unique as a book. Often it is like the lighthouse sending messages of warning, so that we can be spared from danger. Today we are going to look at two warning passages which record the words of two of God's servants – first Amos, then Hosea. We shall discover that the words which they delivered to the people of Israel apply equally to our day and age.

Lesson Outline

Describe the sad decline of the people of Israel (the northern kingdom) in the following five stages:

(1) The enjoyment of prosperity. Describe how the people of Israel had settled into the new land promised and given to them by God. Previous generations had fought and won battles, cultivated the land, planted vineyards, reared healthy flocks, and worshipped the God of King David. Now the younger generation could enjoy the fruit of their fathers' labours. Many people were living in plenty and lavishing on themselves the benefits of their prosperity. Modern Bible versions make this picture particularly vivid *(Amos 6.1-6)*. They lay on beds of ivory, eating tender lamb and choice veal, sipping wine while music was played for their enjoyment, and all the time they smothered themselves in rich oil – or tanning lotion. How like a modern television commercial!

Tell how the Lord chose a country farmer, not an established priest, to deliver His unexpected message of *woe (6.1)* to shock and alarm these people *(7.14-15)*. Amos warned that they would soon be heading the queue of those being carried into exile by a foreign power! They would soon be judged by the Lord. Why? Because their prosperity had been obtained only by:

(2) The neglect of God's laws. Their riches had been gained at the expense of righteousness and justice. Tell the children that although the rich people lived in houses of carved stone, full of ivory ornaments *(Amos 3.15; 5.11)*, they imposed high rents on the poor, living in lowly houses. They also taxed their wheat *(5.11)* and confiscated their clothes if they could not pay *(2.8)*. This was in breach of God's command to return a poor person's cloak before nightfall (when it was very cold – *Deuteronomy 24.12-13*), and to leave supplies of wheat for the poor to glean *(Deuteronomy 24.19)*. As judges and magistrates, they accepted bribes and heartlessly refused justice to the innocent and disadvantaged *(Amos 5.12)*. Evil-doers knew that even a pair of shoes was enough to procure a favourable judgement from these corrupt judges *(2.6; 8.6)*.

Another common dishonest practice was the use of weighted scales as a method of extortion *(8.5)*. Like children bringing stolen money for the Sunday School offering, they proudly donated gifts to religious causes (often heathen) from their ill-gotten gains *(4.4-5)*. Teachers with younger classes can describe the squalid huts that the poor slept in. How cold they were with no cloak or blanket at night! What a mean trick to place weights under the scale pans!

No wonder that the Lord hated their festivals and assemblies and refused their offerings. He said He would not even look at their sacrifices, or listen to their songs and instruments *(Amos 5.21-23)*. The Lord preferred honesty and justice.

(3) Ingratitude to God. While these well-to-do people enjoyed all kinds of luxuries, they forgot it was the Lord Who had provided them with their benefits, and they cared nothing about the state of the Lord's work *(Amos 6.6)*. Their own houses could be magnificently decorated, but it caused them no grief to see the work of God neglected. Even on the Sabbath, and other religious days, they could scarcely wait to get back to their fraudulent schemes and dishonest businesses *(8.5-6)*. At the bottom of this corruption lay the fact that, although they put on a show of worshipping the Lord, their hearts were far from Him. (How many children today turn up to Sunday School but their minds are far away!)

(4) Flirtation with other gods. The Israelites frequently turned aside to the idol-gods of the surrounding nations *(Hosea*

5.4-5), as if their God, the Lord of hosts Who created all things, were no better than these handmade deities. People who worshipped heathen gods practised child sacrifice, witchcraft and other occult activities. Hosea pointed out that Israel was now destitute of truth (including faithfulness), mercy (kindness), and the knowledge of God. Instead, the land was filled with swearing, lying, killing, stealing, adultery and violence *(Hosea 4.1-3)*. (How like the contents of our newspapers!) Explain to the class that worship of false gods (or belief systems) always leads to a throwing away of moral standards. People prefer to worship wooden gods, who are not alive, and obviously cannot see their evil ways. Nowadays they say there is no God at all!

(5) Persecution of the Lord's messengers. The priests of Israel turned a blind eye to all this behaviour in order to remain popular *(Hosea 4.9)*. But when God's true servants, the prophets, arrived at the city gates with condemning and warning messages, they received scorn and fierce opposition from the 'clergy' of the day. Amaziah, the priest of Bethel, complained bitterly to King Jeroboam, and dismissed Amos – the herdsman and grower of sycamore figs – saying, 'Go away to Judah and prophesy there!' *(Amos 7.10-13.)*

Disaster! The last thing that the people thought about was the catastrophe close at hand. While they imagined that they were secure, and their standard of living could only increase, they little dreamed that soon they would be the victims of war! Before long many of them would be marched away to distant lands to serve as slaves to their Assyrian captors *(2 Kings 17.6)*. This was the unpopular message which Amos and Hosea were sent to give *(Amos 6.14; Hosea 5.14; 8.1; 9.7)*. The Lord had sent previous mild warnings *(Amos 4.6-13)*, but these had been ignored. God, Who is holy, could no longer overlook all the wrong, exploitation, and cruelty of a nation that was supposed to belong to Him. They would now face judgement and calamity. The nation was to be humiliated, captured and carried away, never to return. The fruit of their vineyards would be enjoyed by others *(Amos 5.11)*. Nor was this an idle threat of the prophets, for in 722 BC the king of Assyria did exactly as they had predicted. Remind the class that history so often repeats itself. Often periods of immorality and complacency have been followed by the fall of proud empires (such as the Roman empire).

God's tender attitude. Remind the class that Almighty God, Whose power is unlimited (and Who can make a modern city collapse like a toy town in seconds, with an earthquake), could so easily bring our entire Earth under judgement instantly. But it gives Him no pleasure, and He delays judgement in order to plead with men, women and children. The prophet Hosea was sent to express God's 'feelings' to His wayward people in terms which should melt the hardest heart:

(1) A father and son. He likened the people of Israel to His child. Read the tender terms He uses *(Hosea 11.3-4)* – He held them in His arms, held their baby-reins and bent down to caress them. Briefly remind the class of the blessings poured out on Israel since they left the land of Egypt – how God provided their daily needs, protected them from their enemies and guided them safely to the promised land. He loved them as a father loves his son. How tragic and wicked that they should forget, ignore and forsake Him when they reached their new land! God described His sorrow in judging them (vv 8-9). Yet He had no choice for they refused to return to Him (v 5).

Take pains to translate this picture for your class. They too have benefited from God's love and care since birth. They have often been told of His concern for each individual. They also know that God was prepared to send His own Son, the Lord Jesus Christ, to suffer the punishment of every sin (for those who seek His forgiveness) on the cross. But are they grateful to God? Do they believe His Word and obey Him – or do they treat Him as an enemy, and turn away from His lovingkindness with indifference? Do they take His gifts and yet ignore the Giver? If so, how long do they think this can go on? God is kind and patient, but one day He must punish sin and restore His righteous rule.

(2) A husband and wife *(Hosea 1, 2)*. Varying the amount of detail for the age of class, use Hosea's picture of God's love for Israel as that of a husband for his faithless wife. Describe a husband who had married a woman, not noted for her beauty or goodness. He provided her with a home and showed her real affection and love. Imagine his sorrow when he discovered that she had been unfaithful and chased after others. Even so, he would accept her back kindly if she would return to him, with remorse.

Explain that the Lord loves the people He has made just as a husband loves his wife. Even though we deserve none of His love, and are guilty of so much wrong, He wants us to love Him in the same way, and to have no other gods beside Him.

Do we love the Lord with all our hearts? Have we gone after other gods? Have we ever considered confessing our sin and returning to Him? If we refuse, He has no alternative but to hand us over to the gods we idolise, and withdraw all His blessings *(2.11-13)*. Then we shall realise too late how much we owe to the Lord.

The lighthouse of God's Word. We began by comparing the Bible to a great lighthouse which saves lives. The whole of Scripture is full of warnings to us, starting in the book of *Genesis* and continuing through to *Revelation*.

Almost every one of the parables of the Lord Jesus sounds a warning note, and He described hell in the most vivid terms. (For example, *Matthew 13.41-42, 50; Luke 16.19-31*.) Hundreds of years after Amos and Hosea, He stood and wept over Jerusalem, realising that the Jewish people of His day would share a similar fate, for they had refused His words and warnings in the same way as the Israelites refused those of Amos and Hosea.

Urge your class to learn from the Israelites' bitter experience and to heed the warnings of God's Word. No doubt the people of Samaria (the capital city of Israel) wished they had listened to Amos and Hosea when they were marched in heavy chains across the desert at the command of their Assyrian captors.

The Lord Jesus described the horror and remorse that men, women and children will feel on the last day when they finally realise how foolish they have been to reject such a kind and loving Saviour, and face the punishment and consequences of their sin.

Visual Aid

Draw a staircase with five large steps. On each step write one of the five lesson headings from (1) – (5). At the bottom draw an explosion and mark it with the heading – Disaster!

The Word of Defence (143)
King Hezekiah

2 Chronicles 28.24 – 32.23; 2 Kings 18.13 – 19.37

Aim: To show in a very practical way that if God is for us, nothing can be against us.

Teachers' Introduction

The best way to prepare this lesson is to read slowly through these chapters. Begin with the *2 Chronicles* account and supplement it with the detailed account of Sennacherib's invasion from the record of *2 Kings 18.13-19.37*. The narrative itself says so much. It not only describes what happened, but speaks across the centuries to our own situation. The narrative divides into two main sections: the revival, and Sennacherib's threatened attack.

Object Lesson – Security Lights

We suggest for our 'light' illustration this week the way in which many families now leave a light on if they leave the house or flat at night. Burglars are far less likely to break in if they think someone is in. (Older children may be fascinated by time-switch devices which can be set to operate the light as desired.)

In this case, light offers *protection*, and today we are going to see how God's Word protects all those who trust it. All of us face one great enemy whether or not we know it. Satan, since the beginning of the world, has worked to seize the souls of men and women. He is an experienced enemy and no one can resist him with mere human strength. How can he be withstood? Our lesson today provides the answer and illustrates it with a true-life example.

Lesson Outline

A godless generation. Set the scene by explaining that our generation is not the first to turn against God and to ignore His house. When Hezekiah first became king, the people of Judah

were living godless lives, and the Temple doors had been closed
(2 Chronicles 28.24-25).

Hezekiah's reforms. Describe how Hezekiah was a believer
in the Lord who wanted to bring the people of Judah back to
their God. Soon some unusual events were taking place. The
priests in Jerusalem began with great enthusiasm to clean and
prepare the Temple (29.18-19).

(1) The Lord's house re-opened. The people of Jerusalem
were called together to offer sacrifices and hold services with
psalm singing (v 30). Remind the children that this was done
suddenly (v 36), meaning that there was a great surge of spiritual concern and feeling from large numbers of people who
had previously been cold and indifferent. Assure the class that
the Lord draws and welcomes young and old, from religious
and non-religious backgrounds, as they come to His house.
Worship and seeking the Lord are not only for those people
who have been believers for a long time.

(2) A national postal campaign. Soon the appeal to return
to the Lord was spread throughout the land. The postmen were
busy carrying letters to every part of the country urging everyone to return to the Lord (30.6). There were two reactions.
Either they were laughed to scorn (v 10) or they were received
seriously. Ask – When you hear God's message, what is your
reaction?

(3) The Passover celebrated. Describe the enormous crowd
which gathered in Jerusalem for the Passover, perhaps as many
as, or more than, gather for modern national sporting events.
This was not a boring religious ceremony but an occasion of
great gladness and rejoicing. The priests did not mutter prayers
to themselves, but addressed the Lord and, because their
prayers were sincere and earnest, God heard them (v 27).

(4) Idols destroyed. Next the people returned to their own
cities to smash down the altars of any other gods which had
been worshipped instead of the Lord (31.1). If we are really
repentant and earnestly seeking the Lord, we too shall destroy
all our 'idols'. Recount incidents of Christians who have
destroyed bad videos and books, left clubs, poured away 'drink',

and got rid of other unsavoury things as a token of their love for the Lord.

(5) Giving to the Lord. Lastly, as a token of their real desire to return to God, they began to give to the Lord a share of their possessions *(31.2-19)*. This revival was more than words. It began to show itself in deeds. Describe the heaps of corn, wine, oil and honey and the animals which they gladly brought to Jerusalem (a huge harvest festival, week after week).

Their tithes enabled God's servants to proceed with their work unhindered by material needs. Have you ever given anything to the Lord? He sees our hearts and knows immediately if we have given Him something which is of value to us – whatever it is and however small it may appear to others.

The enemy attack. All seemed to be going well, but God's enemies were not pleased. Sennacherib – the mighty king of Assyria, the greatest nation of those days – was angered when King Hezekiah refused to submit to him and pay him homage. He planned to attack Jerusalem thinking that it would be child's play after his other victories *(32.1-15)*. Give an account of the enemy's plan. Warn the class that the devil leaves us in peace whilst we comply with his wishes, but once we begin to seek the Lord seriously, his anger is aroused and he begins to tempt us away.

(1) His demands increased. Sennacherib's army moved towards Jerusalem; he was not satisfied with the treasure given him to persuade him to turn back *(2 Kings 18.15-18)*. Point out that Satan is never satisfied with what we give him. As soon as we give in to him on one point, he demands another, so one sin leads on to another.

(2) He undermined the Lord's servants. The enemy deliberately tried to undermine the morale of the people, speaking their language and aiming to threaten and frighten them so that Hezekiah would lose their support *(2 Kings 18.28-35)*. Describe how Satan appeals to us in a language we understand. He aims to turn us against those teachers and leaders who have brought us to the Lord. How he loves to ridicule those who stand for God. He, lyingly, represents them as out of date in their teaching.

(3) He mocked the Lord. Above all, the enemy mocked the Lord and compared Him with other gods. Satan always presses us to doubt God and His Word (and he entices us by drawing dishonest, rosy pictures of the pleasures of this world). Summarise the vicious threats and taunts made by Rabshakeh. Warn the class to ignore the devil when he tries to turn them away from God. The people of Jerusalem were silent. They obeyed the king and refused to be drawn into the debate. We should never enter into debate with Satan.

Hezekiah stood firm. Hezekiah went to Isaiah, his pastor, and together they prayed to the Lord; not a long, pointless prayer but one which was very earnest and to-the-point. Later Hezekiah took the enemy's letter (which threatened him with extermination) into the Temple, and we can read his prayer *(2 Kings 19.15-19)*. He pleaded God's help, not to save his own skin, but so that God should be seen as the true and living God by all the nations. Real prayer is not for things we want, but for things that honour God. We pray to be forgiven and converted, and for strength to please Him, and for others to be converted also. These are the kind of things that please the Lord. Real prayer is asking something *for God.*

Hezekiah encouraged the people to take a stand. *With him* [Sennacherib] *is an arm of flesh; but with us is the Lord our God to help us, and to fight our battles (2 Chronicles 32.8).* However great our difficulties in life the Lord will enable us to stand for Him. The sooner we learn to trust Him, the sooner we shall prove His power to protect and sustain His children.

Hezekiah discovered the enemy destroyed. The result of the battle seemed almost an anti-climax. Just as Isaiah had prophesied, the people of Jerusalem did not need to lift their swords *(2 Kings 19.32-35)*. 185,000 of Sennacherib's army were destroyed in their own camp. Next morning Jerusalem faced an army of dead corpses! Sennacherib returned home humiliated, and was later assassinated by his two sons (vv 36-37).

Lessons for today. Ask the class to consider if they have experienced Satan's attacks. Has he made them frightened to turn to the Lord? Has he made them into cowards, wanting to be converted but unwilling to stand with the Lord's people?

Why don't they learn from Hezekiah? What more frightening position could a person be in? Let them imagine their town or city surrounded with tanks and armaments, and with enemy soldiers jeering at the top of their voices. Perhaps the enemy has captured the television studios, and is broadcasting threats to the people of their town. Yet Hezekiah and the people of Jerusalem trusted in the power of the living God to deliver them, and very soon their faith was amply rewarded.

Young people today must not fear the scene around them – so many people sneering at faith in God, and wanting to draw them into a life of sin. If only we would turn to Christ, and trust His Word, He would convert us, keep us and surprise us with so many blessings.

The Word Authenticated (144)
Archaeological Evidence from the Time of King Hezekiah
2 Chronicles 32.9; 2 Kings 18.13-35; 19.37; 20.20

Aim: To show that, contrary to what many children are led to believe, the Bible has been demonstrated to be accurate and reliable both from the records of secular history and from archaeological research. This will be an encouragement to them to trust the Word of God.

Teachers' Introduction

This lesson will provide an opportunity to challenge the view, projected by many schoolteachers (and the media in general), that the Bible is not to be taken seriously as history. Far from presenting it as an historical record, they give the impression that it is a book of ancient myths and legends with little more integrity than the story of Cinderella and other fairy-tales.

During the course of this lesson we shall deal with four aspects of the biblical record which have been vindicated by the discovery of very substantial slabs of stone. Our evidence is not based on the word of one scholar, contradicted by another, but it is based on unassailable facts, available for the members of your class to see with their own eyes at national museums. We shall have to restrict our survey to the four major items in the narrative covered last week. Before preparing this lesson teachers are advised to look carefully at the suggested visual aid.

Object Lesson – Daylight

Show the class a picture or photograph of a city, taken by night, and another of the same city taken in daylight. How much more can be seen once the sun comes up! (Or, if easier to find, use instead a picture of a searchlight locating a war-plane at night, and change the 'light' illustration to that of a searchlight bringing into view that which was concealed by darkness.)

Explain that the evidence for great portions of Bible history had lain buried for thousands of years, but was then found by archaeologists, and brought into the daylight. The picture of Bible events is now 'as clear as daylight', and passages from the Old Testament once doubted by cynical people have been proved true in a remarkable way. This has proved once again that the Bible deals with facts and real history, not with theories and myths.

Lesson Outline

Describe how archaeologists excavating in Iraq at the close of the nineteenth century and at the beginning of the twentieth, unearthed huge pieces of evidence which prove that Bible facts are most certainly *historical* facts. The Bible is reliable in everything it says.

(1) **The battle of Lachish.** Show your class photographs of some of the slabs of stone displayed in the Lachish room of the British Museum, depicting Sennacherib's army routing this fortified city of Judah. Explain that King Sennacherib was a proud man who liked to record all his victories. He was not content to have his successes recorded in his country's annals or historical archives. He insisted that skilled artists and sculptors record his successful battles on walls of stone placed throughout his palace at Nineveh (600 miles away from Lachish 'as the crow flies', but even further for people in those days of travel by foot). Huge sheets of stone were erected, and enormous pictures, in minute detail, engraved upon them, all over 2,500 years ago!

These sculptures were discovered by a British archaeologist, Sir Henry Layard. In the nineteenth century they were transported from Iraq to England and erected in the British

1 START with your Bible

2 Visit Jerusalem and nearby Lachish in Israel, where...

3 Visit the remains of Sennacherib's palace in ancient NINEVEH (now in Iraq) where...

4 Fly to LONDON, England, where...

5 Return to your HOME

Copy this 'board game' on to stiff card, make five circles as above, with tabs, and cover the circles on the board. As the lesson proceeds, uncover the wording underneath by hingeing up the circles.

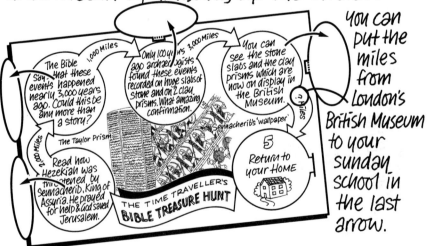

1,000 Miles

The Bible says that these events happened nearly 3,000 years ago. Could this be any more than a story?

The Taylor Prism.

3,000 Miles

Only 100 years ago archaeologists found these events recorded on huge slabs of stone and on 2 clay prisms. What amazing confirmation.

You can see the stone slabs and the clay prisms which are now on display in the British Museum.

Sennacherib's 'wallpaper'

2,000 Miles

Read how Hezekiah was threatened by Sennacherib, King of Assyria. He prayed for help & God saved Jerusalem.

? Miles

5 Return to your HOME

THE TIME TRAVELLER'S BIBLE TREASURE HUNT

You can put the miles from London's British Museum to your sunday school in the last arrow.

VA 2 – Visual Aid for use with Lesson 144 → 'The Word Authenticated'.

Museum.* Today, we can see for ourselves these sculptured pictures of the 'stronghold of Lachish with its stout, high walls'. Here the defenders of Judah fought desperately, showering hails of arrows upon their attackers, and hurling down upon them stones and burning torches. We can see the pictures in stone showing the armour worn, the ramps piled up against the city walls and the siege-engines (the first 'tanks' in history) which were used by the Assyrians. At the site of Lachish the holes and breaches made by the Assyrian 'tanks' can be seen to this day.

Now ask your class to read *2 Chronicles 32.9*, which records these very events. They took place just before Sennacherib's army planned to besiege Jerusalem, where King Hezekiah and Isaiah the prophet were seeking God's protection (as we heard last lesson). Lachish was the last fortified town on the road before Jerusalem. Very few other ancient battles are so vividly and graphically recorded. Sennacherib's record in stone gives solid confirmation of the Bible account. Why should we doubt any more the accuracy of God's Word?

(2) The Taylor Prism. Last week we heard how Senna-cherib's army moved to Jerusalem, confident that they could easily defeat and humiliate Hezekiah. Perhaps you thought it was just an exciting tale. Other people thought so too until the discovery one day of a hollow, six-sided, brown prism, bearing tiny rows of neat Assyrian writing. It was acquired by Colonel Taylor in 1830 in Nineveh. This prism was Sennacherib's official record, written by his officers. It gives the Assyrian king's version of what took place at Jerusalem in 701 BC (the events recorded in the Bible in *2 Kings 18.13-19.35*).

'As for Hezekiah the Jew, he did not submit to my yoke. I laid siege to 46 of his strong cities, walled forts and countless small villages in the vicinity and conquered them by means of well-stamped earth-ramps and battering rams brought thus near to the walls . . . Himself I made a prisoner in Jerusalem, his royal residence, like a bird in a cage. I surrounded him with earthworks in order to molest those who were leaving his city's

---

*Children may be interested to know that one of the winged bulls from the palace of Nimrud (near ancient Nineveh where Sennacherib lived) weighs 16 tonnes – the equivalent of two double-decker buses!

gate . . . I reduced his country but I still increased the tribute and the presents due to me as his overlord which I imposed upon him beyond his former tribute to be delivered annually . . . Hezekiah did send me later to Nineveh . . . 30 talents of gold, 800 talents of silver . . . '

Sennacherib's account confirms that the siege recorded in the Bible is an historical fact. It is true the two accounts differ in several respects. Sennacherib has exaggerated the amount of money he was given. He also feebly claims to have put earthworks up around the city, but he never got that far. He was never able to mount a siege, because his army was destroyed. No pictures of the siege of Jerusalem appear in Sennacherib's picture gallery, for it never happened! And Sennacherib's record says nothing about how it all ended, because it was a humiliating disaster for him, as we learned last week.

The baked clay prism on which all this is recorded can be seen today. It occupies a glass case in the British Museum, London, where it has been on display to the public since 1855.

(3) The Siloam Inscription. Read out, or tell, the Bible record of what King Hezekiah did to re-route his water supply *(2 Kings 20.20)* between the time of the fall of Lachish and Sennacherib's return from quelling rebellions elsewhere in his empire. Hezekiah took this precaution:

(a) so that Sennacherib's army would not benefit from it *(2 Chronicles 32.2-4)*;

(b) so that the people of Jerusalem would have a supply of water during any siege of their city.

An underground tunnel was cut through solid rock to take the water from the Gihon Spring (outside the city) to the Pool of Siloam safely inside the city walls. Its total length was 534 metres (1,777 feet). Work was started from both ends to hasten the procedure (describe the sense of panic as they thought Sennacherib may return at any time). Then came an astonishing engineering feat for the time, because the two sections of hand-hewn tunnel met exactly in the middle. Help the children to imagine the triumph of the workmen digging with nothing more than picks and shovels, when they heard the voices of the team in the other portion of the tunnel.

Go on to relate the astounding discovery of a boy in 1880 who ventured from the Pool of Siloam into a dark passageway and came across an old plaque bearing mysterious words. When the plaque was later cleaned and deciphered these were the words found on it:

'The boring through is completed. Now this is the story of the boring through. While the workmen were still lifting pick to pick, each toward his neighbour, and while 3 cubits remained to be cut through, each heard the voice of the other who called to his neighbour, since there was a crevice in the rock on the right side. And on the day of the boring through the stone-cutters struck, each to meet his fellow, pick to pick; and there flowed the waters to the pool for a thousand and two hundred cubits, and a hundred cubits was the height of the rock above the heads of the stone-cutters.'

Experts confirmed that the type of writing and the age of the plaque placed it at about 700 BC – exactly the right time. Obviously, these words were chiselled in the underground water passage by Hezekiah's triumphant drilling teams. Like engineers today they wanted to leave a record of their great achievement for generations to come. They might have been proud and surprised to learn that two and a half thousand years later their plaque would be removed and put on show in a famous museum in Istanbul. What better proof could we ask? People who dismiss the Bible as fairy-tales can be made to look very silly by these amazing discoveries. When you are next tempted to doubt God's Word, remember the evidence.

(4) A record of Sennacherib's death. The Bible tells us that Sennacherib was assassinated by his own family *(2 Kings 19.37; Isaiah 37.38)*. Is the Bible right about this piece of Assyrian history? Some historians doubted it. But when the Assyrian record was found, this is what it had to say:

'Disloyal thoughts inspired my brothers . . . They rebelled. In order to exercise royal authority they killed Sennacherib. I became a raging lion, my mind was in a fury.'

This is the record of Esarhaddon, the son who *reigned in his stead.*

Why do people doubt the Bible? We have seen how true

and reliable is one small portion of Bible history. We could quote many, many more examples. However, people do not refuse to believe in the Bible only because they have heard others say that it is a book of myths. They reject the Bible because they do not *want* to believe it, because it speaks to their hearts and exposes their sin *(Isaiah 6.9-10, quoted by Paul in Acts 28.25-27)*. It tells them they must seek the Saviour for forgiveness. This damages human pride, and so people resort to excuses for not believing what God has said.

We have demonstrated God's Word to be reliable in every way. If we can trust its history, how much more can we trust its teaching? Have you listened to it speaking to your heart?

Visual Aid

Bring the lesson to a close by revising and re-emphasising its chief points in the manner suggested in the visual aid (VA 2, pages 40-41). This suggests an imaginary treasure hunt from London to the Middle East and back, to bring home the remarkable vindication of the historicity of the Bible account in an exciting way. If the children know people who scorn or doubt the Bible, suggest that they are invited to join the hunt!

The visual aid will help everyone to appreciate: (a) the long *distances* which lay between Jerusalem (and Lachish), where these historical events occurred, and Nineveh, where the Assyrian evidence for them was found; (b) the long period of *time* which passed between the events of *Kings* and *Chronicles* (701 BC) and the discovery of their parallel Assyrian records by archaeologists in recent times (around 1850); (c) the fact that many of these remarkable confirmations can be seen by the children themselves in London.

The Word of Promise (145)
The Prophecies of Isaiah

Isaiah 3.8; 7.14; 9.1; 44.28; 53; and other references quoted in lesson

Aim: To demonstrate simply from the *Book of Isaiah* one of the most remarkable features of the Bible – its detailed and accurate prophecies of future events. Also, to highlight Isaiah's description of the coming Saviour, fulfilled perfectly in Christ, so that the children will respect all that the Bible teaches about things to come, and seek the Lord while He may be found.

Teachers' Introduction

Children, especially the youngest, have very little perspective of time. To them a person is either young or old. Their thirty-year-old Sunday School teacher might just as well be a pensioner! In their minds, events which happened a hundred and a thousand years ago are muddled together. To help them have a clearer picture of the significance of Isaiah's prophecies we suggest a simple graphic aid, which will help clarify the picture not only for younger classes but also for the teenagers and even teachers. We suggest a diagram in the form of a 'telescope of time' which will present time periods and events in a careful and historical manner, and make it easy for all to understand. (See VA 3 on page 47.)

As we begin to follow Isaiah's vision of a coming Saviour, let us imagine he lifts to his eye something like a telescope, and watches future events present themselves to him. He is shown some events that are to be fulfilled in his lifetime, and others that will occur within 200 years. Yet other pictured events will take place some 700 years in the future, these being the detailed views he sees of the life and sufferings of the coming Saviour. But the vision does not stop there, and we can go on to see his wonderful view of world history after the coming of Christ, especially the unexpected inclusion of the gentile nations in the Saviour's kingdom.

Once we have shown the children how all these events have already come to pass, we can urge them to consider Isaiah's predictions of things which are still to come. We may ask, in so many words – 'Having seen how accurate Isaiah was in describing events which have occurred during the past 2,700 years, should we not trust the Bible with our own future?'

Object Lesson – Infra-Red Light

Describe infra-red cine photography to your class. This has enabled badger-watchers to observe the movements of badgers as clearly as if it were daytime. Teenagers may be more

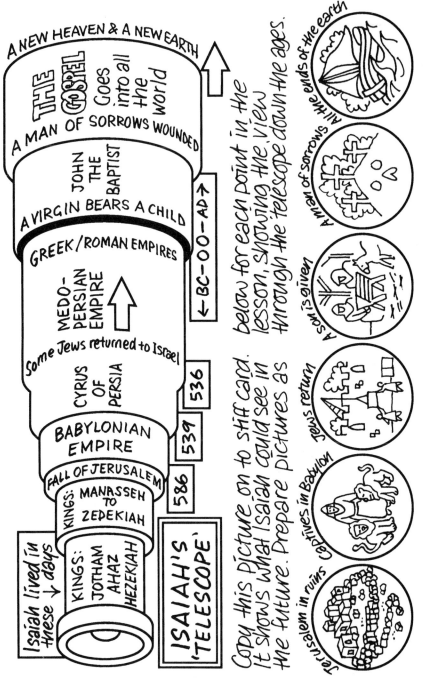

A NEW HEAVEN & A NEW EARTH

THE GOSPEL Goes into all the world

A MAN OF SORROWS WOUNDED

JOHN THE BAPTIST

A VIRGIN BEARS A CHILD

GREEK / ROMAN EMPIRES

MEDO-PERSIAN EMPIRE

Some Jews returned to Israel

CYRUS OF PERSIA

BABYLONIAN EMPIRE

FALL OF JERUSALEM

KINGS: MANASSEH TO ZEDEKIAH

KINGS: JOTHAM AHAZ HEZEKIAH

Isaiah lived in these ↓ days

← BC—00—AD →

536

539

586

ISAIAH'S 'TELESCOPE'

Copy this picture on to stiff card. It shows what Isaiah could see in the future. Prepare pictures as below for each point in the lesson, showing the view through the telescope down the ages.

All to the ends of the earth

A man of sorrows

A son is given

Jews return

Captives in Babylon

Jerusalem in ruins

VA 3 – Visual Aid for use with Lesson 145 – 'The Word of Promise'.

interested to know that the army can now equip front-line troops with infra-red viewing equipment so that they can watch enemy movements even in total darkness. Things which were once obscure and hidden can now be observed clearly. Indicate that, in today's lesson, we shall see how the Bible similarly brings unseen future events clearly into view.

Lesson Outline

Show that the future is unknown as far as humans are concerned. We may have some indications of what to expect. We may hazard some guesses, and calculate future trends based on past patterns, but very little is certain. Give examples, varying with the age of the class, of events about which we speculate, such as the weather, winners and losers in any field of sport, and economic performance.

Then explain that the Bible is a unique book which has a proven success-record in making detailed and accurate predictions of the future. (Older classes may be interested to know that many Old Testament predictions – such as those of Jeremiah and Daniel – proved to be so accurate that cynical scholars thought that they must have been written after the events! However, the discovery of the Dead Sea Scrolls – some of which pre-date the events of which the prophets spoke – exploded this idea.)

History before it happened. Using the visual aid, outline the events which the Lord showed in advance to Isaiah and which he predicted in his book. For children old enough to read the Bible for themselves draw attention to the words *in that day* which Isaiah frequently uses to show that he is prophesying about future things. Explain that these words are a 'cue' or 'code' signalling the giving of a prophecy.

Isaiah lived in the days of the good kings Uzziah and Jotham. These were succeeded by King Ahaz, who turned from the Lord and introduced other gods with grossly immoral ways, even sacrificing children *(2 Chronicles 28.3)*. During the subsequent reigns of Hezekiah and Josiah there was a period of reformation, but the tide of immorality was to surge on amongst the ordinary people. These rejected the Lord (especially during the reign of Manasseh) supposing they could break His laws and get away with it *(Isaiah 1.4)*. But as Isaiah looked into his 'telescope of time' he saw:

(1) **The punishment of Judah** and Jerusalem by an oppressor. *Jerusalem is ruined, and Judah is fallen (Isaiah 3.8)*. The princes and people did not take Isaiah's warnings seriously when he gave them. But a hundred years later his words came true, as Nebuchadnezzar, king of Babylon, besieged and stormed Jerusalem, carrying its finest young men a thousand miles to his capital, and leaving Jerusalem a subject city. More surprisingly, Isaiah predicted that following a period of captivity the Lord would bring about:

(2) **The restoration of the Jewish captives** to their own land. Another Bible prophet (Jeremiah) even foretold the length of the captivity as 70 years *(Jeremiah 25.11-12; 29.10)*. Isaiah warned the Babylonians that their empire would be toppled *(Isaiah 47)*. It would be a new Persian ruler, Cyrus, who would be used by the Lord to set free the Jews, and return them to Judah where they would rebuild the Temple in Jerusalem *(Isaiah 44.28 – 45.4)*. Help the class to appreciate the amazing accuracy of this prophecy given around 170 years before it happened, and quite out of character with the times. (Powerful nations in the time of Isaiah did not release captives and encourage them to rebuild their temples.) Help the class also to understand that Cyrus, who was appointed by the Lord as a 'shepherd' *(44.28)*, was also a picture of an even greater 'Shepherd' Who would come still later in history. God gave Cyrus, the liberator, to encourage the Jews to know that a time was coming when the Messiah, the greatest Shepherd and Liberator (of souls), would come. In chapters seven and nine of his book, Isaiah records what God revealed to him about this special Shepherd.

(3) **A virgin bearing a child** – a unique event in history. The name of the child indicated that He was no mere mortal. It was *Immanuel* [God with us] *(Isaiah 7.14)*. At this point teachers could explain that the Jewish nation had long been told that God intended to send them a Saviour; a Messiah; a Christ; a Deliverer. They tended to think that He would be a great and glorious earthly king, who would save their nation and make it a

powerful empire, with riches and power. They assumed He would be born in a kingly palace in Jerusalem, but Isaiah discouraged their speculation by telling them that the Messiah would appear first to the people of Galilee, a lowly, cosmopolitan, northern province *(Isaiah 9.1-2)*. We now know that, although the Lord Jesus was born in Bethlehem, He grew up in Nazareth and was known as a Galilean. Show the children how accurate the prophet was in this matter.

(4) **A stem of Jesse,** a Branch out of his roots *(Isaiah 11.1-10)*. Isaiah's next picture was of a tree stump. The trunk had been felled, and the tree appeared dead. Suddenly the seemingly dead root put out a new shoot, indicating new life from the tree. Tell the class that this turned out to be a perfect description of the Lord Jesus Who was born in Bethlehem to Mary, a virgin, at a time when His nation seemed to be finished, in the sense that God no longer blessed them and the Romans had taken control of their land. But Christ (the new stem) arose to draw people throughout the world to the God of the Bible. John the Baptist was sent to announce His arrival.

Pass on quickly to the chief and most important prophecy. As Isaiah looked into his 'telescope', the shadows disappeared and he began to see very clearly the picture of the coming Messiah. But instead of a great and majestic figure, he at first saw a quite different person:

(5) **A man of sorrows,** from Whom people turned away. Teachers should read verses from *Isaiah 53*. Emphasise the words – despised, rejected, wounded, bruised, chastised, bearing the marks (stripes) of beating, oppressed, afflicted, dumb, cut off, and buried with the wicked (vv 3-9). Aim to shock the class with this distressing picture. Summarise it with feeling. Ask the class if they recognise the description. Ask Who this suffering Person might be. Ask why the Saviour, the Lord Jesus, was treated so. Point out (a) the extreme accuracy of this prophecy, though so unexpected. (Surely only the Lord God could have put this vision into the mind of Isaiah 700 years before the events, for no human being could have guessed that God's Messiah would appear in such a manner.) And then point out (b) the importance of the words that follow,

explaining precisely why the Saviour had to bear such great suffering. It was for our transgressions; He was bruised for our iniquities, healing us from the stripes of our sins (vv 4-8).

Remind older classes that the Lord Jesus did not die unexpectedly, or by accident, but He intended to allow this to happen. From early in His ministry He identified Himself as the Messiah of *Isaiah (Luke 4.17-21)*, and frequently spoke of His death as the great purpose of His coming. He allowed Himself to be arrested in apparent weakness, and to be crucified. Why?

Go on to describe the next scene to be witnessed and predicted by Isaiah as his vision takes him well into future history. Once again he foretells events completely unexpected and unwanted by the majority of his nation, the Israelites or Jews. He sees:

(6) The Gospel preached to gentiles *(Isaiah 49.22; 60.3; 62.2; 66.12, 19)*. Tell the children how Isaiah described that the Gospel would be taken to *the ends of the earth (Isaiah 45.22)*. This task was given by the Lord to His disciples, and its beginning described in the *Book of Acts*. In the twentieth century, with the Bible now translated into over 2,000 languages, and with the Christian church witnessing internationally, we see the prophecy fulfilled. But at the time of Christ, the idea must have seemed impossible, and at the time of Isaiah, even more impossible! Yet, Isaiah's vision turned out to be true.

Bring the lesson to conclusion by looking very briefly at the closing chapters of Isaiah's book. Emphasise to your class that the six previous points are now fulfilled. It only remains for these last events predicted by Isaiah to come to pass. Should not people prepare for them? As we peer into Isaiah's 'telescope' for a summary of Earth's closing days, we see his vision of the time when the Lord would create –

(7) New heavens and a new Earth *(Isaiah 65.17; 66.22)*. (These were seen again in a vision by the writer of the last book of the Bible.) Ask the class if they are ready for that great day, when the Saviour, Who once came to suffer and die for those who would be saved, will return for the day of judgement. Tell how at that time He will destroy this old, sinful world, and create a new one. Warn them never to ignore the prophecies of

God's Word, so many of which have already been fulfilled. Urge them in the words of Isaiah to – Seek the Lord while He may be found, call upon Him while He is near, forsake their wicked ways and thoughts, and return to God, for He will have mercy and abundantly pardon (see *Isaiah 55.6-7*).

Visual Aid

See VA 3 on page 47.

The Word for Sinners (146)
King Manasseh

2 Chronicles 33.1-20; 2 Kings 21.1-16

Aim: To show how God saved one of the vilest sinners that ever lived. Also, to teach the meaning of the Bible's great themes, grace and mercy, and to persuade the children of their need of these.

Teachers' Introduction

Manasseh's life seems to be little known to present-day Christians. Yet his conversion must qualify as one of the most amazing ever recorded. His father, Hezekiah, had an almost unblemished record as ruler of the Lord's people, so Manasseh's sins were the blatant conduct of one who had the advantage of a wonderful example. Yet his life of vice and idolatry was such that it matched the worst abominations of the heathen who had been expelled from the land (*2 Chronicles 33.2-3*).

Today, when we hear of so many supposed converts whose testimonies reflect so little conviction of sin, we are bound to notice the great humbling which preceded Manasseh's return to the Lord. This lesson will enable us to describe the nature of real repentance, so necessary as part of a true work of grace in any heart.

Object Lesson – Lightning

Today's lesson reminds us of the power of God, which could be compared with the most dramatic and powerful form of light – a flash of lightning. Children will remember the eerie darkness which precedes a storm. Suddenly the lightning strikes. At night the whole sky is lit up. One bolt is charged with 100 million volts of electricity. One stroke of lightning has sufficient latent power to supply the average household for two years!

The Word of God similarly has great power, as today's lesson demonstrates. Hardened, wicked sinners can be changed and transformed by its power in a moment of time (eg: Manasseh, the apostle Paul, Martin Luther). Proud empires have fallen in days at the command of God (eg: Belshazzar's Babylonian empire), and the effect of the Bible on the world's history cannot be measured.

Lesson Outline

A rebel. Remind the class about Hezekiah, and how he turned the nation of Judah back to worship the Lord. Because he served the Lord and prayed to Him, even the mighty Sennacherib could not defeat him. Ask what kind of son you would expect such a king to have. But instead of young Manasseh being a devout believer as we might expect, we discover that from an early age he flagrantly rebelled against everything his father stood for.

(1) He worshipped pagan gods (2 Chronicles 33.1-3). All the altars to heathen gods which Hezekiah had destroyed, Manasseh rebuilt. Not content to restore Baal alone, he worshipped *all the host of heaven.* He became involved in the worship of numerous pagan gods. This was a deliberate insult to God, as if he was trying to say, 'I would rather worship anything than You!'

Show that men and women, boys and girls, have always been guilty of this attitude towards their Maker and Creator. Jesus described it in the parable of the Prodigal Son. When the prodigal had accepted his father's money, he moved as far away from him as possible. Show how even from earliest childhood we prefer almost any other novelty or activity to serving and knowing the Lord our God.

(2) He erected heathen altars in the Temple (2 Chronicles 33.4-5, 7). Help the children to feel real disgust at Manasseh's behaviour by describing how he went to the extreme of erecting pagan altars and images in the Temple itself! This could only be interpreted as calculated abuse of the God to Whom Manasseh owed all – his lofty position and his kingdom. It could be compared to a husband committing adultery in his wife's own bedroom. Remind the class that these gods and idols were worshipped for all the sensual orgies that went with them. This encouraged every extreme of vile behaviour among the people.

(3) He opened the flood-gates of wickedness (vv 6, 9). Go on to list all the other evils and vices which were practised by those who worshipped these idols. Witchcraft flourished, with all the fear, extortion and evil that went with it. (Manasseh's own children were victims.) Tell your class that one sin always leads to another. We may feel quite good as children, never having been involved in serious wrongdoing, but if we are living away from the Lord, all our faults will develop and enlarge either in outward sins, or in the hidden rottenness of the personality.

(4) He abandoned justice. Alongside all this, Manasseh was such an unjust tyrant that he allowed people to get away with all kinds of injustice in his kingdom. The guilty had their wrong-doing overlooked, while their victims were left unprotected. Many innocent people suffered hardship and even death *(2 Kings 21.16)*.

(5) He ignored God's warning *(2 Chronicles 33.10)*. God was disgusted with Manasseh, and had every right to judge him immediately. But such was His kindness that He *spake to Manasseh, and to his people.* But *they would not hearken.* We do not deserve that God should have any dealings with us after the way we have treated Him either, but He appeals to us to seek His mercy and love, and also warns us through His Word. Above all, He sent His Son to die for us.

The work of grace. Draw up a charge list against Manasseh. Ask the class what their verdict would be. Never was there a clearer case of a sinner deserving judgement. Yet by the end of our lesson we shall see that Manasseh *knew that the Lord he was God* (v 13), and he began to try to put things right when he returned to Judah. What brought about this amazing change? The answer is – God had worked in his heart in an act of *grace*.

Ask the class, what does the word *grace* mean? It is easy to learn and remember. It means *undeserved and unearned favour.* Even a criminal would be disgusted by Manasseh's record. But when a person is saved by the Lord it is not because he deserves it or earns it, but because God in His love takes pity upon him and freely pardons and blesses him. How did the Lord so dramatically save this hardened sinner?

(1) The Lord afflicted him, and brought him into desperate trouble (v 11). The Assyrian army took him captive, chained him up and took him off to Babylon. Manasseh was dragged like a slave through the streets of Babylon to the sneers and jeers of the people, and then he was dumped into the city gaol. Only then did his stony heart begin to crack. As he sat day after day in the dark cell, he remembered how the Lord had protected his father from a far larger force. Then he began to see that he deserved only punishment from God.

He thought with horror of the way he had treated the Lord. Why? Had he any reason to insult the Lord? Was it not God Who had given him a kingdom and a rich inheritance? And what had he done with these? He had used them to mock and to bait his God. His sin had affected others too. Little children had been sacrificed to idols and women terrorised. Many had been drawn under the spell of religious prostitutes. Manasseh must have thought deeply about all his many sins while in his prison. How he must have wished that he had never rebelled against God.

(2) The Lord humbled him. As a young man, his sin had all been a joke – a way of boasting of his independence. Now with horror he saw the vileness and the ugliness of his deeds and he *humbled himself greatly before the God of his fathers* (v 12). He was so deeply ashamed he could scarcely think. He realised he had also betrayed the trust of his father and so many others. What a wretch and a worm he was! It began to dawn on him that the Lord never overlooks sin, and even devout men like his father had been rebuked by the Lord for their shortcomings. What would God do to him?

(3) The Lord forgave him. Help the class to visualise the way in which the Lord dealt with the repentant Manasseh, following the account from *2 Chronicles 33.13-19*. Explain how God's Spirit moved in the prodigal king's heart:

(a) He *remembered* the God of his fathers, the God of the Bible, the God Whose mercy endures for ever. In his prison cell far from home, far from any servant or prophet of God, far from the Temple, he doubtless remembered the sermons of the prophet Isaiah, and the words of the psalms he had learned as a child. Perhaps some of the verses of *Psalm 103*, a psalm written by King David, came into his mind, *Bless the Lord, O my soul . . . who forgiveth all thine iniquities; who healeth all thy diseases . . . He hath not dealt with us after our sins; nor rewarded us according to our iniquities. For as the heaven is high above the earth, so great is his mercy toward them that fear him* (vv 2-3, 10-11).

(b) What we are certain of is that he began to *pray* to David's and Hezekiah's God, entreating Him to forgive him and answer his supplications *(2 Chronicles 33.13)*.

(c) He *confessed all* his sin and guilt, remembering the wicked and treacherous things he had done. Then he pleaded with the Lord to forgive him.

(4) The Lord changed him. The Bible account then tells us how God heard Manasseh's prayers. Not only did the Lord forgive him, but He brought him back to Jerusalem. Ask the children what they would expect him to have done once he returned home. Tell them how he strengthened the city and its walls, and took away the pagan gods and their altars from the Temple courts, casting them out of the city (vv 14-16). He then repaired the Lord's altars and recommenced the sacrifices to the true God. Help the class see that this was the outward proof of his inward conversion. Perhaps they might have thought that his repentance in prison was a passing phase. His willingness to make a public and open reversal of his policy when he returned to old surroundings proves the opposite. He had become a new man. Conversion really does entirely change people.

Learning from Manasseh. Apply the experience of Manasseh by pointing out the lessons to be learned. Above all, the forgiveness and restoration of Manasseh is unquestionably an example of the Lord's lovingkindness and mercy to one of the vilest offenders. In no way did Manasseh deserve to be numbered amongst the Lord's people. Yet he was. As we apply his testimony to our classes we shall be able to – (a) Encourage those who may consider themselves outside the scope of salvation because of the sinfulness of their behaviour, or that of the circle in which they move. Assure them there is 'none too vile or loathsome for a Saviour's grace'. (b) Remind ourselves and the children from Christian families that no one deserves God's kindness. It is always a matter of His wonderful mercy and grace that any human is saved, for none of us is righteous, no, not one *(Romans 3.9-19)*. (c) Emphasise that should any child, sadly, turn away from the Lord in years to come, and then be convicted of their sinful ways in later life, it is still possible for them (as it was with Manasseh) to repent and be forgiven.

Ask the children if they have prayed to God as Manasseh prayed, a real and earnest prayer, begging forgiveness and admitting the wrong things they have done. Ask if they have ever known what it feels like to be forgiven and changed by the Lord. Remind them that God still reaches out in mercy and grace to sinners of all kinds. His grace is always undeserved and unearned, and is very powerful.

The Word Rediscovered (147)
King Josiah

2 Kings 22 – 23.28; 2 Chronicles 34 – 35

Aim: To open the eyes of our children, enabling them to see that our modern, atheistic society, with its scorn of morality, has much in common with the 7th century BC. It is a step backward, not forward. Also to describe how King Josiah sought the Lord from an early age and fought evil. Finally, to remind the class that the way back to God begins at Calvary's cross.

Object Lesson – A Torchlight for Searching for Lost Items

Sometimes we use a torch to search for an item we know is lost, perhaps in a shed, an attic, a cellar, or in the depths of a large, dark cupboard. Remind the class of the woman who searched for her lost coin, using a candle to find it *(Luke 15)*. Sometimes, however, we make an unexpected discovery while using a torch. Its bright beam suddenly lights up an item which we had lost and forgotten. Today's lesson is about such a discovery.

Lesson Outline

Remind the class that we have seen how the people of Israel and Judah were constantly attracted to the immoral gods of the nations around them. They had experienced a period of godliness under good King Hezekiah, but once he was dead they had quickly returned to the worship of Baal, and to a worse extent than before. This happened under Manasseh, and also under his son Amon. Manasseh's conversion and reforms were not wholeheartedly welcomed by his subjects *(2 Chronicles 33.17)*. When at the age of eight Josiah inherited the throne, Baal-worship was well entrenched.

(1) **Young Josiah seeks the Lord.** Tell the class how, in spite of the prevalent culture, Josiah at sixteen parted company with the evil of his days and *began to seek after the God of David his father (2 Chronicles 34.3).* Remind the class that:

(a) The Bible urges *all* young people and children to remember their Creator. The Scriptures give David, Samuel, Josiah, Daniel, Timothy and others as examples of young believers.

(b) This could not have been an easy step for Josiah to take – a young person (even a king) who refused to join in the sinful pleasures and pastimes of his age-group would be ridiculed and hated. Encourage your class to follow his courageous example.

(c) Josiah died aged 39 years, yet he had done great good in Judah. If he had postponed his search for the Lord until he was middle-aged, he would have missed that opportunity to influence others for good. Warn the class that death sometimes comes suddenly and unexpectedly. Urge them to make the best use of childhood and early years.

(2) **Josiah's campaign against evil.** Make this lesson very relevant to the children by demonstrating that the present surge of atheism (with its vicious campaign against morality) is nothing new. These chapters from the Old Testament show how similar that moral climate was to the state of affairs today.

The evils which confronted Josiah have a very familiar ring about them. Practices which he outlawed as evil and barbaric are now back.

Following the account from *2 Kings 23*, we read of:

(a) The worship of Baal (v 4). Explain that the people of Judah gathered at the high places and the special copses where they indulged in the fertility rites of Baal worshippers. Ask the children whether in our day it is necessary to travel to hilltops and tree-surrounded altars to witness immorality. Point out that nowadays people can sit at home and have these things paraded before them by video and on television. Or they can go to see an immoral type of film. In addition, they are encouraged to get together to stir up their lusts by the beat of erotic music, with their senses dulled by lights and drugs. Today people are doing much the same as the ancient Baal worshippers, believing that it is all new and enlightened.

(b) The worship of sun, moon, planets and the host of heaven (v 5). Josiah's subjects had abandoned the serious and rational worship of the God of the Bible, the Maker of Heaven. They went outdoors to worship non-existent 'gods' with a superstitious fervour. Draw parallels with our society. The children will be familiar with the emphasis on environmental issues and New Age propaganda. Although it is right that the human race should take good care of the environment, this worthy aim is ruined by people who think the Earth is part of God. They are trying to lure people into thinking that the universe is God, and *we* are God too! This is what they want people to think. They do not believe in the real God, Who made us and the Earth, and Who is above us. Warn the children to watch out for this brand of 'green' and 'ecology' teaching! Show them magazine cuttings. Point out that whereas such articles insist that the environment is to be preserved and protected, there is a deafening silence about the Creator Himself. This new cult has also promoted a return to astrology even among educated people, including a recent president of the USA. Once people turn away from God they soon plunge into superstition and occult thinking.

(c) How Josiah broke down the houses of the sodomites which were near to the house of the Lord (v 7). Whereas as Sunday School teachers we would prefer not to have to mention this subject, yet we have a duty to older classes to at least indicate that all such behaviour is inexcusable and sinful in the sight of God. It is condemned in the Bible *(Leviticus 18.22; Romans 1.26-27)*. We may owe it to our young people, who are the victims of a lying campaign on this theme, to make a brief, careful statement, so they learn the truth about God's standards. It will probably be wisest to tell younger groups how Josiah banished those involved in unspeakable evils.

A brief summary for younger classes. Teachers of younger classes may like to approach this part of the lesson by telling the class briefly that Josiah had horrible and evil things to forbid and deal with. People were dancing and singing to the invented god, Baal. This religion did not mind how much people sinned. In addition, rather than yield to the true God, they worshipped the things He had made, imagining the sun and the moon could help them! Tell the children that they will come across many shameful things done by adults today. Urge them not to be drawn into things of this nature but to be like Josiah, and to serve the true God.

(3) Josiah leads a return to the Bible. Describe the wonderful change that came about in Jerusalem as the priests and people set about cleaning and restoring the Temple. Mention that no financial accounts had to be kept of the offerings, for the priests and workers could now be trusted *(2 Kings 22.7)* – a practical proof of their return to the Lord and His ways.

A great discovery. It was as the people demonstrated their real sorrow for past behaviour, and their desire to put things right, that they made a wonderful discovery. Hidden, perhaps in a dusty corner of the Temple, the priests came across a very old copy of the Scriptures, a book of the law of the Lord given by Moses *(2 Chronicles 34.14)*. Their response was not to wrap it up or put it in a museum, but to take it urgently to the king. Josiah was deeply troubled to learn that for many years the nation had forgotten and neglected the instructions of the Lord given in this book. He immediately set about putting the matter right, asking for the Lord's pardon, and calling the people to hear the book read *(2 Chronicles 34.19-33)*. Describe the solemn promises which Josiah made to the Lord in the presence of the people, and their willingness to follow his lead.

Ask the class when they last read the Bible seriously and asked the Lord to help them obey its teaching. Explain that the Bible alone has power to change the hearts of men, women and children.

(4) Josiah returns to 'Calvary' *(2 Chronicles 35.1-19)*. This point enables teachers to explain that although we cannot be saved without earnestly repenting, yet repentance cannot and will not save us. Only faith and trust in the Saviour and His death on Calvary can take away guilt, and make us fit for Heaven.

(a) Judgement. Describe Josiah's horror as he listened to God's Word. He realised that he and his people had so often disobeyed and neglected God's ways and laws. He heard how the Lord warned of judgement and punishment for those who were guilty of breaking His covenant. He feared the great anger of God upon them. Point out to the children that the reading of the Bible can make us tremble as we realise that the sins we treat so lightly and do so frequently (lying, stealing, hating, etc) will one day be judged by God.

(b) Salvation. Thankfully, Josiah also heard how Moses had instructed the people to keep a yearly feast – the feast of Passover *(Exodus 12.24)*. Depending on the knowledge of your class, ask or remind the children briefly how the feast of Passover taught the people about the grace and lovingkindness of the Lord God towards His chosen people:

(i) That way back in the days of their sin, slavery and weakness in the land of Egypt, He had taken pity and come to their rescue mightily by judging the Egyptians and setting His people free.

(ii) That the Lord had said it was only those houses which carried the marks (blood stains) of a spotless lamb, which would be passed over by the angel who brought death to the God-provoking Egyptians.

Soon after they heard the Scriptures read, Josiah and his people gathered in Jerusalem to keep solemnly the Passover feast in a way not observed since the days of Samuel. They acknowledged their dependence on the Lord's grace and willingness to forgive, and the Lord was true to His promise and postponed His judgement on the nation until after the days of Josiah.

Assure your class that the same God is willing to pardon and forgive them too. Remind them that the Lord Jesus Christ said that He was the spotless Lamb of God, Who had come to bear away sin for all who trust in Him. It was His death which would enable a holy God to punish sin and save them.

However repentant we might try to be, we can never make up for our past and future sins. But, just as for Josiah, the Lord wonderfully reveals to us that He has provided us with a Saviour, the Lord Jesus, Who has taken the punishment of sin for all who repent.

Visual Aid

(1) A scroll from which the teacher can read about the forgotten Passover can be hidden before the lesson and 'discovered' at the appropriate point in the lesson. (2) Pictures of the Passover feast.

The Word Under Attack (148)
Jeremiah the Prophet

2 Chronicles 35.25-36.32; Jeremiah 1.1-8; 2.1-13; 4.3-31; 7.1-16; 19; 20.1-9; 26.7-15; 31.31-34; 33.1-18; 36.20-23; 37.11-21; 38; 39.15-18. (Teachers are advised to read *2 Chronicles 36* first which will give a brief overview of the events which took place during Jeremiah's ministry.)

Aim: To summarise the importance and trustworthiness of God's Word even in years of great opposition, and to urge the children to take its message to heart.

Teachers' Introduction

We could not conclude a series on the Word of God without demonstrating its resilience to the attacks made on it down the running centuries. Over and over again we see mankind's irrational rejection of God's call of grace and mercy, and its bitter hostility towards the message of salvation.

Jeremiah could not have presented his warnings and pleadings more tenderly, yet his message was met with scorn and

derision and he was persecuted cruelly. Despite all the antagonism the Word of God proved unassailable, and we see how
Jeremiah's predictions were completely accurate not only in the
immediate future but also in the long term. We can indicate to
our classes that this is a pattern which has often been repeated
in the annals of history. God's own Son met with a similar attitude when He came to Earth, but although He was crucified,
His words have and will achieve all that He planned they should
(Isaiah 55.11).

Object Lesson – The Sun – An Inextinguishable Light

At the conclusion of this series show the children a dramatic
picture of the sun, the source of all our light. Encourage them to
think for a moment what a massive source of light it is. Imagine
trying to turn the sun's light off! Imagine trying to black out a
modern city at noon! Almost impossible!

Point out that throughout history people have tried by
various means to black out and hide God's Word, but such
plans are doomed to failure. The Bible, and its message, has
been despised, ridiculed, forbidden, burned, and even kept in a
classical language so that most people would never be able to
read it. Those who have believed it have been imprisoned,
stoned, put in labour camps and persecuted in many cruel ways.

However, the light of God's Word, like the sun, shines just as
brightly. Today's lesson describes the futile efforts made to
smother the light of God's Word in the days of Jeremiah.

Lesson Outline

(1) **God's love refused.** Remind the class of the special
favour and love of God to the people of Israel for over a thousand years. From the days of Abraham to the reign of David,
and then to the time of their remarkable preservation under
King Hezekiah, they had experienced God's kindness in many
ways. But no matter what He did for them, the vast majority
turned away from Him, and worshipped the pathetic gods of
the surrounding nations, gods made of wood and stone. Pagan
religions overlooked and encouraged all kinds of sin and moral
perversion, including even the sacrifice of young children.

(2) **God's warning ignored.** At this time a young man
named Jeremiah, the son of a priest, was sent to deliver the

Lord's message. He courageously took his stand in a prominent, public place close to the Temple, where some of these pagan atrocities were carried out, and denounced them. He warned the people of Judah that the Lord was about to send King Nebuchadnezzar, the king of Babylon, with his powerful army to overthrow, destroy and burn their city *(Jeremiah 4.3-31)*. However, they took no notice, hiding behind a superstitious belief that God would never allow the Temple to fall into enemy hands. Far from taking Jeremiah's warning seriously, they continued to flout God's laws and ignore the threat of military siege *(7.1-16)*.

Jeremiah saw catastrophe drawing closer daily, and he tried every means to persuade, plead with and urge them to change course. Once he used a very down-to-earth illustration which no one could fail to understand. Living in days before running water was on tap in every home, he compared them with people who lived close to a fountain of fresh, cool, clean water which gushed out of the hillside and was freely available. However, in Jeremiah's 'parable', those people behaved in a way that was beyond belief and explanation, for they ignored that nearby fountain, and instead scraped pails of polluted water from the bottom of a dug-out cistern or tank, which had become broken *(Jeremiah 2.13)*.

Jeremiah reasoned that forsaking the Lord, Who made Heaven and Earth, for gods which were not gods was just as foolish. As he condemned them, their consciences were pierced, and they knew inwardly they were guilty. However, they would not admit it. And to avoid Jeremiah's challenging preaching, they turned against it and tried to silence the messenger. This is what happened:

(3) God's servant tortured. (a) Describe how Jeremiah was struck by Pashur, chief governor of the house of the Lord, who put him in the stocks in order to humiliate and ridicule him. This was done in a public place at the gate leading into the Temple *(Jeremiah 20.1-6)*.

(b) Tell how the priests and prophets campaigned for his death *(26.7-11)*.

(c) Picture the scene as Jeremiah's words were read to King

Jehoiakim by Jehudi, and this king cut the scroll leaf by leaf, and contemptuously tossed it into the fire *(36.20-24)*.

(d) Explain how the princes imprisoned Jeremiah, where he remained in a dungeon cell for many days *(37.15-16)*.

(e) Stir the children's indignation by telling how they took Jeremiah and threw him down a dried-up well in a dungeon, the bottom of which was mire, where they hoped he would soon die of starvation *(38.1-6)*. He was rescued through the action of a gentile believer named Ebedmelech, who made ropes of rags and worn-out clothes and lifted him out of the well *(38.7-13)*.

(4) God's Word opposed today. Discuss with your class – according to their age – the methods which have been used in the centuries since the time of Christ to silence God's Word.

(a) By violent means (force). You could tell them something of Tyndale's experiences. Bring the survey up to date by informing them of the persecution of believers in countries behind the Iron Curtain in recent times, and the vicious punishment of Christian evangelists in Moslem lands today.

(b) By derisive means (scorn). Ask how God's Word is silenced in our land. Describe the devil's subtlety in discrediting the Bible and giving it the image of an out-dated book of myths. This is done by some schoolteachers. It is also done in television programmes. Instead of fighting the Lord's people with physical threats, the devil nowadays aims to prevent anyone listening to their message.

(c) By counterfeit means (deceit). Describe the devil's subtlety in using false religions – whether 'Christian' or non-Christian – to divert attention from the only Truth which can save souls. It is still the case that many religious leaders are the most vicious opponents of the Bible's message, yet they pose as the advocates of God!

Jeremiah's words come true. After his rescue by the Ethiopian, Jeremiah spoke to King Zedekiah and gave him a graphic account of the capture and burning of Jerusalem which was soon to happen. He pressed the king to surrender, but Zedekiah lived in fear of his princes and stubbornly remained in the capital. Before long the mighty Nebuchadnezzar besieged

Jerusalem, burned houses, including the king's, and broke down the walls. He killed Zedekiah's sons, and he removed Zedekiah's eyes, leading him in fetters to Babylon. Only a few were left in Judah including Jeremiah who was set free from the prison house by the Babylonians *(40.1-6)*. Most of the Jews were taken captive to Babylon. Some went to Egypt, against Jeremiah's advice, but even then they did not repent or seek the Lord and further humiliation ensued.

Still Jeremiah pleaded with them to see the error of their ways. *Because ye have burned incense, and because ye have sinned against the Lord . . . therefore this evil is happened unto you (44.23)*. Convey this same message to your class. All kinds of evil and suffering have overtaken our world. When will we acknowledge that it is because we have forsaken the Lord?

Jeremiah's message of hope: (a) Of a Saviour to come *(Jeremiah 33.15)*. Tell the children how a plant or tree which seems to be dead can suddenly send up a new, vibrant shoot, which brings it back to life. As Jerusalem was overrun and humiliated in defeat, Jeremiah was able to reassure all who looked to the Lord that in future days He would raise up a *Branch of righteousness*, the Lord Jesus Christ, Whose kingdom would last for ever. God's promises never fail.

(b) Of a better covenant *(31.31-34)*. In these future days, the Lord would make a new and better covenant. Instead of it being a matter of outward, national religion, God would make a covenant written in the hearts of individual people, who would love and know Him in a personal way. However much the world opposes the Lord and His Word, a great company of people *will* believe in Christ.

(c) To Ebedmelech *(39.18)*. In closing, remind the children that, even in days of national disaster and defeat, God's purposes of love and kindness were never forgotten. As the enemy closed in, God, through Jeremiah, gave wonderful promises to this Ethiopian believer, *I will surely deliver thee . . . because thou hast put thy trust in me.* Encourage young believers to stand for the Lord, no matter what other people may do. To seek and find Him is the most important issue in life. He gives to believers a new nature, and He guides and blesses them greatly all through life. Then, when He comes to judge our world, believers will rejoice. Remember also that nations and empires come and go, but God's Word will shine on to the end of time, and its predictions will be proved correct for ever.

Visual Aid

Refer to the map of Jerusalem (VA 10, page 145) and provide a picture of the Temple gates where Jeremiah delivered many of his messages. Brightly coloured pictures of stocks, a roll of 'paper', a penknife, a blazing fire, and a dungeon/well will interest the children and help them appreciate the hostility Jeremiah faced. Use three arrows to show the devil's three-pronged attack today [see section (4), above].

The Word Fulfilled (149)
Revision

Lesson references and Jeremiah 31.31-34

Aim: To discover how much the children have learned from this present series, both factually and spiritually.

Teachers' Introduction

This series has covered a long period of Bible history filled with strong salvation themes. Revision is therefore particularly important and this lesson should be utilised fully. It can be adapted by each teacher to suit the needs of the class. It could be based on the different kinds of light which the Bible provides for those who love it, as we have shown. (If teachers prefer, they can use VA 1, page 19, and base their questions on this.)

(140) **Runway lights** – which guide. The kings we learned about give us an example of how to love and trust the Lord. What did the Lord do for them? Describe the amazing battles He enabled them to win. How can the Lord help us?

(141) **My own light** – which enables me not to rely on others. Name the king who appeared to love the Lord but whose love disappeared when his godly guardian-uncle died. How old was he when he became king? Why had he been hidden? Do we have a place in Heaven just because our parents

or our Sunday School teachers are Christians? How can we tell if we ourselves are true Christians? How many tests can you remember?

(142) A lighthouse – which warns of danger. Which prophets were sent to warn the people of Israel that their godlessness would be followed by judgement? Name some of the evil practices which they condemned. How did the Lord bring about judgement on the northern kingdom? Will God overlook our lying, stealing and cheating?

(143) Security lights – which protect. Hezekiah put his trust in the Lord and was protected in the most frightening of situations. What king was threatening him? What happened to this king's mighty army? Who and what are *our* worst enemies? How can we escape their power?

(144) Daylight – which brings to light unseen facts. The Bible deals with facts, and can be archaeologically and historically authenticated. Describe at least one tablet of stone which lay hidden in the sand for many years but which can now be seen in the British Museum, and which verifies the Bible's account of Hezekiah's times. What did a boy discover in the tunnel leading from the pool of Siloam? Which king recorded his battles on stone 'wallpaper'?

(145) Infra-red light – which enables people to see in the dark. What hidden events of the future did Isaiah clearly 'see' and predict? How many have already taken place? Which events are still to come? How can we prepare for them?

(146) Lightning – which is unexpected and powerful. Manasseh was a man who had committed foul sins. Whose power alone could cleanse and save him? Where was Manasseh when the Lord's Spirit struck home to him? Think of ways in which the Lord may humble us, before we acknowledge our need of a Saviour. What does the word 'grace' mean when it is used in the Bible?

(147) Torchlight – which is used for searching. Which king discovered portions of God's Word in the Temple as it was being restored? Why was he concerned? What did he do? Why did he please the Lord more than any other king *(2 Kings*

23.25)? When did he first seek the Lord? When should we seek the Lord?

(148) The sun – which is an inextinguishable light. It is impossible to shut out sunlight from the world, and impossible to frustrate God's Word. Which prophet did the people of Judah try to silence? What did they do to him? Tell how his words came true. Can we afford to ignore God's Word?

Conclusion. From these lessons the children should be equipped to appreciate for themselves how foolish and misinformed it is to be critical of the Bible. If we have succeeded in our task, those who give the impression that it is nothing more than ancient myth and legend will be seen as ignorant and prejudiced.

Remind the children that all will still be lost if they have nothing more than mental respect for the Scriptures. So often the Jews, about whom we have been hearing, respected God's Word outwardly, but failed to act on it. This is not enough for the Lord. Turn the class to Jeremiah's prophecy in *Jeremiah 31.33*. Explain how God is only satisfied when His Word is written on our *hearts*, and we believe what it teaches about our sin, our need to repent and our need of a Saviour.

The following verse (v 34) suggests a very practical test. If we have truly believed and received God's Word then we shall know the Lord, and our sins will be forgiven. In case the children think this is only possible for adults, remind them that this verse says that it includes the least to the greatest. Even a young child can come to know the Lord. Ask the children – Have they taken God's Word to heart? Have they asked the Saviour to forgive their sin? Do they know Him for themselves? If not, urge them to continue their search, using God's Word as a lamp to their feet, and a light to their path.

Series 18
Matthew's Gospel (Part II)

THE LIFE, DEATH AND RESURRECTION OF THE LORD JESUS CHRIST

150 – The Saviour – Confessed

The Saviour knows that His work in northern Galilee is almost complete and soon He must travel to Jerusalem. He has some important questions to ask the disciples (for *their* sakes, because He already knows the answers) – Who do the public think He is? Who do they say He is? Who do *you* say Christ is? Will you be willing to follow Him even when the way is hard?

151 – The Saviour – Confirmed

When the Lord goes to a high mountain to pray, He is transfigured into His heavenly glory. Moses and Elijah appear and speak with Him, and the voice of God the Father is heard saying, *This is my beloved Son . . . hear ye him.* Peter, James and John never forgot this remarkable event. We can learn from it too.

152 – The Saviour – Welcomed

There is great excitement in Jerusalem as the miracle-working prophet from Galilee approaches the city, and great crowds come out to welcome Him. He is more than a prophet and miracle-worker. The events of this great day have been predicted hundreds of years beforehand. Some days later the Lord Jesus weeps over Jerusalem as its people and leaders refuse His message. Will you refuse His lovingkindness too?

153 – The Saviour – Returning

The Lord Jesus pictures Himself as a bridegroom Who will return to take His bride home. When the day finally arrives, some people will be caught unprepared. Will that include you? Or will you be one of those ready and waiting for the great day?

154 – The Saviour – Rejected

The Lord Jesus pictures our world as a vineyard which has been taken over by a bunch of violent, greedy workers. He predicts that people will soon kill Him and complete their 'take-over'. People today imagine they can take over God's world, but they will not succeed for long!

155 – The Saviour – Arrested and Condemned

He is betrayed with a kiss, tried at dead of night, slandered by false witnesses, and sentenced for being called *the Son of God* – which He is! He undergoes a travesty of a trial. One day the tables will be turned and men and women will all appear before His judgement seat. The trial will be open, fair and just. More wonderful still, the Judge has already paid the punishment Himself on behalf of all who desire His mercy.

156 – The Saviour – Sentenced

'A murderer they save, the Prince of life they slay.' What madness drives these people to demand the crucifixion of the Lord of Glory? Whose fault was it that Jesus died? There are several answers to this question, but over and above them all is the fact that the Lord Jesus laid down His life for His 'sheep'. Are you moved by such love?

157 – The Saviour – Crucified

No deeper disgrace could be devised in Jewish eyes than to be hanged on a tree outside the city boundary. The Lord Jesus is forsaken by His beloved Father until the price of our sin is paid. Why did He endure such agony and pain? What did He gain for us? How much do His children owe Him? What language can we borrow to thank Him?

158 – The Saviour – Risen

The fact that the Lord's dead body has been placed in a stone tomb, under guard, makes it hard for the disciples to believe the words of the angels – *He is not here: for he is risen.* But after appearing to many people on many occasions in a real body, it becomes obvious to all that He is the risen Saviour, the Son of God. He has fought the fight and won the battle against sin and death and hell for all His people. Why refuse to believe any longer?

159 – The Saviour – the Son of God Indeed (Revision)

People today still speak of Christ as though He were a mere man. Some supposed Christians discuss which aspects of His teaching they can accept, foolishly imagining that He was limited in mind by the education and knowledge of those times. Have we been convinced by Matthew's record that the Lord Jesus Christ was the second Person of the Godhead, the Saviour to Whom every knee will one day bow?

Teachers' Introduction to the Series

Before beginning this series, teachers should reread the 'Teachers' Introduction to the Series' from *Lessons for Life 3*, at the start of 'Matthew's Gospel (Part I)' (pages 195-196).

The Saviour – Confessed (150)
Peter's Answer at Caesarea Philippi

Matthew 16.13-28

Aim: To set the scene for the series with a brief review of the highlights of Christ's life up to the days at Caesarea Philippi, and to challenge the children with the same question that He set His disciples.

Lesson Outline

Using the map in the visual aid (VA 4, page 75), begin by quickly revising the key events which we have already seen in Matthew's Gospel, each of which goes to prove that Jesus was *the Christ, the Son of the living God*, the promised Saviour.

(1) Bethlehem. Varying the question with the age of the class, ask where Christ was born. Remind the children of the uniqueness of His birth – that He was the son of a virgin, because He was the Son of God. Explain that following their escape to Egypt in the dangerous years of Herod's reign, Jesus' parents returned with Him to their home town of Nazareth in the province of Galilee.

(2) Galilee. Remind the class of the outstanding events about which they have heard, which took place in this northern region. (This may be done by means of questions.) Depending on the age of the class mention certain key events:

(a) The miracles – the healing of the sick and disabled, the stilling of the storm, the raising of Jairus' daughter, the feeding of the five thousand, etc.

(b) The teaching of the Lord Jesus, which held huge crowds spellbound, and the wonderful parables so full of meaning, yet so simple, which pointed to the need of forgiveness and a new life as the only way to Heaven.

(c) The opposition of the professional ministers and clergy – the scribes and Pharisees – to Christ's teaching, because He exposed their hypocrisy and drew away their audiences.

(d) The popularity of Jesus with the people, who, in the days before television and modern medicine, walked miles to listen to Him and to be healed by Him.

(3) Caesarea Philippi. Show the children how, after these busy days, the Lord Jesus turned aside to this area where He could talk alone to His disciples. The first question He asked them was, *Whom do men say that I the Son of man am?* The disciples reported that many people thought He must be John the Baptist, Elijah, Jeremiah or some other prophet. This was the most common way of explaining the remarkable powers of the carpenter's son of Nazareth, as they thought of Him. These explanations avoided facing up to the obvious one – that He was the promised Messiah.

(a) 'But whom say ye that I am?' But then the Saviour turned the question towards the disciples themselves, asking, *But whom say ye that I am?* What a question! Can the class imagine what it would feel like to be so directly asked by the Lord Jesus Christ? It is the great question which we must all answer some day. Think of some of the answers people give today. Some think He was one of the world's great religious leaders. Some say He was a good man who set us all an example of gentleness. Some consider Him to have been a misguided and weak person. And some have never given the question any serious thought.

(b) What did Peter reply? Then describe how Simon Peter, so often the spokesman for the twelve disciples, gave his reply clearly, precisely and without hesitation: *Thou art the Christ, the Son of the living God.* They had come to the conclusion that Jesus was none other than the Son of God, the Saviour promised from the beginning of the world. The Lord Jesus effectively told Peter that this certain conviction, given him by His heavenly Father, was the best knowledge he could ever have received. Peter was the first to assert it openly and unashamedly but there would be many others to follow.

(c) How did the Church start? This wholehearted trust in the Lord Jesus as Saviour and God would be the starting point (the rock, the foundation) for all Christians in the years to come. It would be only those people who believed as Peter did that Jesus was the Son of God, the second Person of the Trinity, the Saviour promised from the beginning of time and throughout the Old Testament, who could truly belong to Him and constitute His Church. On this certain rock, namely faith in Christ, the Lord would gather people out of every day and age, out of every land and nation to form His Church, and no enemy would be able to bring it down, not even the powers of hell. Two thousand years later we realise how true these words have proved to be. Despite all the opposition and persecution down the centuries, millions of people the world over know and love Christ, believing in Him just as Peter did at Caesarea Philippi.

The keys of the kingdom. Ask the class if they are yet trusted by their parents to have their own key to their home. It is a sign of trust when the day comes, and adults judge children to be sufficiently responsible to take a door-key and keep it safely. Describe how in Bible times the chief servant or steward was the person trusted with the keys of the house, able to decide who would be admitted and who refused. Show how this illustrates Christ's words to Peter. In the years ahead, Peter and the other

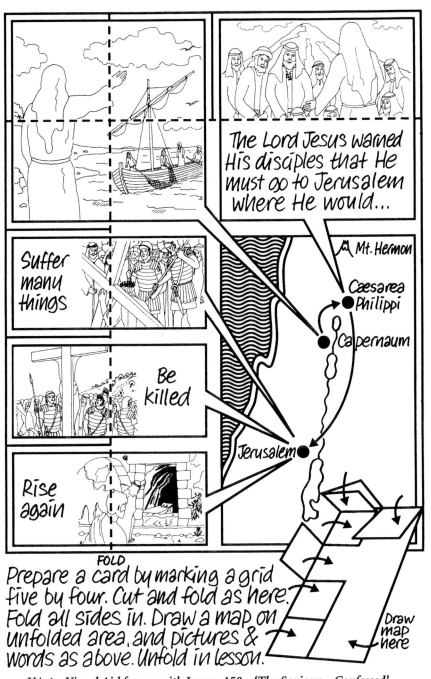

The Lord Jesus warned His disciples that He must go to Jerusalem where He would...

Suffer many things

Be killed

Rise again

Mt. Hermon

Caesarea Philippi

Capernaum

Jerusalem

FOLD

Prepare a card by marking a grid five by four. Cut and fold as here. Fold all sides in. Draw a map on unfolded area, and pictures & words as above. Unfold in lesson.

Draw map here

VA 4 – Visual Aid for use with Lesson 150 – 'The Saviour – Confessed'.

apostles would be entrusted with preaching this soul-saving message of Christ as Saviour, first to the Jews *(Acts 2.14)* and then to the gentiles *(Acts 10)*. Their message, preached and then written as part of the Scriptures, would unlock the kingdom of God to millions who would trust Christ to save them.

For the present, Christ warned His disciples to keep the 'secret' of His real identity as the Messiah. For the moment, when crowds gathered they must see His miracles, and hear His teaching, and come to that same conclusion for themselves. The disciples must not, just yet, tell anyone that Jesus is Christ, because that would bring them under severe persecution from the leading Jews, when in the months ahead they were due to be taught many things which they would need to know for their future work and teaching.

(4) Jerusalem: (a) The disciples' plans. Peter had reached the greatest conclusion in the world, but now the Lord Jesus had to teach him some hard lessons. Peter imagined that to be the Son of God would mean nothing but greatness and glory. He and the other disciples supposed that the Lord would soon claim His kingdom and assert His power in Jerusalem, the capital. They imagined they would receive positions of privilege in that kingdom *(Matthew 20.20-26)*.

(b) The Saviour's plan. Instead, the Lord Jesus began to inform them that He must indeed go to Jerusalem but there He would suffer cruelly at the hands of the religious leaders, be killed and then rise again. Peter was horrified and took Jesus to one side and expressed His abhorrence. This was the last thing he wanted to happen to the Person of Whom he thought so highly, and he told Jesus in no uncertain terms. It was at this point that the Lord Jesus turned to Peter and called him 'Satan'. Can the class think why? What could be wrong in trying to save Jesus from pain and suffering?

(c) The Lord God's plan. Help the class to see that the great purpose of God in sending His Son (predicted so often in the Old Testament, especially clearly in the sacrifices of the Pentateuch, and in *Isaiah*) was that He should offer His life as a sacrifice for our sins. Had there been any other way of forgiving sinful people, the Lord God would have taken it, but such was the foulness of our sin that only the perfect Son of God could bear it away, paying the price for us and setting us free. To suggest that He should avoid this ordeal, would be to frustrate and spoil God's will.

(d) **Satan's plan.** Jesus explained that Peter's plan to save Him from rejection and death would be playing into Satan's hands, ensuring that no sinner would ever be freed from his power, that evil would triumph and our world remain unredeemed. Remind the class that the Lord Jesus knew precisely what must happen to Him when He went to Jerusalem and He went knowingly and willingly to the cross of Calvary.

(e) **A chosen plan.** Children may have heard the idea that the Lord was taken by surprise by His arrest and unpopularity, and that His death was an unexpected setback to His plan. People who say this have never read their Bibles carefully, or they would realise from this passage alone that the reverse was the case. Our Saviour, the Son of God, knew all the things that would happen to Him. How greatly He must have loved us to endure the pain and agony which awaited Him, and deliberately to set His face towards Jerusalem in order that we might be saved and redeemed from our sin!

(f) **A plan to follow.** We must bring the lesson to a close by reminding the class that before the Lord Jesus made any move towards Jerusalem, He began to warn His disciples that if they were to follow Him there, they must also be prepared to forget themselves and their ambitions and be willing to suffer with Him. They must, as it were, take up their cross and be willing to give up themselves.

Ask the class if they would be willing to follow the Saviour on these terms. Tell the children that those who trusted in Him were not disappointed. They also glimpsed His glory (as we shall learn next week), and His resurrection. They received forgiveness and new lives, and even after He had finally returned to Heaven, they continued to know His wonderful power so that even in times of trial they could rejoice *(1 Peter 1.3-6)*.

Visual Aid

See VA 4, page 75. [Pictures from take-home leaflets.]

The Saviour – Confirmed (151)
Christ's Transfiguration

Matthew 17.1-9; 2 Peter 1.15-18

Aim: To describe this remarkable event so that the children are given a glimpse of the Saviour's glory. Also to urge them to 'hear Him' too.

Lesson Outline

Fact not fables. Open the lesson by telling how the apostle Peter, many years after the events we heard about in last week's lesson, wrote to other Christians reminding them of one of the great events in the life of Christ – the very event we shall learn about in this lesson. Such events had made him certain that the Lord Jesus was the Son of God, the Saviour. The faith of Christians was not based on cunningly devised fables of religious cranks, but on the eyewitness accounts of apostles like himself. Peter, remember, was an ex-fisherman (not the kind of people known for gullibility) who had heard and seen the Father's endorsement of His own dear Son.

Encourage young believers in your class. They too must believe in Christ, though they have never seen Him. Some people may think them foolish, and mock saying, 'How can you believe and serve a person you have never even seen?' But in fact they have very good grounds for believing. Take, for example, the event which Peter mentioned in his letter.

Three eyewitness accounts. The Bible carries three clear accounts of this event, witnessed by men who were present on the occasion. Matthew, one of the inner band of twelve disciples, Mark, who was related to Peter, and Luke, the physician and historian, all write of this event. Peter reminded the early Christians that the authors of Scripture were moved by the Holy Spirit, and their words were guaranteed to be God's words *(2 Peter 1.19-21)*. Let us hear what happened on that remarkable day.

Amazing events on a high mountain. Explain that within a week of Peter making his great confession of the Lord Jesus, and

Jesus' warning (that He must shortly go to Jerusalem where He would be rejected, suffer at the hands of the religious leaders, be killed and then rise again), Jesus took Peter, James and John up into a lonely mountain place (thought to be Mount Hermon). There they were to witness an event which they would never forget. Suggest that – (a) this was God's own confirmation of Peter's profession; and (b) it was a great encouragement to the disciples, who had been shaken and surprised by Jesus' forecast of future, frightening events.

Provoke and keep the children's interest by posing and answering the following series of questions:

What did they see? The Lord Jesus, with these three closest disciples, went to pray to His heavenly Father *(Luke 9.28)*, and as He did so, suddenly He was changed, transformed, transfigured. It was as though the three disciples saw Him for a moment as He really is – as the Lord of Glory. From the time He was born as a babe in Bethlehem, He had veiled His glory in a body of flesh, but for a brief time they saw something of His true splendour and majesty. Point out to the class the radiance of His face, and the shining whiteness of His clothing. These spoke of His glory, His holiness and purity.

Who did they see? To add to the wonder of the occasion two figures then appeared and were seen speaking to Christ. Although Peter, James and John had never seen these men of the distant past, they immediately realised who they were, no doubt because God gave them special understanding. From boyhood these fishermen had known the Old Testament Scriptures which were made up of two parts: the law, given by Moses, and the prophets. One of the chief prophets was Elijah. It was these two who now spoke with Jesus, as if to confirm that *He* was the sacrifice of Whom Moses had so often written, and the only Person Who could perfectly keep the laws of God which Moses had delivered to the people of Israel. And He was the Saviour Who had been promised by all the prophets.

What did they hear? Luke tells us what they were speaking with the Lord Jesus about. Can the class guess? What was it that the Lord Jesus had come into the world to do above everything else? They spoke about His departure (His death) which He would accomplish at Jerusalem. Remind the class that many people today regard this as a tragic event, a sign of failure. Even some so-called Christians rate it as unimportant compared to Christ's teaching and example. But the death of Christ was the only event spoken about when Moses and Elijah were with Him on that mountain. To them it mattered more than anything else. Had the Lord Jesus not died, there would have been no atonement for sin. Had He not willingly laid down His life and suffered the greatest agonies ever known, there would have been no forgiveness for anyone. Had He not accomplished this task, there would have been no message of peace or reconciliation between God and man. This was the only matter discussed. It was the very heart of God's purpose, unfolded by Moses and Elijah and others in the Old Testament.

What did they do? Explain that the disciples, wakened from sleep to see these extraordinary events, were taken aback. On the spur of the moment Peter could only think of making three tabernacles, or tents, one for Christ and the other two for the great visitors. Children will know what it is to react nervously to events beyond their normal expectations, but Peter was spared the embarrassment of having his suggestion declined, for, as he spoke, something even more amazing took place.

What did the Lord God say? As Peter was stumbling with his words, an unusual and bright cloud overshadowed them. It was from this glorious cloud that they heard a voice which they realised immediately was the voice of God the Father. His words were clear, His instruction plain: *This is my beloved Son, in whom I am well pleased; hear ye him (Matthew 17.5).*

Now Peter knew that the confession he had made a week before was echoed from Heaven itself. The Jesus Whom he loved *was* the beloved Son of Heaven, and he was right to give all his attention and trust to this same Lord. The knowledge that they were hearing the very words of God Almighty filled the disciples with terror and alarm and they fell to the ground in fear and awe – the natural reaction of all those who truly meet with God the Maker of all things.

What can we learn? Apply the lessons of this wonderful occasion to your class:

(1) The Lord confirms Himself to those who put their trust in Him, strengthening their weak faith. In the twentieth century, when we are bombarded with atheistic propaganda and cynicism, it is hard for a child to be sure of Christ, and to follow Him. Often they are plagued with doubts. Assure your class that just as Peter had his faith confirmed, so we shall also have ours confirmed.

If only we will come to Him saying, *Lord, I believe; help thou mine unbelief (Mark 9.24),* we shall soon have many wonderful experiences of His closeness and His power to bless us. Explain that when people repent of their sin, and yield their lives to Christ, He changes them. They know they are different, with a new nature. Then they walk daily with the Lord, pray to Him and are overwhelmed with many remarkable answers to their prayers. Give some examples of your own. As believers get older, they become even more certain of their Saviour and His love.

(2) The Lord knows what lies ahead and He prepares us for it. The three disciples who saw this amazing sight were soon to travel to Jerusalem where they would see the Lord Jesus in His agony in Gethsemane. Soon they would watch His arrest and crucifixion. This experience on the mountain top would help them to face those dark days of bitter sorrow and doubt. How kind of the Lord to sympathise with them and prepare them for those days ahead! Ask the class if there is any other guide or friend in life who so kindly bears our needs in mind.

(3) We must hear Him. This is the message of God from Heaven to lost sinners. It is very clear and simple. Leave behind the conflicting and doubtful advice of this world and put your trust, along with so many others, in the Lord Jesus Christ, the powerful, eternal Son of God.

Say to Him:

Jesus, I do trust Thee,
  Trust without a doubt;
Whosoever cometh
  Thou wilt not cast out.

Faithful is Thy promise,
  Precious is Thy blood:
These my soul's salvation,
  Thou my Saviour God!

Visual Aid

See VA 5 on page 89.

The Saviour – Welcomed (152)
Christ's Entry into Jerusalem

Matthew 21.1-17; 23.37-39; Psalm 24 and other Old Testament references quoted in the lesson; see also Luke 19.28-44

Aim: To describe the great pity that the Lord has, even for the most rebellious people. To show that He will certainly draw many people to Himself and show mercy to them. Also, to use these great events to challenge the class, and to describe the joy which comes to those who welcome Him as their King.

Lesson Outline

Talk to the class about the excitement which people, and especially children, derive from visiting a great capital city. As the plane flies over the suburbs, or the car approaches famous buildings seen only on postcards and advertisements, the tension mounts. The jostling crowds and the opportunity to visit sites full of the nation's history, all contribute to the thrilling sensation which only such visits can produce. The atmosphere was something like this in Jerusalem whenever thousands of pilgrims gathered for the great feasts. On the occasion covered by our lesson, there was another factor generating special excitement. The 'prophet' and 'miracle-worker' Whom they expected to take power, and liberate the nation from Rome, was to come to the city. (This was *their* idea, not *His*.)

Today's lesson describes the day when the Lord Jesus and His disciples reached Jerusalem, the capital of Israel. On the way to the city, Jesus had again reminded the disciples in detail of the suffering that lay ahead *(Matthew 20.17-19)*, but on the day He entered the city, His astonishing reception must have caused them to feel sure He would not have to suffer.

(1) A long expected event for Jerusalem. It was more than ordinary excitement which erupted as the crowds came out to welcome Jesus of Nazareth. There was a sense in which Jerusalem welcomed home its long-promised King and nothing could stop this. Give the children a *brief* résumé of Jerusalem's remarkable history, and in particular the expectation and promises of a coming Saviour:

(a) **The hill of Abraham's sacrifice (2000 BC).** Remind the class how it was here on Mount Moriah that Abraham had been tested by God, and commanded to offer up his son Isaac. To his great relief, as he obeyed, the Lord called to him to stop, and provided a substitute, a ram *(Genesis 22.1-14)*. 2,000 years later, the Lord came to the city where Mount Moriah was located, having said that He would *give his life a ransom for many (Matthew 20.28)*.

(b) **The site prepared by David for the Temple (1000 BC).** Then explain that it was this same mountain to which the Lord directed King David to prepare for the building of the first Temple, to be constructed by his son Solomon *(1 Chronicles 21.18 – 22.5* and *2 Chronicles 3.1)*. It was in the Temple that sacrifices had been offered, which pointed to the coming Saviour, Who would be the true sacrifice. It was in the Temple that the people had gathered to hear the Scriptures which spoke so frequently of the coming Messiah.

After so many years of promises and expectation it was not surprising that Jerusalem cried out with welcome when the Saviour made His special entry, even though most of the people acted without realising what kind of a Saviour He would be. The leaders, of course, were simmering with hatred and resentment against the Lord. As the Lord Jesus said, had the people not welcomed Him, even the very stones would have cried out in welcome *(Luke 19.40)*.

(c) **The people prepared by Zechariah (500 BC).** The prophet Zechariah, though he lived five hundred years before Christ was born, described the Saviour's arrival with great precision, saying: *O daughter of Jerusalem: behold, thy King cometh unto thee . . . lowly, and riding upon an ass, and upon a colt the foal of an ass.* He went on to predict that this same *lowly* King would one day have a dominion which would be *from sea even to sea, and from the river even to the ends of the earth (Zechariah 9.9-10)*.

(2) **The great day begins.** Describe the events of the great day, noting particularly (a) the triumphant, royal aspect, mingled with (b) the humble, lowly, unostentatious character of Christ's entry.

(a) **Lowly transport.** Explain how the Lord Jesus prepared to enter Jerusalem. Just as Zechariah had indicated, He sent the disciples to a nearby village to 'requisition' an ass, and her foal, which was to be His humble 'limousine'. The lowly workhorse was willingly handed over by its owner once he heard the now-famous message, *the Lord hath need of him.*

(b) **Humble carpeting of the way.** Then describe how the crowds (some of whom had accompanied Him from Galilee, others of whom had come to believe in Him as a result of His raising Lazarus from the dead after being in the grave four days), along with the residents of Jerusalem who had heard Him before and seen His deeds, gathered along the roadside. Many disciples took items of their own clothing to make a carpet for their King. They could not provide rich and lavish decorations, but these personal items indicated more truly their esteem. As the word got round, and very large crowds gathered, others, looking for some means of decorating the streets, cut down palm leaves and laid them in the road. The crowd included many children who no doubt joined enthusiastically in this great and triumphant event.

(c) **A genuine welcome.** Those who walked before Him and those who followed after burst into cheers of welcome – *Hosanna to the son of David: Blessed is he that cometh in the name of the Lord; Hosanna in the highest.* This was no officially organised civic occasion laid on at the taxpayer's expense, but an entirely spontaneous and genuine reception. Before long the whole city was filled with rumour and speculation. *Who is this?* was the question everyone was asking; the most common answer given by the crowds being – *This is Jesus the prophet of Nazareth of Galilee.* Many began to hope that this Jesus would be the Jewish Messiah sent, as *they* thought, to free them from the Romans and to make their nation great again, a hope which was soon shown to be a mistake and a wrong interpretation of the Scriptures.

So it was that the Lord Jesus, despite the hostility and rejection soon to be shown, entered Jerusalem as its King of Glory, as *Psalm 24* had so beautifully pictured many years before.

Conclusions for us to draw. Urge the class to consider

carefully these remarkable facts prophesied so many years before they took place. Which other kings or world leaders have had their accession described in such detail hundreds of years before the event? Which other city has been the setting for so many historic events which reached their fulfilment very obviously in a Person, born centuries later? Could this possibly be explained merely in terms of coincidence? What answer therefore would the class give to the great question, 'Who was this Jesus?' Are they ready to join the band of disciples who believed that He was the Son of God, the Lord of Glory Who came to be the Saviour of the world?

(3) Jesus' visit to Jerusalem's Temple. (Those with younger classes, or those short of time, could omit this section and close with section 4.)

(a) The authorities exposed. Just as the Lord had predicted, the religious authorities refused to join in the scenes of jubilation. They remained sullen, suspicious and full of hate. Indeed, they continued to plot the Lord's arrest and death *(John 11.47-53)*. Nor did their hostility abate when the Lord made His way, first of all, to the Temple. Shock the children by explaining how the priests were running it like a tourist attraction and 'ripping off' the visitors. They had turned it into a market-place where poor worshippers were swindled, having their money changed for so-called Temple money at grossly unfair rates, and being sold animals for sacrifice at exorbitant prices.

Help the children picture the surprising scene as the Lord Jesus turned those involved out of the Temple, throwing their tables of ill-gotten coinage to the ground and unseating their dove-sellers, and publicly accusing the religious authorities of having turned His Father's house of prayer into a den of thieves. The Lord, though humble in manner, was majestic and powerful when He confronted men who used God's work to make fame and fortune for themselves.

(b) The priests hostile. As the chief priests and scribes went on to see the Saviour healing the blind and paralysed, the children singing His praises and the crowds hanging on His words, they were incensed and demanded indignantly that He tell them on what authority He did these things. Unable to accuse Him of wrongdoing, they dared not seize and arrest Him immediately as they dearly longed to do. Instead they applied their minds to how they would trap Him as soon as possible (eg: *Matthew 22.15*).

Many children today are unaware of these events. It is good that they should know about the head-on conflict between Christ and the religious hypocrites of the day. There are still many such hypocrites around and it remains Satan's aim to muddle false religion with the true Gospel.

(4) The Saviour's grief over Jerusalem. As the lesson closes, explain how Christ reasoned with these men and warned them of the consequences of their attitude and behaviour *(Matthew 23)*. He knew that they would soon persuade the people of Jerusalem to turn against Him, their Saviour. Help the children picture the Lord looking over the city with tears in His eyes (see *Luke 19.41*), and broken-heartedly (to use a human expression) lamenting its fate – its humiliation and destruction by the Romans (which took place in AD 70).

Uncover the heart of the Saviour as He expressed His great longing to gather together the people of Jerusalem *as a hen gathereth her chickens under her wings.* But they had refused! Feelingfully ask your class if the same could be said of them. Is it possible that you, as their teacher, have told them of the Saviour and His great love, His willingness to save and rescue them from the onslaught of their sins – both in this world and eternally – but they have wilfully, stubbornly and coldly turned away, preferring to live life without Him? Ask them if they are not causing grief to the Saviour just as the people of Jerusalem did as that week progressed. Urge them to see the danger of dismissing the love of such a Saviour and to turn to Him in their great need, asking His forgiveness and His care.

Visual Aid

Provide or draw a map, model or picture of Jerusalem in the days of the Lord Jesus (Nehemiah's map – VA 10 on page 145 – could be adapted). This will help the children see these events in their mind's eye. Add lesson headings at appropriate points.

The Saviour – Returning (153)
The Parable of the Ten Virgins
Matthew 24.1-30; 25.1-13

Aim: To raise the subject of future events, both for the individual and for the world, and to urge the children to listen carefully to the words of the Lord Jesus Christ, Whose predictions have proved so accurate.

Teachers' Introduction

Without getting into details of varying eschatological views, we should aim to present the chief features of future history as outlined by the Lord so as to set the scene for this much-loved parable. Teachers of classes already familiar with the parable itself may wish to spend longer with this introductory theme, while teachers of younger children may prefer simply to make the point that the Lord Jesus always promised to come again and take His people to the heavenly home, and proceed to the parable.

Lesson Outline

A never-ending world? Point out to older classes that evolutionists are compelled to assume that the Earth is many millions of years old, in order to accommodate an impossible process of evolution. One of the effects of the Earth being thought of as so very old, is that people imagine it will also go on for millions of years into the future. Although nuclear wars, food shortages, global warming, and so on, are seen as threats to a long future history for mankind, people still think things will continue. Why bother about the end of the world? Arouse the children's curiosity by saying that the Lord's prediction for our world was very different:

(1) His accurate short-term forecast. Take them back in their imagination to the scene as we left it in the previous lesson. The Lord Jesus Christ was sadly surveying the city of Jerusalem. The people were about to reject Him and crucify Him, and as a result He could foresee its doom. The disciples were trying to interest Him in the buildings of the Temple, when He surprised them by predicting that before long not one stone of this magnificent building would be left standing on another (*Matthew 24.1-2*).

Later, whilst on the Mount of Olives, the disciples asked the Saviour when these things would happen and what events might occur beforehand. The Lord gave a careful answer with detailed warnings and instructions. Not many years later (AD 70) His words proved true as the armies of Rome sacked and destroyed Jerusalem, razing the Temple to the ground. The Lord Jesus was proved completely accurate in this prediction.

(2) His accurate long-term forecast. Point out to the class that at the same time as the disciples had asked the Lord to give them the signs to be expected before the fall of Jerusalem, so they had asked for the signs which would occur before the end of the world (v 3).

Outline the chief predictions made by Christ in answer to their question. (a) Wars, famines, epidemics and earthquakes would continue (vv 6-8 – note the pessimistic tone, in contrast with frequent human predictions that these disasters will be overcome and a period of peaceful co-existence eventually come to pass). (b) The preaching of the Christian Gospel throughout the world would be accomplished (v 14). Note that *we* are not surprised by this prophecy which has come to pass, but to the twelve disciples it must have seemed an impossible vision. (c) The rise of many false religions and prophets would occur (vv 11, 24-26). This is another point the fulfilment of which no one would dispute nearly two thousand years later!

Point out to the class that not only has Christ's prediction concerning the Temple been literally fulfilled, but also these long-term prophecies. Each one, contrary to what many expected, has come to pass in an open and indisputable way. So has His prediction that there would be a safe refuge in the mountains of Judea, where Christians could hide safely when the threatened events of AD 70 came. So has His prophecy, made at this time (see *Luke 21.24*), that the Jewish people would suffer great hostility from other nations until the end of time.

(3) Another most important forecast. Next, go on to reason with the children that if the Lord Jesus has proved so accurate in

Cut out these shapes and write the words here. This V. aid shows those who were present at the transfiguration. Prepare a large board and draw a mountainside. As the lesson proceeds place the shapes on one by one.

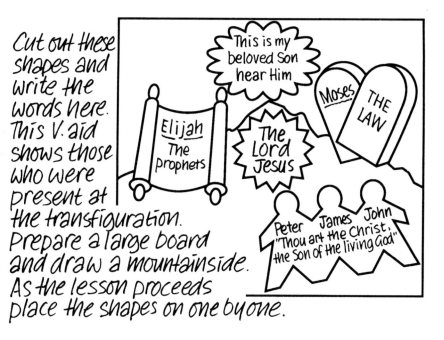

Make jigsaw as shown. Construct in lesson on a base board. End with the fifth piece placed in.

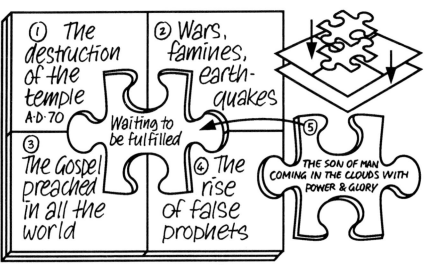

Top: VA 5 – For use with Lesson 151. Bottom: VA 6 – For use with Lesson 153.

His predictions of events and trends which have already taken place, should we not trust His words about events which are still in the future? Chief of these was His promise that He, the Son of Man, would return to Earth in a dramatic way *(Matthew 24.27-31)*, so that no one could possibly miss it. However, He said that great numbers of people would be 'caught out' by His second coming, being totally unprepared for the great day towards which our world is hurtling.

Looking ahead to that time, the Lord Jesus pictured it in one of His remarkable parables – so very simple yet so profound – beautifully capturing the scene in a way which causes us all to ask – Will I be ready for the Lord Jesus when He returns? Will I be caught out like the foolish bridesmaids of whom He spoke? Am I waiting eagerly for His arrival, or dreading such a day and hoping against hope that it will never come?

Proceed with the parable of the ten bridesmaids in the following way:

(a) **Weddings are weddings** the world over – joyful occasions when relatives and friends gather to witness the happy union of a young man and woman for life. Ask the class about the chief features they would expect of any wedding – the beautiful bride, the solemn vows, the presents, the celebrations, etc.

(b) **Cultural differences** affect the *form*, but not the substance of marriage celebrations. In this particular case, part of the proceedings took place at night (lamps being needed). It was the custom for the bride to be taken from her own home in a torchlight procession by her husband to his home where the reception and celebrations were held.

(c) **The bride** and her party had looked forward to this day, possibly for years. Explain that in those days the bride lived for the day when, at last, she could go to be alone with her dear husband. She would have spent many weeks (even years) making clothes and furnishings for her new home. In times before women worked independently, they could only expect to find their fulfilment in marriage and all its attendant joys and tasks. The wedding itself was a much looked-forward-to occasion for all. In days before television, videos and travel, life could be very dull in the average village. A wedding was eagerly awaited and meticulous preparations were made months in advance. Relatives travelled long distances and stayed for days in order to be present for these joyful family events. To be chosen as a maid to wait on the bride, was an honour indeed.

(d) The negligent bridesmaids. Explain the unbelievable foolishness of the five bridesmaids who attended this wedding without any reserves of oil for their lamps. Anyone would expect to take the simple precaution of a spare jar of oil on any day of the week, but it was particularly vital on so special an occasion.

(e) The bridegroom's arrival. Tell the class what happened – the delay of the bridegroom (in days when primitive travel made journey times unpredictable); the sleepiness of the ten bridesmaids (no doubt they had risen early in their excitement for the great day); the midnight arrival of the groom; the panic of the five when their folly was realised; their expedition to buy oil; the start of the celebrations; the shutting of the door; the arrival, too late, of the foolish five; the anguish and tears as the groom refused to recognise them despite their desperate cries; the brief but appealing application of the Lord Jesus, *Watch therefore, for ye know neither the day nor the hour wherein the Son of man cometh (Matthew 25.13).*

The parable's message. Varying with the age of the class, make some of the following applications:

(a) Christ, the bridegroom – the wonderful fact that the Son of God views His return to our Earth at its close as something to be compared with a bridegroom coming to fetch his beloved bride. Despite our rebellion and unworthiness in His sight, He loves us and regards all people who have yielded their lives to Him, and repented of their sin, as His beloved bride! He gave His very life to save and to restore us to this wonderful position. He wants us to look forward to His coming with anticipation and eagerness.

(b) 2,000 years delay? Because His return is 'delayed', unconverted people assume He will never come, or, at the least, they behave as if there is no likelihood of His imminent return.

'Let us do as we like,' they say, 'eat, drink and be merry, assume that death is the end, and that there is no day of judgement, and no chance of going to hell.' Remind the class that 2,000 years may seem a long time to us, but in God's sight it is as nothing *(2 Peter 3.8).*

(c) The foolishness of those who become convinced of this cynical view. Looking down from above, the Lord must wonder how people can become so careless and foolish with their eternal souls, and give up the opportunity of eternal joy. He not only describes them as foolish, but as guilty *(Matthew 24.48-51).*

(d) The belief in universal salvation is the equally foolish assumption that if Christ is real, and we are not ready to meet Him when He returns, then we will be able to find some way out at the last moment. The five bridesmaids no doubt thought they would find some way to get out of trouble if they should be caught out. Many 'Christians' imagine that everyone will be saved in the end, no matter how they treat the Lord, but this parable teaches the very opposite. The warning of the parable is clear. Those not known to the Lord, and not waiting for Him when He returns, will regret their error too late. They will be shut out of His kingdom.

(e) The wisdom of those who, overwhelmed at the privilege of being brought to love and serve (by conversion) the King of Heaven, prepare with great thought and care for the day of His return. Describe Christians as those who live in the light of that coming day. No one but God knows its date, and they should never believe anyone who claims to know it, as many strange cults have done. The Lord said that He would return at a time we would not expect *(Matthew 24.42-44).*

Ask your class – At His coming, or should they die before that great day comes, will they be caught out like the unprepared and foolish bridesmaids? Or are they those who prepare for that great day by seeking the Saviour and living for Him so that His coming will be the amazing meeting to which they have long looked forward?

Visual Aid

Pictures of weddings and bridesmaids can be used to good

effect. See also VA 6 on page 89 which illustrates the points made at the beginning of the lesson.

The Saviour – Rejected (154)
The Parable of the Vineyard Owner

Matthew 21.23-46

Aim: To demonstrate Jesus' perfect knowledge of future events, and to urge the children to take seriously His warnings about losing their Gospel privileges.

Lesson Outline

Remind the class that the Lord Jesus Christ had predicted that the chief priests, elders and scribes would be responsible, humanly speaking, for His death. The children should remember that when the Saviour rode triumphantly into Jerusalem, they were not amongst the welcoming crowds. When crowds of people, including children, gathered to see Christ healing the lame and the blind, and to listen to His teaching, this same group of leaders demanded to know by what authority He did these things. Often they appeared pleasant and courteous towards the Lord in public, but in private they schemed His death.

Often they asked questions deliberately designed to trick Him into saying something unlawful (so that they could report Him to the authorities), or something which would turn the people against Him and break His popularity with the crowds. However, as Jesus is God, He could see into their hearts, and He knew exactly what they were thinking and planning (just as He knows everything we think or plan to do). Instead of confronting them head on, and accusing them publicly, He first told a parable in which He exposed the wickedness of their plans and the awful consequences, so that they might be warned, and have the opportunity to repent. If they were guilty of these things, they would recognise themselves in the parable, and sure enough they did. Also, the Lord gave them the opportunity to pass judgement on the villains in the parable. He asked, *What will he do unto those husbandmen?* In answering, they sentenced themselves!

Having put the parable in context, the children will be impressed by the means the Lord employed to challenge and warn those who opposed Him. They will also respect Him for so accurately predicting the events ahead of Him, and will be challenged to consider whether they also are identified with the villains in His parable.

The method. We suggest that teachers relate the entire parable before applying its message. With older classes, the skill will be to draw the class to suggest how the parable related to the Jews and then for the teacher to apply it to unbelievers in our day and age. (This is similar to the plan of Nathan, who allowed David to condemn the rich farmer in his parable before pointing out that David was the man.) With younger classes it will be wiser to apply the parable directly to the class, with only a passing reference to the Jews. As with all of Christ's parables, the chief point is to enable the class to grasp the key for themselves. This parable is full of drama. Imagine something like this happening in our own time. Help the children to be outraged at the way the husbandmen treated the owner of the vineyard.

(1) The vineyard owner. Unlike some of the heads of big companies today, who sometimes achieve their highly paid positions by jumping from one company to another, this vineyard owner had spent his life working to make the vineyard what it was. He had planted it, made it secure by building a protective wall round it at great expense, and equipped it with processing equipment, namely a winepress. In addition he had gone to the expense of building a high tower from which a security guard could watch for thieves and vandals. This beautiful vineyard had no doubt been planted with the finest vines, and was a delight for the husbandmen employed there.

(2) The wicked husbandmen. Describe how pleased these men had been in the first place to be able to rent such a fruitful and pleasant vineyard, where they could benefit from the labours of the owner and the success of his enterprise. After a time, however, they had come to take their privileged position for granted and began to be envious and resentful of their landlord. They wanted to behave as though *they* owned the vineyard.

(3) The servants were sent to fetch the fruit. The owner was entitled to a portion of the fruit. But when the representatives of the owner arrived, these greedy and rebellious tenants beat one, killed one, and maimed a third by stoning. Other servants were treated in the same way.

(4) The son was then sent, the owner feeling sure they would respect him, but he was hurled out of the vineyard and then killed. Explain that in the culture of those days, the son in a family business was normally given much more respect than might be the case in modern society. The tenants, however, seized on his death as their opportunity to take over the vineyard.

(5) The owner returns. Wealthy enough to protect himself with an army, the landowner returned. At this point the Lord broke into His parable, to invite His audience, which included the chief priests and Pharisees, to say what should be done to those tenants. They could hardly suggest anything other than that those wretches should be destroyed, and that the beautiful vineyard should be let to others more worthy, who would hand over the proportion of fruit due to the owner.

Suggest that the class will have realised by now where this was all leading. They will have realised that the chief characters in the parable were easily identified as:

(1) The vineyard owner – The Lord God Who made this Earth and Who sustains it and its people. We can picture the Lord as the landlord of the universe to Whom we all owe a debt of rent for the life He has let out to us, together with the necessary gifts of health and all that makes our lives sustainable. (In particular, the Jewish people knew that they had enjoyed special privileges from God, and had been treated by the Lord [as in *Isaiah 5*] as the people of His own vineyard.)

(2) The wicked husbandmen. We are told by Matthew that the chief priests and Pharisees – *perceived that he spake of them (Matthew 21.45).* They knew that many of the prophets of the Old Testament had been rejected and persecuted by the Jews. They also knew that *they* were planning to kill 'the Son', as Christ frequently called Himself. The parable was beginning to get very uncomfortable for them to listen to, especially with others listening in.

Once the children see this point, turn the spotlight in their direction. Tell them how the story also pictures all men and women, boys and girls, who reject the Lord Jesus in whatever day and age. The husbandmen or tenants stand for all of us, if we rebel against the Lord and pay Him nothing for all the good He bestows on us.

(3) The servants, as the children by now may realise, stand for God's messengers. Nowadays the Lord sends out missionaries, preachers, church workers, and Sunday School teachers with a message of forgiveness, and of judgement to come. Yet many people turn against them, ridicule and ignore them, and reject their message. Instead of listening, they behave as if they owned the world, their bodies and lives, and as if they owe nothing at all to God, their Creator.

(4) The son was killed. The crucifixion of God's Son took place within a few days of His telling this parable. He was indeed taken out of the city (vineyard) and killed. But it was not only those religious rulers who were guilty of His death. All those who resist God and His laws, and refuse to give Him His rightful recognition in their lives, are in a sense 'crucifying' the Lord for themselves. But we believe that we have killed Him in an even greater way. The guilt of all of us who believe in Him was placed upon Him when He died, and the Father punished Him instead of us. We may say, 'My sin was placed on Him. My sin was the cause of His pain. He suffered for me.'

(5) The owner returns. The Jewish leaders had to confess, in answer to Christ's question, that the wicked husbandmen deserved to be punished, and have their privileges taken away and given to others. History shows that this is just what happened. The Jewish people, so long privileged and protected by God, found their special status taken away and their nation scattered. The new Church in the future was to be mainly a gentile Church, though God is still gracious to Jews as well.

We must all remember that the Lord in this parable warned that He would eventually return to judge the world and its people. Those who oppose Him now will tremble on that day when they see Him return in glory and great power. Urge your class to ask themselves if they are ready to face their Maker.

Visual Aid

Pictures of vineyards in Bible times will help the children to follow the lesson. A bunch of grapes would also set the atmosphere. See also the *Bible Learning Course* sheet.

The Saviour – Arrested and Condemned (155)
The Jewish Trial

Matthew 26.1-5 and 47-68

Aim: To make the children aware that if Christ is not their Lord and Saviour, they must one day face Him as the Judge of all. To show that the trial of every unbeliever will be scrupulously fair, but that it will lead to certain condemnation. To show, in the light of this, how important it is to seek the Lord's forgiveness now.

Teachers' Introduction

Children are always intrigued by trials. Perhaps they have seen court-room dramas on television. The trial of the Lord Jesus Christ was highly unusual. In fact, it was a travesty of justice. Help the children to see this as you describe it. The visual aid will be particularly helpful as you come to compare and contrast the trial of Christ with the trial of men and women on the day of judgement, at the end of time.

(Christ's agony in the Garden of Gethsemane and His denial by Peter have been the subject of previous lessons and are referred to only briefly in this presentation.)

Lesson Outline

Show the class pictures or word-cards which indicate the chief characters present at a trial. List (and if necessary explain briefly) the roles of the judge, the accused, the defence, the prosecution, and the jury. Explain that the object of a good trial is to come to a fair and just verdict, either side having been given an opportunity to state its case in an open court before an impartial judge. Explain that, if the accused is found guilty, the judge pronounces the sentence.

Introduce the class to the subject of the trial of the Lord Jesus by the Jewish authorities. Show that the events recorded in the four Gospels make it clear that the Saviour was accorded a shockingly unfair trial. Why?

(1) The arrest. (a) The Lord Jesus was arrested under cover of darkness. During the daytime He had been openly teaching in the Temple, yet the authorities were so cowardly they arrested Him at night, knowing that public opinion was in support of the Lord Jesus and would not allow them to hunt down such a good person.

(b) They paid one of His disciples, the traitor Judas, to give away His Master's location at night.

(c) They sent hundreds of armed men to arrest Him, although He was known for His kindness, humility and avail-ability. Stress, however, that Christ gave Himself into their hands, despite His great power. Although He made them all fall backwards at a word *(John 18.6)*, showing that He could easily have walked away, He knew that He must allow Himself to be taken and treated as He was, for *our* sakes.

(2) The trial. The trial, in two parts, was held at the dead of night, and at the break of day, and the proceedings were all over before the public realised. They were, in effect, held in secret. The verdict had been decided before the trial! For a long time these religious leaders had tried to kill the Lord. Their final, determined plot to kill Him is recorded in *John 11.53*. Now, at last, He was in their custody, and the trial, with its two hearings, was a mere formality. First the Lord was taken to Annas, a former High Priest who was the real head of the Jewish council, who had proposed His killing. What an impartial judge! Annas had even allowed his officers to assault Jesus physically in the open court *(John 18.22)*. Annas was more interested in finding out about the disciples in order to take action against them, than to do justice. After this initial hearing, the Lord was taken to Caiaphas.

(3) The judge at the second hearing was the High Priest,

THE LAST Judgement

TIME — When the Lord Jesus returns

EVIDENCE — The Books will be opened

The Prosecution — God's Law in the Bible and in our hearts

CHARGE: SIN
VERDICT: Guilty
SENTENCE: Death
ACQUITTED — All who trust the Saviour

The Judge — THE LORD JESUS

WE must ALL appear — The Accused

The Defence — We shall be Speechless — without excuse

THE JEWISH TRIAL

TIME — Before daybreak

Evidence — False Witnesses (could not agree)

The Prosecution — THE JEWISH COUNCIL

THE LORD JESUS — The Accused

CHARGE: BLASPHEMY
VERDICT: GUILTY
SENTENCE: DEATH

Jewish Judge — CAIAPHAS — Wanted Jesus dead

The Defence — MISSING

Here we compare the unfair Jewish Trial with the perfectly fair Last Judgement. Draw up a board for the Jewish Trial as above left. Prepare separate cards for the Last Judgement (above right) and in the lesson, place each one on the board to cover each point one by one.

VA 7 – Visual Aid for use with Lesson 155 – 'The Saviour – Arrested'.

Caiaphas, who was also far from impartial. How fair was this trial? It was absurd, as we shall see, and here also the Jewish leaders spat in the Lord's face and punched Him *(Matthew 26.67)*.

(4) The prosecution set out to find people willing to lie, and to misquote the words of the Lord. They could find no real case against Him. Tell the children they could hardly condemn someone for healing sick people or teaching the love of God!

(5) The defence did not exist. The Lord Jesus stood alone in the 'dock'.

(6) The charge was blasphemy, because the Lord had declared Himself to be *the Christ, the Son of God.* Ask the class – Would Jesus deny this? No. Why not? Because it was true, as we have seen throughout this series of lessons. However, the intense hatred and prejudice of the Jewish leaders caused them to shut their eyes to all the evidence that Christ was the Son of God. They saw His astonishing miracles, and they could not account for them. But still they *would* not believe. In their eyes, therefore, the Lord was guilty of blasphemy when He called Himself the Son of God.

(7) The sentence. Having rushed through the farcical trial, the High Priest moved to the verdict – *He is guilty of death.* Help the children imagine how pleased those evil men were. The crowds awoke to discover that the Lord had been arrested and tried, and that the verdict was published and beyond appeal. Only one problem remained for the Jewish leaders. They did not have the power to execute the death sentence! Only the Roman governor could pass a death sentence. Explain that those were the days of the great Roman Empire, and Palestine was an occupied country, governed, taxed and ruled by the Romans. So they rushed their prisoner to the judgement hall of Pilate at earliest light, and in the meantime they subjected Him to further torture.

Another trial. On the surface, the cause of the Lord Jesus seemed lost. Indeed He was crucified before long. (But the lesson cannot be closed at this point. This is a good moment to anticipate the future.) Explain that during His trial before the

Jews, the Saviour warned His accusers that, because He was indeed the Son of God, He would one day return to this Earth in power and glory, and then the greatest trial in history will take place – the final judgement of all people. Using the visual aid, show the class how the two trials will vary. On that great day the situation will be entirely reversed.

(1) **A good Judge,** once so maligned and ill-treated by the two 'judges' Annas and Caiaphas, will return as the supreme Judge. Appointed by His Father, He will judge the world in righteousness *(Acts 17.31)*. He will judge the living and the dead *(Acts 10.42)*, and as He returns in the clouds *every eye shall see him, and they also which pierced him (Revelation 1.7)*. Annas, Caiaphas, the chief priests and elders, will be brought from their place in hell, where they await this day. They will tremble before the Lord, along with all who never obtained forgiveness and new life *(Revelation 6.15-17)*.

(2) **An open trial.** Unlike the trials of the Lord Jesus, held at night and in secret (so that people could not see what happened), the trial of sinners will be held in the open *(Mark 4.22)*. Also, we shall have an opportunity to answer for ourselves – although there will be no point, for we shall know to our shame that we have done all the things with which we are charged. We shall be speechless and unable to excuse ourselves *(Matthew 22.12)*.

(3) **A fair trial.** The Lord Jesus will not base His judgements on the biased and false witness of others (as happened in His trial). He will go by the *facts* recorded by God Himself. The books will be opened *(Daniel 7.10; Revelation 20.12)*, and the records consulted. His judgements will be *true and righteous (Revelation 19.2)*. He will judge us according to our *works* (what we have done) rather than on what others say about us *(Matthew 16.27; Romans 2.6)*. He will judge us, not by whim or prejudice, but by the *laws* of God, revealed to us throughout the Bible and written on our consciences *(Romans 2.12-15)*.

(4) **Millions acquitted.** Whereas the Saviour encountered a wall of hatred and antagonism when He was tried, a vast number of guilty people will never have to go through the great

trial at the end of time, for they will already have been acquitted. Indeed, they will help the Lord in that day. Why will they be left out of that judgement? Because Christ Himself has already borne the punishment of the sins of all who trust Him. In amazing love He has already paid the penalty (the price) of their sin – *the just for the unjust (1 Peter 3.18)*. Did the children ever hear of such a judge – so kind, so merciful, so sympathetic. Help them imagine the shock that a guilty man or woman would feel in an earthly court, if, having been sentenced to a heavy fine, they discovered the judge had paid it from his own pocket! Explain that this is just what the Saviour has done for all those who will receive His mercy, and acknowledge that He is their only hope. He has not 'let them off' their sins, or turned a blind eye to their evil ways. Instead He has been punished Himself for all their wrongdoing, and so He has the power to forgive and renew them so that one day they will see Him and become like Him.

Urge the class to consider the great day of judgement, when we shall all stand before Him. Will He be their Saviour and Friend, loved and adored by them – or their Judge, before Whom they will tremble, with those others who pierced Him?

Visual Aid

See VA 7 on page 99.

The Saviour – Sentenced (156)
The Roman Trial

Matthew 27.1-25

Aim: To give a factual account of the Lord's trial before Pilate and to help the children see that, had we been there, we too would have been responsible for His death. To show them, however, that it was the Lord Jesus Who chose to lay down His life in order that He might save us.

Lesson Outline

Events at daybreak. Describe the scene in Jerusalem as the day dawned. The people of Jerusalem awoke to hear the news that Jesus, 'the prophet of Nazareth', had been arrested, tried and found guilty during the night hours. Any who were out and about early may have seen Christ, with His hands tied, being rushed along like a criminal amidst a heavy guard on the journey from the palace of Caiaphas, the High Priest, to the palace of Pilate, where the Roman judgement hall was located. As the crowds heard the news and gathered in the streets, the religious leaders set about persuading them that Jesus was not the hero they had thought, and that He had been found guilty of a grave crime by the Jewish authorities. Many Jews were disappointed that Jesus had refused to take political power, and alleviate their troubles, so the exciting thing to do that day was to join the frenzy of hatred stirred up against Him.

The need to obtain a death warrant. Describe the frustration of the religious leaders who, having sentenced Jesus, could not administer their verdict. Help the children grasp the other problem which stood in their way. They had sentenced Jesus for the crime of blasphemy. But the Jewish leaders did not want the people to blame them for rejecting such a great miracle-worker. They wanted the Lord executed as an ordinary criminal.

A new charge – treason! Encourage the class to follow the cunning plot of these wicked men as they schemed another way. They would accuse the Lord of treason against the Roman government! After all, He had often spoken of the kingdom of God and Heaven and presumably He imagined Himself to be the king. The Romans would certainly wish to punish anyone found to be setting himself up as a king and planning the downfall of their regime. Pilate would be bound to take this charge very seriously! Help the class to see how ridiculous it was for them to accuse the Saviour of stirring political unrest, when He had refused any such course and confined Himself solely to the spiritual needs of the people. On the one occasion that a crowd in Galilee had attempted to make Him a king, He had left them and gone alone up a mountain. Later He offended many of them by insisting that His purpose was to bring life to their souls, not their bodies *(John 6.15, 26-27, 66)*.

The trial before Pilate. Tell the class the course of the trial as outlined by Matthew:

(a) The charge – Pilate put it to the Lord, 'Are you the king of the Jews?' He was, of course. He was their Maker and their Messiah. But in the sense in which Pilate understood the term – an earthly ruler intent on opposing the Roman power, and seizing independence – He was not. The Lord simply answered (in modern terms), 'You've said it.' Pilate no doubt realised that the Lord was no revolutionary. He saw through the false charges brought by the Jewish leaders. However, the Lord refused to answer the false charges of the Jews, just as the prophet Isaiah had predicted 700 years before *(Isaiah 53)*.

(b) Pilate's plan – to release Christ without shaming the Jewish leaders. Pilate decided to use a legal loophole to release Christ by exercising his annual right to show goodwill and set free a prisoner. Would this be acceptable?

(c) Refusal by the Jews. Far from accepting Pilate's compromise, the Jews immediately demanded the release of another prisoner, a violent criminal named Barabbas, guilty of murder, rebellion and robbery. They would much prefer to have him released.

(d) A wife's warning – added further tension to Pilate's concern over the execution of a miracle-working prophet of such dignified bearing. *Have thou nothing to do with that just man,* was the guidance Pilate received from his agitated wife.

(e) Yielding to pressure. Pilate, increasingly helpless to oppose the Jewish leaders who had begun to accuse him of protecting an enemy of Caesar *(John 19.12)*, asked, *What shall I do then with Jesus which is called Christ?* Help the class see the irony of the situation as Pilate, supported by the might of Rome (his soldiers and bodyguard around him), finally submitted to the threats of the Jewish leaders. Anxious to avoid trouble and tension, he sacrificed justice. Attempting to relieve his own conscience, he washed his hands before handing over the prisoner Whom he had publicly acknowledged to be innocent of the crime of which He was accused, saying, *Why, what evil hath he done?*

(f) Cruel treatment. Varying the degree of detail with the age of the class, list the horrific physical cruelty handed out to the Lord of Glory, the Saviour of the world, the Friend of sinners. Mention particularly the scourging at Pilate's command, which meant being whipped with leather strips into which were tied

VA 8 – Visual Aid for use with Lesson 156 – 'The Saviour – Sentenced'.

pieces of bone and metal calculated to rip deeply into the flesh. Many criminals died from this, because the wounds could be so deep and severe. Mention also the stripping and mockery of Christ by the Roman soldiers, and how they spat at Him and punched Him about the head, before preparing Him for the long walk to crucifixion, carrying the wooden cross on which He was to be nailed, to the hill of Calvary, outside the city. Throughout, He knew that He would finally bear the punishment of the sins of millions of people.

By way of application, we suggest that teachers (using VA 8, page 105) ask the question: Who was responsible for this dreadful pain and suffering, borne so uncomplainingly by the Saviour? Give three answers, and help the children see how they are involved in all three.

(1) **The proud, religious leaders,** who planned and schemed these events, and who persuaded the crowds to support them, were responsible. Those who should have known most about the promised Messiah were His greatest enemies. They were jealous of the Lord Jesus Christ. He drew the crowds and spoke with an authority they did not have. He exposed their pride and hypocrisy. *They* were responsible for His pain and death. But it was not only them. Remind the class that self-righteous pride is not confined to the Jewish leaders of that time.

Today many people refuse Christ and fight viciously against His teaching. They believe that they can manage life without God. They refuse Him any of their time or obedience. They ridicule His warnings about hell, and they condemn His moral code. If the Lord Jesus were alive today, they would ban Him from the television screen and whip up a frenzy of hostility and ridicule against Him, just as they do against His followers. Warn the children that they also may become too proud to see their need of a Saviour.

(2) **Pilate** knew Jesus was innocent, but was too concerned to safeguard his own position and power to care what happened. Tell the class that there are still many people like Pilate, who acknowledge in their heads that Christ is to be respected, but who are unwilling to part with their plans and ambitions and lifestyle in order to identify with Him. Many boys and girls are

reluctant to give up their Sunday afternoons to come and learn about the Saviour. If they are likely to be scoffed at because of their belief in the Lord, they act like cowards, and give up. There are many Pilates today!

(3) The people, who only a week previously had cried, *Hosanna to the son of David,* had foolishly allowed themselves to be swayed by evil men. Without the support of the people the priests would never have succeeded in their plan to kill the Lord. Some weeks later the apostle Peter confronted a vast crowd of these people and condemned them for what they had done to Christ. As if they had slain Him with their own hands (although in reality the Roman soldiers did it), Peter said, *Ye have taken, and by wicked hands have crucified and slain (Acts 2.23).* Today, if we just follow the crowd, and do the popular thing, and copy our friends in ignoring or disowning the Saviour, then we are responsible before God. If we allow ourselves to be influenced and led to oppose Christ, we share the guilt of the ringleaders.

Ask the class – Are they amongst those who are 'ashamed' of Jesus, preferring to stay with the crowd?

But the Lord went willingly. Surprise the class by reminding them that the Lord Jesus Christ went willingly to His death. Though it would be the most terrible suffering in the history of the universe, He was ready to go through with it for our sakes. He had spoken often of laying down His life for His sheep. He had said, *No man taketh it* [my life] *from me, but I lay it down of myself (John 10.18).* Just before He was arrested He had said, *This is my body which is* GIVEN *for you (Luke 22.19).* He was indeed the Son of God and He had assured Peter that He could have prayed to His Father for twelve legions of angels (72,000) to protect Him from being arrested *(Matthew 26.53).* But He chose not to do so in order to fulfil His Father's will, described so clearly in the Bible.

Explain very simply that the Lord Jesus deliberately laid down His life in order that we might be saved. He knew from His early days that this was the reason for His coming. Even His names (Jesus Christ) tell us He came to save us. He bore all the malice and insults in order that He might go to Calvary in our place. He *made himself of no reputation . . . humbled himself, and became obedient unto death, even the death of the cross (Philippians 2.7-8).* Ask the children to go home and think about this seriously and to consider their response. Were they aware that they had such a Friend in Heaven?

Urge them to find it in their hearts to respond like this:

> *And from my smitten heart with tears*
> *Two wonders I confess –*
> *The wonders of His glorious love,*
> *And my own worthlessness.*

Encourage those who are not yet Christians to find a quiet place where they can pray to the Lord, to express their appreciation of His great love and their desire to leave behind their sin and follow Him. Encourage young believers to think often of their Saviour's mighty grace and the debt of love they owe Him.

Visual Aid

Two visual aids are suggested; the first is particularly suitable for older classes and the second for younger classes.

(1) Adapt VA 7 (see page 99) as follows:

Judge – Pilate
Time – A.M.
Evidence – Crowds shouting 'Crucify Him'
The Prosecution – Chief priests and elders
The Defence – Jesus made no answer
The Scroll – Charge: Treason; Verdict: What evil hath He done?
Sentence: Crucifixion

(2) Use VA 8 on page 105. Draw three large arrows marked: (1) RELIGIOUS LEADERS, (2) PILATE, (3) THE PEOPLE. Use these as you discuss the question, 'Who was responsible?'

The Saviour – Crucified (157)
Why Did the Son of God Die?

Matthew 27.26-50

Aim: To provoke the children into considering and appreciating the great and amazing love of the Saviour in laying down His life for His people.

Teachers' Introduction

Teachers should adapt the lesson for the age of the class. Where the reasons for Christ's death are given, teachers with younger classes may wish to use only the first text provided in each section. Those with older classes should use more. The widest range of texts will serve to challenge and convince the most senior classes. This subject matter lies at the heart of the Gospel, and teachers are urged to prepare the lesson with particular care and prayer. (Elsewhere in this syllabus the subjects of the veil of the Temple being torn, the dying thief, and the Saviour's cup of sorrows have been the main theme of a lesson, and are therefore referred to only briefly here.)

Lesson Outline

Show the class the outline cross suggested as a visual aid. Tell the children how, very shortly after Pilate handed the Lord over to the Jews, He was led out of the city and crucified. As He hung on the cross, He was taunted by the religious leaders – *If thou be the Son of God, come down from the cross.* In this lesson we shall ask the question – Why did Jesus not save Himself? Why did He die? Were the priests and scribes right to say that if He were the Son of God, He would have saved Himself? Opposite answers may be given to these questions. The first (wrong) answer is that the death of Jesus was proof that He was only a weak man who had miscalculated in his bid for public attention. The second (correct) answer is that His death displayed the power and wisdom and mercy of God.

Suggest to the class that as we learn about the events which took place at Calvary almost two thousand years ago, it will be obvious that the first answer is absurd, and the second is true.

The journey to Calvary. Remind the children of how Pilate had washed his hands of the Lord's case and handed Him over to the Jews. They will remember the brutal and humiliating treatment handed out by the soldiers just before the guard and prisoner set out for the place of crucifixion. Teachers can make two points, which may be seen as insignificant, but which are important.

(1) Jesus was taken *outside* the city to be crucified. To be thrown outside the city indicated that someone or something

was considered to be loathsome and obnoxious. This was the place where criminals were banished, lepers sent, and refuse tipped out. The fact that the Lord suffered outside the city identified Him as an outcast, a rejected person *(Hebrews 13.12)*. Could He really be the Lord of Glory – the Holy One? Yes, because God had given an order to Moses (in *Leviticus 4.11-12, 21; 16.27*) that the sin-offering for all the people must be carried outside the camp where it would be burned. The sacrifices all pointed like acted-out prophecies to the great sacrifice that Christ would make. And when He died, although the authorities did not know the significance of what they were doing, they offered Him up outside the city, and so 'prophecy' was fulfilled.

(2) The Lord was executed on a cross, made from a tree. To Jews this was particularly abhorrent for they had been taught, *He that is hanged* [on a tree] *is accursed of God (Deuteronomy 21.23* and *Galatians 3.13)*. This mode of death signalled God's particular displeasure. Would God allow His own Son to die such a death? 'No!' thought the hostile Jewish leaders. 'Yes!' say believers, because He was *accursed* on our behalf.

Bearing these two points in mind, describe (or read directly from *Matthew 27.32-50*) the events of that day:

(a) The journey to Golgotha. Simon of Cyrene was ordered by the guard to carry Christ's cross. Perhaps by now His state of physical exhaustion was evident to all.

(b) The spectacle of the three crosses. The centre one bore the title, THIS IS JESUS THE KING OF THE JEWS. On the other two, common thieves were hanged.

(c) The spite and cruelty of the religious leaders. They ridiculed Christ's sad state. Help the children to identify with this agony and unfairness. He became a dying man to release millions of people from eternal punishment, and in the process was scorned for 'weakness'!

(d) The darkness which came over the land for three hours. The immense agonies of the Saviour as He bore our eternal punishment were too precious and profound to be on constant public view. When God the Father heaped upon Him the punishment of human sin, He shut out the sun.

(e) The terrible, heart-rending cry of the Lord Jesus, *My God, my God, why hast thou forsaken me?* Part of His suffering was to experience separation from His Father and to feel abandoned, forsaken, condemned and alone as He bore away our sin. He felt just as we must feel if we are ever cast away by God into everlasting terror. He suffered what we deserve to suffer, in order to buy our freedom.

(f) The final cry of the Lord Jesus. John tells us His final words – *It is finished (John 19.30)*. He was satisfied that He had completed all that was necessary and so He gave up His spirit.

Explain that Jesus was indeed the Son of God, and that He died for the following reasons. (We limit ourselves to four reasons in order to make the best impact in a short lesson.)

(1) Because He loved us. The amazing fact is that, although we do not deserve it (for we would have joined the crowd who cried, *Away with him, crucify him*), the Son of God loved, and gave Himself for, His people *(Galatians 2.20)*. He Himself explained that He would be 'lifted up' (just as Moses had lifted up the serpent for the sick people in the wilderness) so that whoever would believe in Him should not perish (die eternally) but have everlasting life *(John 3.16)*. He pictured Himself elsewhere as the Good Shepherd Who lays down His life for His sheep *(John 10)*.

Ask the children to try to take this in. They may have heard of someone donating a kidney to save the life of a relative – a wonderful 'gift' – or even of another person risking his or her life to rescue a friend. But the Lord's sacrifice went far beyond any other human act of kindness and sacrifice. The willingness of the Son of God – the sinless One – to come to our sin-sick world and submit to the awful punishment of sin for His people, is beyond our comprehension.

(2) Because He was paying the price of our sin. The Bible tells us He was purchasing us with His own blood *(Acts 20.28)*. He was paying the debt which we owe to our Maker (see *Matthew 18.32*). He was redeeming us from the curse of having broken God's law *(Galatians 3.13)*. By giving Himself as the Lamb of God, He was making the *perfect sacrifice* for all our sinful and evil thoughts and deeds, and taking them away *(John 1.29)*. He was giving His life as a *ransom* for many by bearing our sins in His own body on the tree *(Matthew 20.28; 1 Peter 2.24)*.

Ask the class to imagine the price which would be asked for the secret of a wonder-drug which would cure cancer, or for a new lethal weapon which would bring its owners all that they wanted without the dangerous effects of radioactivity, or for an amazing invention enabling people to view in 'total reality' the wonders of the world without leaving their armchair! The price would be astronomical! No wonder then that the price (ransom) which the Lord Jesus paid to free us from the punishment of sin and to give us everlasting life was so very great for Him.

(3) Because He was opening the gate of Heaven for us. The Bible has many ways of expressing this. It tells us that the Lord Jesus died to *bring us to God (1 Peter 3.18)*. He came to seek and save the *lost (Luke 19.10)*, and to bring near those who were *far off* (the children remember the far-off prodigal who returned home). He came to *reconcile* us to God *(2 Corinthians 5.19)*, to act as our *mediator* (negotiator), our priest, our 'go-between' *(Hebrews 9.15)*. Remind the children of the hymn verse which puts it very simply and touchingly.

> *There was no other good enough*
> *To pay the price of sin;*
> *He only could unlock the gate*
> *Of Heaven, and let us in.*

Tell the class that ever since the first man and woman sinned, we, who are sinners just like them, have been shut out of Eden; of Paradise; of Heaven. God made it clear that sinners could not enter into His holy presence. Hell is a place far from God, where all His blessings that we enjoy on Earth are withdrawn; a place of *outer darkness.* How wonderful, then, that the Lord Jesus came into our doomed world to find lost sinners and return them to the fold *(Luke 15)*.

(4) Because He had to make us fit for Heaven. Use an illustration along these lines. Supposing a boy or girl is applying to the top school or college in the area, which has only one place left. It will not be good enough just to say, 'I have never been in trouble at my first school; I have never failed an exam; I have never been sent home.' Instead it would be necessary to be able to say, 'I was head prefect at my junior school; I have 10 grade A's; I was captain of the sports team!'

Show the class, by this means, that in order to enter Heaven it will not only be necessary to show that we are washed clean from all sin (because the Lord has borne it away for us). It will also be necessary to have positive merit which will commend us to God. But what do we have? Nothing! Once again, we shall have to depend on the Saviour Who not only took away our sins as He died, but Who offered up His righteousness and goodness on our behalf. In other words, He earned for us our 'entrance money'. He gave Himself to enable poor, outcast sinners to enter Heaven. And on top of that, by His power He *makes* us better. He supplies all those who know Him as their Saviour with a new heart *(Ezekiel 11.19)*. He earns Heaven for us, and then begins the work of making us *continually* more fit for that glorious place.

No wonder! Close the lesson on a triumphant note. Tell the children that it was:

exactly what was intended – that the Lord Jesus suffered very greatly, to bear the punishment of our sin;

exactly what was intended – that the sun was darkened and other strange upheavals took place;

exactly what was intended – that He cried with a loud voice, *It is finished,* for He had achieved what no one else could ever achieve.

No wonder the centurion who saw all these things close at hand said, *Truly this was the Son of God.*

Visual Aid

To illustrate points 1 – 4, which give four reasons for the Saviour's death in the words of believers (based on the hymn, 'There is a green hill far away'), provide:

(1) The outline of a cross – print over it the words, HE DIED TO SAVE US.

(2) A replica banknote or cheque – print on it the words, HE DIED TO PAY THE PRICE OF SIN FOR US.

(3) The outline of a doorway with two gates that open – print

behind the gates the words, HE DIED TO UNLOCK THE GATES OF HEAVEN AND LET US IN. Open the gates to reveal these words as you tell how Christ died.

(4) The outline of a gown or robe – print on it the words, HE DIED TO MAKE US GOOD.

The Saviour – Risen (158)
The Resurrection

Matthew 27.57 – 28.20

Aim: To tell the children how the Saviour, despised and rejected as He had been, rose triumphantly from the grave, proving beyond all reasonable doubt that He was the Son of God, so that (a) children who are doubters may come to believe in Him, and (b) young believers can be assured that they have a living, all-powerful Saviour.

Lesson Outline

Describe to the children how things must have seemed as Jesus died on the cross. It seemed that:

(1) The religious leaders had been successful, and that their enemy was dead.

(2) Satan, death and evil had been victorious. Jesus Christ, thought by His disciples to be the Son of God, had died in apparent weakness, so that His teaching, His promises, His example, now carried no credibility.

(3) 'Christianity', and the new church of which Christ had spoken, was finished. His little band of disciples were shaken, sad and disillusioned. They had scattered as He was arrested.

Relate the events of the evening:

(a) Mention *the courage* of Joseph of Arimathæa, a disciple, who previously had been a secret disciple *(John 19.38)*, to ask Pilate for the body of Jesus. Joseph was a rich man, who had recently had a handsome grave built, which was so far unused. Point out to the class that the Lord Jesus had no earthly home of His own, and certainly no grave reserved for Him. Describe how Joseph had the body wrapped in long linen bandages, with much ointment of myrrh and aloes, as was the custom, and laid it gently in his tomb.

(b) Mention *the devotion* and loyalty of the women, who would not leave the Lord, though perplexed and distressed. They followed His body to the sepulchre and sat opposite until the Sabbath called them away, but it was their intention to return at the earliest possible moment, at daybreak following the Sabbath, to embalm the body.

(c) Mention *the determined hatred* of the religious rulers who remembered that Christ had said that He would rise again. Although the disciples had not fully registered these words, and had forgotten them, the Jewish leaders had remembered, and arranged for Roman military guards to be stationed at the tomb because they thought the disciples might steal the body and claim that Christ had risen from the dead. Now they felt relieved in the knowledge that their enemy was dead and His body secure in a rich man's tomb, sealed by a heavy stone door that had been rolled across its entrance.

But God . . . Suggest to the class that this was the ultimate moment of testing. If Jesus were only a man this would indeed have been the end of Him. His body would have remained in the grave, dead and decaying. But if He were the Son of God, we should expect to see surprising things, for how could the eternal God perish and die? Now that His great mission was accomplished, His time of humiliation was at an end and the time was right for Him to be highly exalted, and given a name above every name *(Philippians 2.9)*. And this was just what happened. Summarise the events that took place on the Sabbath morn and afterwards.

(a) Christ rose. Death, no longer able to hold on to the perfect, sinless Son of God, yielded Him to life. The Lord Jesus Christ, by His own power and by the power of His Father and of the Holy Spirit, rose from the dead to become the Giver of life to all who believe in Him *(Acts 2.24)*.

(b) The stone was rolled away. An angel was sent, accompanied by an earthquake, to roll back the great stone from across the entrance to the grave, so that when the women arrived, wondering how they would move it, they found it already out of the way. The soldiers, shaken by these amazing events, were numbed and lifeless *(Matthew 28.4)*.

(c) An angel announced – *He is not here: for he is risen. Why seek ye the living among the dead? (Matthew 28.6; Luke 24.5.)* Would anyone look for the latest computer equipment in an antique shop? Would they expect to find an Olympic-class athlete being cared for in an old people's home? Why then were the women looking for Christ, the eternal, all-powerful Son of God (Who had said He would rise from the dead), in a tomb?

(d) Christ appeared to Mary *(Mark 16.9; John 20.11-18)*, the women *(Matthew 28.9-10)*, to Peter *(Luke 24.34)*, to the two disciples on the road to Emmaus *(Mark 16.12; Luke 24.13-31)*, to the ten disciples and others who saw His hands and feet (not those of a ghost) and saw Him eat fish and honeycomb *(Luke 24.33-43; John 20.19-23)*, to the eleven, now including doubting Thomas *(John 20.24-29)*, to seven disciples fishing at the Sea of Tiberias *(John 21.1-14)*, to the eleven in a mountain of Galilee *(Matthew 28.16-20)*, to 500 disciples at once, to James *(1 Corinthians 15.6-7)*, and to the disciples at the Ascension *(Mark 16.19; Luke 24.51; Acts 1.9)*. Comment on the fact that these appearances were recorded by eyewitnesses in the days when those involved were still alive to check the accuracy of their records *(1 Corinthians 15.6)*. (After the Ascension the Lord appeared to Stephen, to Saul, and to John on Patmos – making fourteen appearances in all.)

His resurrection was soon talked about all around that part of the world, and throughout the Roman Empire.

What the resurrection teaches us. Using a simple visual aid, make the following points. The resurrection teaches that:

(1) Jesus Christ is the Son of God, to Whom all power in Heaven and Earth is given *(Matthew 28.18)*. Who else has returned victorious from the dead? The world has produced countless wealthy people, many mighty rulers, deep thinkers, great soldiers and so on, but they have all died as mere mortals. Only the Lord Jesus rose again to bless His people. The resurrection shows Him to be the source and fountain of life – the mighty God.

(2) Jesus Christ is the Saviour Who was promised from the beginning of time to this lost and fallen world. God has kept His promises in every detail. In the very first promise of a Saviour *(Genesis 3.15)*, God said that a descendant of Adam would suffer because of the devil, and He would break the power of the devil. In other words, the Saviour would suffer, but would be victorious. Isaiah tells of how the Saviour would be slaughtered, cut off, stricken and buried when He offered Himself for sinners. But then the prophet also said that the Saviour would see the fruit of His work, and see the people whom He would save, and receive the spoils of the battle – in other words He would live again *(Isaiah 53.10-12)*. The resurrection shows that Christ fulfils all the prophecies of a Saviour.

(3) Jesus Christ fully succeeded in atoning for the sins of His children. The fact that our Redeemer lived again makes us certain that His work on Calvary was a total success. The debt of sin has been paid.

(4) Jesus Christ's resurrection shows what will happen one day to all who belong to Him. They will also be raised with new bodies. When Christ returns to end this present world, He will bring with Him all believers who have already died and gone to Heaven. Of course, they will be *souls* only, having left their bodies at death. But when the Lord returns, their bodies will be raised in new and glorious form, like His. Christ's resurrection body gives an insight into this glorious future event.

1 Thessalonians 4.16-17 reads: *For the Lord himself shall descend from heaven with a shout, with the voice of the archangel, and with the trump of God: and the dead in Christ shall rise first: then we which are alive and remain shall be caught up together with them in the clouds, to meet the Lord in the air: and so shall we ever be with the Lord.*

We can say in the words of a hymn:

> *Lives again our glorious King:*
> *Where, O death, is now thy sting?*
> *Once He died our souls to save;*
> *Where thy victory, O grave?*

What harm can death do to us? It is now only the gateway to an eternal life of bliss with our Saviour. Remind the class that unbelievers fear death, whereas Christians look forward to being *with Christ; which is far better (Philippians 1.23).*

Visual Aid

Draw the outline of an Eastern grave with a large stone which can be rolled aside. As the lesson proceeds, draw out, from behind the stone, cards on which the four lessons of the resurrection are printed, eg: (1) Jesus Christ is the Son of God.

The Saviour – the Son of God Indeed (159)
Revision

Aim: To touch the hearts of the children by drawing together all the information they have heard about the Lord Jesus which points to the fact that He is the Son of God Who gave His life to save sinners. To urge them to take the step of faith which will lead them to Him as their Lord and Saviour.

Teachers' Introduction

Each of this current series of lessons includes references to Christ as the 'Son of God'. Most use these exact words. In testing the children's memories and understanding it will be helpful to highlight these sentences and then to clothe them with the surrounding events.

Lesson Outline

(1) **'Thou art the Christ, the Son of the living God.'** Who said these words to the Lord Jesus? Where did he say them? Whom did the ordinary people say Jesus was? What did the Saviour predict would happen to Him when He reached Jerusalem?

(2) **'This is my beloved Son, in whom I am well pleased.'** Add the last three words spoken by the voice out of the cloud. Who heard them and where? Who else appeared with the Lord Jesus and talked to Him on this occasion? How did He look?

(3) **'Hosanna to the Son of David:** Blessed is he that cometh in the name of the Lord.' Who called out these words, and when? What other unusual things were done on this day? Later the people of Jerusalem rejected the Saviour. As the Lord wept

over the city, how did He picture Himself and His desire to protect them?

(4) 'Behold, the bridegroom cometh.' Who, in this story told by the Lord, was not ready for the bridegroom? How many bridesmaids were ready? What lesson did the Lord teach from this parable?

(5) 'This is the heir [son]; come, let us kill him, and let us seize on his inheritance.' Who spoke these words in the Lord's parable of the vineyard? Who else had been killed, earlier in the story? What did the vineyard owner finally do? Who does the vineyard owner stand for? Who, in real life, was put to death? Whose return should we prepare for?

(6) 'Tell us whether thou be the Christ, the Son of God.' Who said these words to Jesus, and when? At what time of day had Jesus been arrested? Who had betrayed Him to the chief priests and elders? How did the trial of the Lord Jesus differ from the day when God will judge each one of us?

(7) 'Art thou the King of the Jews?' Who asked the Lord this question? Which notable prisoner did the crowd prefer to have released, rather than Jesus? What did they demand should be done to Jesus? In what way did the soldiers mockingly treat the Lord as a king?

(8) 'If thou be the Son of God, come down from the cross.' Who insulted and mocked the Lord Jesus with these words as He hung on the cross? Why did He not come down from the cross? Why did He cry, *My God, my God, why hast thou forsaken me?* What did the Saviour achieve for all who believe in Him by His death? What did the centurion, and those that were with him, say about Jesus immediately after He died?

(9) 'He is not here: for he is risen.' Who said these words? On what day of the week were they said? As the women who heard these words went to tell His disciples, Who met them? Who else saw the risen Saviour?

Conclusion. Draw the lesson and series to a close by telling the class that, after appearing to the disciples with many infallible proofs for forty days, and teaching them all they needed to know for the Gospel work ahead, the Lord ascended into Heaven *(Acts 1.2-3)*. Express your regret in the spirit of the hymnwriter at having to end this wonderful 'biography' of the Saviour:

> *Here might I stay and sing,*
> *No story so divine;*
> *Never was love, dear King!*
> *Never was grief like Thine.*
> *This is my Friend,*
> *In Whose sweet praise*
> *I all my days*
> *Could gladly spend.*

Urge your class never to be satisfied until they can say with once-doubting Thomas, 'This is *my* Lord and *my* God.' Then they will be amongst that great company of people from around the world and throughout the centuries of time, who will welcome His return to Earth, and, having been saved by Him, will go to spend eternity praising their Saviour and their God.

Visual Aid

This visual aid suggestion is based on the star used in VA 10, *Lessons for Life 3*, page 197. In the six segments of the star print six of the lesson headings (we suggest those for headings 1, 2, 3, 6, 7 and 9). On the circle at the centre print, WHO SAID? Use the folded star to keep the children guessing and interested throughout the lesson and only unfold each point as you question them on the related lesson.

Series 19
CHARACTER STUDIES FROM DANIEL AND NEHEMIAH

160 – Loyalty
As a young man in a foreign land, Daniel stands firm for the Lord. What is the secret of his success? His loyalty, which at first threatens him with disaster, results in promotion and lasting good. Truly converted young people will make similar discoveries themselves.

161 – Pride
King Nebuchadnezzar is given several dramatic warnings from the Lord, but he allows pride to take hold of him. Finally the Lord has to humble him dramatically. Countless people have to learn the hard way at the end of life's journey. Will we?

162 – Contempt for God
Belshazzar sins without a qualm against Almighty God in the most extreme and provocative way. Suddenly God interrupts his feast to announce a terrible sentence. Within hours, the great Babylonian Empire and Belshazzar's own life are finished. The Bible warns about contempt for the Lord.

163 – Faithfulness or Spiteful Jealousy?
This lesson provides a vivid contrast between the ambition, jealousy and cunning which motivates one group of men, and

the faithfulness of Daniel. Thrown to the lions as a result of their intrigues, Daniel is rescued by the Lord. Which set of values will control and determine the course of our lives?

164 – Unselfish Concern

Living far away from Jerusalem, and surrounded by pomp and power, Nehemiah might have forgotten his homeland. Instead, his only concern is for the Lord and His work. All those who know the Lord as their Saviour feel the same way.

165 – Determination and Courage

Nehemiah, under constant threat and attack, is able to rebuild the walls of the city in fifty-two days because of his unswerving loyalty to the Lord. Satan uses all kinds of devices to threaten and frighten him, and he uses similarly cunning methods against souls today. Learning about Nehemiah can be a great help to us.

166 – Kindness

Nehemiah's selfless devotion and personal sacrifice enables Jerusalem's walls to be built and the city to be made strong in every sense. His kindness reminds us of the love of the Lord Jesus in coming from Heaven to rescue lost sinners, at great cost to Himself.

167 – Fickleness

The *Book of Nehemiah* closes on a sad note. While Nehemiah is away the people of Jerusalem go back to their old sinful ways. Satan is always watching for an opportunity to make us fall back into his ways. Are we ready to resist him?

168 – Revision

I have more understanding than all my teachers (Psalm 119.99). Children who have followed this series thoughtfully will have more insight into character than many adults.

Teachers' Introduction to the Series

This series will be helpful in presenting the children with a challenge in the area of character studies. It is obvious that from an early age children pattern their behaviour on people they observe in the adult world. Even Beginners and Infants decide they would like to become fire-fighters, air stewardesses, etc!

Yet the secular world of education has largely abandoned any character training by means of positive examples written into books and films. Moral tales are despised. On the contrary, most entertainment available to the young today perverts and depraves.

Sunday School teachers see great significance in the fact that the Lord has arranged much of His Word in narrative form, presenting a great variety of character-types for the instruction of the young. How we glorify Him for such shining role models as Daniel and Nehemiah! How important it is that we should present them as men of conspicuous character, who shone out in their generation as towers of strength, and who secured (with God's help) great benefits for the people they served.

Loyalty (160)
Daniel Refuses the King's Food

Daniel 1

Aim: To show that true Christians can stand firm for the Lord in the face of great adversity and danger because they really do know Him and have personally felt His love and mercy. To urge the children to seek such an experience in conversion.

Lesson Outline

(1) **Babylon – a great city.** Help the class to picture young Daniel arriving in the magnificent city of Babylon, the greatest city of the world in those days. He would have passed through the great Ishtar Gate, with its breath-taking and ornate decorations, and admired the massive, double walls which fortified the city (see VA 9 on page 127).

Once inside, Daniel would have seen the vast network of roads, laid out like a modern American city in long, straight parallels, designed to show the greatness and glory of the Babylonians and their king, Nebuchadnezzar. High above the palaces he would have seen one of the greatest sights ever, the hanging gardens of Babylon.

(2) **Babylon – why was Daniel there?** Explain that Daniel had come from the land of Judah where he had been brought

up from a young child to know the Scriptures and to believe in
the God of Whom they spoke. Probably he had a very godly
mother who from his earliest days had taught him to pray and
to trust the Lord, her Saviour.

Describe the tragic days through which Daniel had recently
lived. He had looked out from the walls of Jerusalem with
horror as the mighty king of Babylon and his army had
surrounded the city and cut it off until, nearing starvation, it
had been forced to surrender to his demands. Daniel's father, a
prince, may have been killed trying to defend the city. His
efforts would have been in vain for, as the prophets had
predicted, God was about to punish the king and people of
Judah for their evil ways. Recent kings had turned away from
the Lord, broken His commands, worshipped other gods and
allowed the most vile and evil practices to go on even within the
Temple itself. Now they were to suffer the consequences.
Instead of receiving divine protection, as in previous years, the
king of Judah was humiliated and ordered to hand over everything of value. From now on he must carry out the orders he
received from Babylon. Daniel had been lined up with other
Jewish boys of his age and selected for the thousand-mile (1,600
km) journey to Babylon.

(3) Babylon – a great opportunity. Describe how, out of the
many thousands of Jewish young people sent to the world
capital of those days, Daniel and a few others had been selected
by Nebuchadnezzar's civil service for special training at the
king's court. It was part of the imperial policy to hand-pick and
train exceptionally able young nationals to administer the
colonies, and also to enrich the cultural understanding of the
king's government.

Daniel was one of the few Jewish youths who scored so highly
in fitness, physique, intelligence and knowledge that he was
chosen to join this elite team. They were to study the literature
and language of the Chaldeans. Their daily food and wine
rations were to be supplied direct from the king's own larders
and cellars.

At the end of three years' intensive academic and physical
education they were destined to enter the king's personal
service. Many other teenage captives from Judah would be used

as slave labour or expendable manpower in the Babylonian armies, but Daniel and a select few had abilities so outstanding that they were to receive the training of a prince.

(4) Babylon – the king's retraining programme. Children will readily appreciate how easily Daniel might have been over-awed by this magnificent capital city, with all its might and modern development. It could easily have stolen his loyalty and devotion from the God he worshipped. After all, his own country had been humiliated and lay in distress. Study in the world's most advanced academy, and the experience of Chaldean life and cuisine would surely cause him to forget his family and former ties, including his religion, and adopt the new culture as his own.

Dreams of the future might easily have danced before Daniel's eyes. Having become a senior trainee in the king's court, he would be guaranteed the highest kind of office in the empire. He might well have pictured himself returning home as governor of the whole region.

This dream was a real possibility. There was only one condition, which seemed easy enough to fulfil – students were to do as they were told.

Daniel's personal crisis. In those days God had said that those who served and loved Him must show it in the following way: they must not eat certain foods, including, for example, pork and food offered to idols. Help the class to appreciate the courage and determination which would be needed by Daniel and his friends if they were to refuse the offending foods. They would most certainly face:

(a) Danger. Daniel loved God, but if he kept this commandment it would put him in danger of angering his new masters and would probably result in his disgrace and death for insulting the king's provisions. Would he dare keep to his principles with so much at stake?

(b) The derision of the other students. Imagine the scorn and merriment they might expect from their colleagues when they announced their decision not to eat of such mouth-watering food for religious reasons. (Remind the class that they might face similar embarrassment if, when out with a group of school friends, they refused to drink alcohol or watch immoral videos.) Young people living today are tempted by the new trends of selfish and immoral deeds advocated on films and television. But the Christian takes a stand for the Lord, preferring to obey Him, no matter what it costs.

(c) Expulsion from this privileged course. Young people around the world in those days would have envied Daniel's place on such a course with all its wonderful prospects and prestige. Was he prepared to put his place in jeopardy? (Tell the class how young believers in communist lands who would not deny their faith were refused university places until a few years ago.)

Daniel's decision – to stand for the Lord. What was Daniel to do? Who was he to obey? Far away from home and parents, it would have been easy for him to fall in line with the other students and obey his new master who had so much to offer him. But no amount of promised promotion or tempting novelties could persuade him to disobey the Lord. Daniel did not try to hide his problem or take the coward's way out. He spoke openly to the commander of the officials and made his position clear – he could not take the king's food and wine.

Why make such a decision? Help the class to puzzle out why a young man, a thousand miles away from home, would place himself in such danger and put aside tempting opportunities. If God was only a figment of the imagination, would he show such bravery as this? The answer is – no. Daniel's God was a real God Whom he knew and loved, a God to Whom he prayed every day, and Whose blessing and help he frequently experienced. Daniel knew and read the Scriptures which explained so many things far better than the literature of the Chaldeans. Its explanation of our world and the reason for human behaviour rang so true to the facts. Its laws and commands were so wise and beneficial. And Daniel had believed, and experienced God's way of forgiveness for sins. Only this real and certain knowledge of the Lord enabled him to stand firm and say, 'I am on the Lord's side! I will not take the king's food.'

Could we make the same decision? Explain to the class that

VA 9 – Visual Aid for use with Lesson 160 – 'Loyalty'.

the same will be true for them. There is no possibility of their resisting the devil's temptations unless they have a personal experience of the Lord. Unless they have known the experience of having their sin forgiven and of receiving a new nature, they will be drawn like a magnet towards sin. The taunts and threats of worldly friends and interests must overpower them. But if they trust and obey the Lord, like Daniel, they will remain calm, knowing that God will use His great power to help them out of all difficulties.

Dangerous days. The Bible account suggests to us that Daniel was such an upright and likeable young man that, under God's good hand, his overseer reacted kindly to his dilemma and was anxious to help him. The overseer had only one problem – he feared for his own job. Should any of these recruits fail to gain sufficient weight and strength, or should they show any signs of ill-health, then not only his position but his life would be at risk.

The ten-day test. Describe how Daniel suggested a ten-day test, during which time he and his believing friends would live on vegetables and water. Daniel believed the Lord would honour their stand and that they would not fall behind the others even physically. After ten days the weighing scales pronounced the verdict. Daniel and his friends were heavier; they also looked more healthy than their colleagues. The officer's fears were quelled and he agreed to give them this diet on a permanent basis. He was not let down.

Chosen for high office. Three years later when the course finished, the four young men from Jerusalem not only won the prizes for fitness and strength, they also achieved great success in their academic work and examinations. Because they had obeyed the Lord, He stood by them and gave them understanding and knowledge far above that of others of the same age, even in the interpretation of dreams, a science which the ancient world highly valued. When the great day for presentation to the king arrived, Nebuchadnezzar picked them for his personal service, and found them to be more useful and able than all his teams of professional advisers.

A life we can respect. The Lord Jesus Christ promised that there is no one who leaves house or relations for the sake of the kingdom of God who shall not receive many times as much in this life and in the age to come, eternal life *(Luke 18.29-30)*. For many years Daniel was to hold an influential position at the heart of the empire. Kings came and went, but for decades Daniel remained as adviser to successive rulers, and as the helper of his own people, the Jews.

He and his three friends were to suffer persecution at the hands of jealous rivals, and on several occasions they were thrown into the very jaws of death – but their stand for the Lord never faltered. The Lord always strengthened and helped them, and in the end vindicated His servants.

Encourage your class to respect these young men and their loyalty to the Lord. Urge them to follow their example and to earnestly seek and find the Lord early in life, so that their lives too may be guided and blessed and made useful.

Visual Aid

Use VA 9 (see page 127) to impress the children with the magnificence of the great city of Babylon in Daniel's day.

Pride (161)
Nebuchadnezzar Commands Everyone to Worship his Image

Daniel 3 – 4; refer also to chapter 2

Aim: To show the children that proud self-confidence is always wrong. To help them face the facts about themselves while there is still time to turn to the Saviour.

Teachers' Introduction

One of the greatest obstacles for children seeking the Lord is *pride*. The devil knows this only too well and seeks to fuel its flames even in young children. Our whole pattern of society is geared to foster a sense of self-confidence and egotism. No wonder the modern child finds it difficult to appreciate the values of humility, honesty, kindness and unselfishness!

Lesson Outline

Introduction. Whet the children's appetite by telling them that today's lesson will describe how God reduced the world's most powerful ruler (at that time) to an animal existence. Only after having been so humbled, did *he* acknowledge the Lord, and His great power.

Inherited privilege. Remind the class of last week's lesson, particularly of King Nebuchadnezzar, his victories in battle, and his magnificent capital, Babylon. We know that most of his success was due to the overruling hand of Almighty God. (Following a remarkable dream, interpreted for him by Daniel, he had acknowledged this – *Daniel 2.47*.) We also know that he had inherited much of his power from his father who was one of the greatest empire builders of ancient times.

(1) Pride surfaces – a golden image. Although Daniel had reminded the king that his power came from *the most High*, Nebuchadnezzar soon began to preen himself and take credit for all his supposed achievements. Before long his sense of pride and achievement had taken such a hold of him that he felt that everyone should be made to acknowledge his greatness. He commanded that a huge image of himself be made in gold, and ordered everyone to fall down and worship it at certain specified times. (If a cubit equals approximately 18 inches, it measured 90 feet high and 9 feet wide. Nelson's column in Trafalgar Square, London, is 145 feet high.)

Remind the children of the excessive pride in today's world:

(a) Pride in nations. Even in our century, nations parade past huge posters of their leaders. They also give immense adoration to their 'superstars'. Suggest ways in which most people indulge in pride.

(b) Pride in children. People love to be admired, flattered and congratulated. But beware! Pride always grows, and like an ugly disease it can take us over completely. Ask the children if they know a boy or girl who has been spoilt by a little success. Perhaps they know someone who used to be a nice person, but who since becoming form-captain, or leading performer in the school play, or a member of a school team, has become big-headed and boastful, even scoffing at others not so talented.

Some people are even proud of their aggressive behaviour, or their efforts at cheating, stealing and other wrongdoing.

(c) Pride in unbelief. Describe how hearts become proud when people stop remembering *how much they owe to God.* Every one of us depends on Him for life itself. We owe our very existence to Him and any gift we have is from Him. How ridiculous it is to be puffed up with pride about our looks and abilities. When we begin to think that nothing matters except what we have, and what we want, then pride is dominating our hearts.

First lesson – from a fiery furnace. Nebuchadnezzar was given a very dramatic warning that his pride had gone too far. Recount the courageous testimony of Shadrach, Meshach and Abed-nego who refused to bow to his command. Describe the terrifying threats made to them, and their refusal to comply. It was not only because they believed that their God would deliver them from the fiery furnace that they refused to obey the king. They would rather have burned than worship the golden idol *(Daniel 3.18).* Help the class imagine Nebuchadnezzar's fury and rage at this insult, and describe the consequences (vv 19-20). Recount the amazing events that followed, and the humbling effect these had on the king (vv 21-29). As the three emerged from the burning fiery furnace unscathed, Nebuchadnezzar recognised that these men worshipped a living God Who had protected them, because they had refused to serve his idol. At that moment he acknowledged that *no other God* could save like Him, and that God's people should be respected and protected by law.

Remind the class that God often sends warnings to us. We may get a pang of conscience about our pride. Or we may suffer bitter disappointments because our proud desire for something is thwarted. (Someone else, perhaps, is picked for the team instead of us.) God may speak to us through a lesson from the Bible, showing us our pride. Sometimes we are very alarmed by a dramatic happening (teachers could give examples suitable for their class) and, like Nebuchadnezzar, we resolve to think much more about God in the future.

(2) **Drifting back into pride.** Nebuchadnezzar made a

similar resolution. After the three men had come out of the furnace, unsinged and not even smelling of fire, he acknowledged the greatness of their God. But there is no sign that he really humbled himself and turned to God. He simply decided to be more reasonable to the Jews.

Warn your class that it is possible for people to become 'religious' without truly becoming Christians. People may even boast of their interest in religion, but unless they are really converted, their pride will continue to grow. Its growth may be halted temporarily, but soon the old self-confidence, self-admiration and ingratitude to God will creep up. We read that before long Nebuchadnezzar was flourishing in his palace.

Second lesson – a warning dream. This time the warning from God took the form of another vivid dream, the meaning of this being explained by Daniel with a sense of foreboding *(Daniel 4.19)*. Teachers should make the dream as enthralling as possible. Its message was clear. The greatness of Nebuchadnezzar's empire was described. It was pictured as a great tree (vv 20-22). But then the tree was cut down, leaving only the stump (vv 23-25). The king was shown in stark detail the disastrous consequences of a further drift into pride.

Have we ever considered how suddenly our abilities and achievements could be taken from us? How quickly a footballer can have his career snatched from him by a leg injury! What good will all our education be if unemployment prevents us from making use of it? How quickly illness can wreak havoc with our plans! What use will success in this life be if it costs us an eternity in hell?

(3) Pride grows again – great Babylon. God was showing kindness to this proud monarch when He issued this warning, but as the days went by Nebuchadnezzar showed still less respect for God, and after only a year he was to be seen strutting around his palace roof, admiring himself for his wisdom and achievements. Help the class to appreciate the stupidity of his action. It was architects, masons and craftsmen who actually designed and built the great city of Babylon! It was the king's father who had laid the foundations for this rich empire! It was above all the Lord Who had enabled Nebuchadnezzar to achieve prominence in order to punish the Jews for a time! Yet Nebuchadnezzar boasted, *Is not this great Babylon, that I have built . . . by the might of my power, and for the honour of my majesty? (Daniel 4.30.)*

Third lesson – with the beasts. Describe how one of the world's greatest rulers was reduced to a gibbering idiot. It would have been bad enough if he had been deposed and reduced to poverty and ignominy. Instead he was *driven from men* and put out with the animals. *How are the mighty fallen!* The higher a man lifts himself, the further he has to fall. The greater our pride, the greater must be our humbling.

God's grace to Nebuchadnezzar. Despite this tragic happening, God did not immediately overthrow Nebuchadnezzar's empire, and when he returned to his senses it was still intact, waiting for him to take hold of the reins again as Daniel had promised (vv 25-26). Now, at last, the mighty ruler was ready to admit that God's ways are full of truth and judgement, and that *those that walk in pride he is able to abase* (v 37).

God's grace to us. Explain to the class that before anyone becomes a Christian he or she must be humbled. Young people who want to live without God could be compared to a little boy who thought he was too clever to go to school. The world teaches us that we are gifted and good, and can do without the Lord. But the Bible teaches that we depend on God for spiritual life and experience, and unless we turn to Him we shall never have these things.

The world teaches us to trust in our own ability and sense, but the Bible teaches that we are poor, lost sinners in God's sight. The world teaches us that we shall somehow win through in the end. The Bible teaches us that we need desperately and urgently to go to the Saviour. Urge the class to see the folly of trusting petty achievements, other people's praises, and the flattering lies of the devil. Tell them how easily we could be humiliated, like the Babylonian king. Encourage them to follow the examples of Shadrach, Meshach, Abed-nego and Daniel, who humbly obeyed the Lord and left their future promotion in His wise and powerful hands.

Appeal to them to join that great company of people down

the ages who have gone to the Cross of Calvary, recognising with shame how sinful they were in God's sight, and trusting in the suffering and death of the Lord Jesus in the place of sinners, as the only means of forgiveness, new life and a place in Heaven. Urge them to pray:

> I am trusting Thee, Lord Jesus,
> Trusting only Thee,
> Trusting Thee for full salvation,
> Great and free.

Visual Aid

Illustrations of the golden image, the fiery furnace and Nebuchadnezzar's humiliation are available in many books. Use them to highlight the three main points of the lesson. Re-use the picture of Babylon from last week's lesson.

Contempt for God (162)
Belshazzar Sees the Writing on the Wall

Daniel 5; see also Jeremiah 51

Aim: To awaken the children from the indifference and complacency which grips every godless generation, and to help them to see the nearness of God's judgement.

Teachers' Introduction

One of our chief concerns in this age of extreme godlessness is that the Lord will return and find our children unprepared to meet Him. The average worldling is so far away from God that he sins and blasphemes without any qualms or fears. Such was the case with King Belshazzar before the Lord disturbed his peace in a most dramatic way. By describing these events vividly, we have the opportunity to put the writing on the wall for our children.

Lesson Outline

Introduction. Some teachers may like to show how up-to-date and relevant our theme is, by telling their class about the disaster of the *Titanic*. In recent history we have this example of disaster striking at the very moment that society was celebrating its ability to build an 'unsinkable' ship. Today's lesson centres on a very similar tragedy, except that, just before the end came, God spelled out the meaning of the events that followed. There was no time for King Belshazzar to take adequate measures to put matters right. But these events are recorded so that *we* might benefit.

The party. At the very moment that enemy forces were silently gathering outside the city walls of Babylon, Belshazzar, king of the Chaldeans, had prepared an enormous feast. His mind was far away from matters of war and of state. He was completely taken up with preparing one of the most magnificent entertainments ever staged – all in his own honour. A thousand guests were to attend this massive celebration. During the course of the evening the king not only boasted of his drinking capacity, but ordered the wine to be served in the gold and silver cups which his grandfather brought from the Temple in Jerusalem. (In the Old Testament the word *father* also indicates a *forefather*.) Belshazzar wanted to add every possible variety of boasting to this occasion, and to insult openly the God of the Jews at the same time. He wanted to vaunt the 'gods' of gold, silver, brass – money, possessions, human craftsmanship and science.

A picture of our generation. Describe how modern man resembles Belshazzar. He loves to boast of his knowledge, his power, his wealth, and at the same time insult and blaspheme God Who gave him all the abilities which he has. Three headings help us to show the children how like this proud king we all are –

(1) Lazy. Remind the class how easy it is for us to be lazy like Belshazzar, to forget our duties, and to think that everything will take care of itself. We even imagine that we will turn out to be honest and decent people without any effort! Instead of working hard at these things and praying for God's help, we concentrate on enjoying ourselves and showing off things which we possess. Belshazzar was too busy boasting to notice that the enemy was at the gate. We, too, are so occupied with pleasure that we fail to notice the guilt which has already built up in our lives, and will shut us out of Heaven.

(2) Boastful. Remind the class that, like Belshazzar, we like other people to admire us. There are different kinds of boasting. Some people who are not successful at anything like to be admired for their daring and wrongdoing. Often the things we boast of are not ours to begin with. Some children do well at exams, but who gave them their brains? Pretty girls become proud of their appearance, but who gave them their good looks? We boast of modern technology but we forget how much it depends on the inventions of the past.

(3) Insulting God. Belshazzar carried his sin to excess when he deliberately insulted and ridiculed the Lord by using the cups from the Temple to praise his evil gods. How often we see this kind of behaviour today. People boast of their atheism and at the same time take delight in using God's name to curse.

The writing. Belshazzar's party was proceeding when a terrifying thing happened. Describe how the fingers of a man's hand began to write on the wall, and how this affected the king (v 6). He was panic-stricken by the divine intervention. He called for his experts and advisers, but not one of them could decipher the meaning of the words. The boastful, bragging monarch had been reduced to a dumbfounded victim of fear within moments. Only the queen could offer helpful advice and as a result Daniel was summoned to appear. (Probably he had been demoted from his former position of trust and respect by this evil ruler.)

Offering rich rewards, the king pleaded with the Lord's servant for an explanation of the handwriting. Relate how Daniel replied fearlessly to the king's request. He reminded the king of the bitter experience of Nebuchadnezzar. But instead of learning from this, Belshazzar had committed even greater evil in mocking the true God, and had given his heart and mind to the 'gods' of wealth, pleasure, greed, and other sensual sins. He had obstinately refused to acknowledge or glorify *the God in whose hand thy breath is.* Then Daniel unveiled the sentences of judgement (vv 25-28).

Mene. Meaning, *God hath numbered thy kingdom, and finished it.* Belshazzar, who proudly imagined that his life and kingdom were his own to do as he pleased with, was reminded that his days were in the hands of God. The God of history, Whom Belshazzar had chosen to ignore, had 'numbered' the last year of his kingdom and finished it. Tell the class that God has often done this through history. Empire after empire has believed that it was indestructible, but God has ended each one in turn! Individuals are the same. Day by day we hear and read about death, yet we do not consider what will happen when it comes. Will we be shocked and dismayed when our life is ended, and we realise we are going to stand before God in judgement?

Tekel. Meaning, *Thou art weighed in the balances, and art found wanting.* Show the class a picture of a pair of balances. These were originally used, we are told, to ensure that gold was pure. Describe how, if gold had been mixed with some cheap metal, it was immediately obvious when it was put on the scales opposite a block of real, solid gold. Belshazzar's value as a person had been put to the test by the Judge of all the Earth, and found to be worthless and sinful. Ask the class if they realise that one day each person must appear before the judgement seat of Christ *(Romans 14.10).* Help them to do their own arithmetic to test their own record. On which side will the scales come down? Their 'bad' will far outweigh their 'good'. Their 'outward manner' can never make up for the mass of sin and selfishness which lies beneath. Do we imagine we can hoodwink the Judge?

Peres. Meaning, *Thy kingdom is divided, and given to the Medes and Persians.* There was no hope for Belshazzar. At the very same time that Daniel was pronouncing this sentence, the Median and Persian troops were pressing through the city gates ready to subdue and capture the city, where all the leaders of the empire were drunk. Within hours Belshazzar was dead and his great kingdom divided.

A day of judgement for us. Explain to the class that just as certainly as Belshazzar was humbled by God, so our sin and shame will be judged by the Lord. God has appointed a day on which He will judge everyone. There will be no exceptions. Those who have proudly lived away from the Lord will be sent away from Him for ever. God had given detailed warnings of the fall of Babylon many years before, through His servant

Jeremiah. Similarly the Bible warns us of God's judgement. Is there any way out? Yes, because God, in all His love and mercy, has found a way of forgiving all those who humbly admit their sinfulness and turn to Him with sorrowful hearts.

Right back before the beginning of time, the Lord Jesus, God's own Son, agreed to come to Earth, and to give His life for all who put their trust in Him. In due time, He came, and bore our punishment on the cross of Calvary. Urge the class to wake up to the danger they are in, and turn to the Saviour while there is time.

Visual Aid

The subject of Belshazzar's feast has been a favourite with artists, including Rembrandt. Use paintings and illustrations which give a worthy impression.

Faithfulness or Spiteful Jealousy? (163)
Daniel Remains Unmoved by Threats to Throw him to the Lions

Daniel 6

Aim: Children often give thought to the kind of people they want to be. Often they will pattern themselves on some particular hero. This lesson will describe various types of character into which they could develop, and urges them to give serious thought to value the best.

Lesson Outline

A man of God – (a) Respected. Describe how the years had passed and Daniel had become a greatly respected man. He had won the confidence of the world leaders of his time. Having held distinguished posts in the Babylonian Empire under Nebuchadnezzar (and having predicted accurately the downfall of his grandson, Belshazzar), Daniel was available to advise the new Median-Persian administration as soon as it took over.

(b) Conscientious. King Darius (who governed as 'king' of the Chaldean region of the Median-Persian Empire) recognised in Daniel a man of immense ability and supreme honesty. He greatly admired his character. Remind the class that men in power, both then and now, often have difficulty finding honest and competent administrators and organisers. They know that so many of their helpers are greedy for power, and capable of treachery when any opportunity for personal advance arises.

(c) Trustworthy. King Darius felt so safe with Daniel that he planned to *set him over the whole realm*. Mention that through the course of history, believers have sometimes been given positions of great trust. (Children will remember Joseph, trusted by Pharaoh.) Even in school, teachers often single out young believers for special tasks, knowing they can be relied upon not to steal or lie or take advantage.

His rivals – (a) Jealous. Despite favour with the king, Daniel experienced great difficulties. His success and favour aroused great jealousy from others. Presidents and princes were angered by his being preferred to them.

(b) Hostile. Daniel's conduct made these presidents and princes feel shabby by contrast, and they hated him all the more, and became determined to do him harm. They called in their 'dirty tricks' department, but search as they might they could unearth no dishonesty or treachery in Daniel. Finding they could not accuse him of corruption, dishonesty or negligence, they resorted to foul play. Describe their plan.

(c) Devious. In describing the scheme hatched by Daniel's rivals, emphasise how important it was that they flattered the king. The idea was that for thirty days no one would be permitted to pray to God (or to ask any priest to do so for him). As a mark of honour to Darius, all prayers must be made to him for that period. This would give recognition to him as being so mighty as to be a god! It would signify that Darius was greater than Daniel's God. (For the benefit of teachers, the mainstream commentators affirm that the word *petition* in *Daniel 6.7* refers strictly to a *religious* request, or a prayer.) Had the king not been so proud, he might have suspected their motives. But instead he fell for their flattering suggestions (v 9).

(It would be good to inform the class that the devil first used this ploy on Eve, and still finds it highly successful. When he flatters people, they believe him. Today, for example, Satan tells men and women that they are far too intelligent to need moral rules and commands. He says that everyone is much too good to need a Saviour, and he watches with satisfaction as people believe his flattering lies.)

Tell how Darius signed the document, and the decree went out that any person making a *petition* (explain the meaning) to anyone except the king would be thrown into the den of lions.

Daniel's reaction – (a) Faithful. How would Daniel respond? He had every reason to fear that the princes would have their way and that the law of the Medes and Persians would be carried out. But Daniel had greater trust in the Lord his God. Daniel did not assume that the Lord would automatically save him from the difficulties and rescue him from death. He knew of many who had been persecuted bitterly for their love of the Lord. But he did believe that if it was God's will for him to continue with his ministry, then no king, no interdict or decree could prevent him from doing so. Whatever happened, he certainly would not renounce the true God, and grovel before a man as a god.

(b) Courageous. Daniel was unmoved by the threats of being thrown into the lions' den. He was determined to remain faithful to the Lord and leave the outcome in His almighty hands. Surrounded by hatred, jealousy and intrigue, he knelt unashamedly at his open window three times a day. Gladly he turned to the Lord just as he had always done, confiding in Him, and asking His blessing.

(c) Close to God. He would not have missed that wonderful privilege, however many lions were waiting to devour him. Explain to the children that when real Christians pray, it is a treasured experience, far removed from the dreary chants and repetitious liturgies which the children might have confused with prayer.

Thrown to the lions. Describe how Darius, unable to discover a loophole in the law, reluctantly assigned Daniel to the den of lions. No doubt the princes saw to it that the lions were very hungry. But such was the impression made by Daniel on the monarch, that Darius felt a certain confidence that Daniel's

God would deliver him. Nevertheless the king had no stomach for food or pleasure that evening and endured a sleepless night. He was greatly relieved and overjoyed the next morning to hear Daniel's voice coming from the pit.

Protected and safe. Daniel had been given a divine escort in the lions' den, and instead of being destroyed he was lifted high in the king's estimation and given even greater influence and respect. The men who had schemed this horrible death were themselves eaten by lions, and a proclamation was made throughout the kingdom that Daniel's God should be recognised and feared.

Our security. Tell the class how the Lord overruled these events many years ago so that all His people anywhere and at any time could be encouraged to put their trust in Him. Daniel's experience does not teach us that Christians will never be in danger. The Lord Jesus warned that His people would often face persecution and even death. There have been many martyrs for the Lord. However, God has promised that He will always be with His people to strengthen and uphold us, and that all things will work together for our *spiritual* good. Once we belong to Him, no one can ever pluck or snatch us from His hand.

Every real Christian can sing –

> *Should all the hosts of death,*
> *And powers of hell unknown,*
> *Put their most dreadful forms*
> *Of rage and malice on,*
> *I shall be safe; for Christ displays*
> *Superior power and guardian grace.*
>
> Isaac Watts

Who will you be like? Remind the children that they are at a very important stage in life, when their whole future is being shaped and decided. Encourage them to look back on this lesson not just as an exciting tale of a brave Daniel facing lions but as a challenge to them. Show them how to weigh up the three chief character-types represented, and to ask what sort of person they want to be. Which of the following three character-types will they be like?

(a) King Darius. Will they be like him – enjoying the benefits of godliness in others, and having a respect for the Christian way, but not going so far as to turn to the Lord for themselves? Will they be caught out by the flattery of this world (as Darius was), and allow it to dictate a way of life they would not altogether choose for themselves?

(b) The presidents and princes. Will they be like them – refusing God and His blessings, becoming embittered and jealous, and resorting to backstabbing, deceit and dishonesty in order to achieve their selfish goals in life?

(c) Daniel. Or will they become like Daniel – earnestly trusting the Lord from earliest days, and throughout life, even when others scorn or jeer? Will they have the wonderful experience of knowing the Lord to be present with them in the most threatening situations, and will they prize above all else a personal knowledge of the Saviour? Will they live in the certainty that they belong to Him, that He gave Himself for them on Calvary's cross; and that He will return one day to take them to His heavenly home, where they will see Him face to face and serve Him for ever?

Warn the class that if they never bother to stop and think about their future course of life, Satan will cultivate in them all the kinds of sinful, selfish and godless patterns of behaviour which will lead them to judgement and hell. How much better to turn to the Lord in early days, and then to look back on life as Daniel did and say:

> *In early days Thou wast my Guide,*
> *And of my youth the Friend;*
> *And as my days began with Thee,*
> *With Thee my days shall end.*
>
>   M. Bruce

Visual Aid

Cut out from stiff card outline figures of: (i) King Darius; (ii) the presidents and princes; and (iii) Daniel. Place a large cut-out question mark beside each as you describe their characters and ask the class, 'Which will you be like?'

Unselfish Concern (164)
Nehemiah's Desire to See Jerusalem Restored

Nehemiah 1 – 3

Aim: To portray a believer who wanted to be useful to God above all else. To use the qualities of Nehemiah to test the spiritual standing of each child.

Teachers' Introduction

The *Book of Nehemiah* will be familiar to very few children, and so this series is full of excitement, intrigue and triumph.

Lesson Outline

Introduction. Open the lesson by describing the splendour of King Artaxerxes'* palace in Susa. Out of all the richly-clad nobles attending court, our 'camera' homes in on the cupbearer to the king. Explain that Nehemiah was like Daniel, a Jew living in exile, but privileged to be a close and respected official in the service of the king. This Persian monarch was surrounded by people who plotted and planned his downfall, and it was essential that his closest adviser should be completely trustworthy. So the king turned to a man who loved and served the Lord. Normally, an alien like Nehemiah would have been content and happy with his position, enjoying as he did the favour of so powerful a man and the glamour of such a splendid court. But we shall soon discover that his heart and thoughts were somewhere far away.

Bad news! Tell how a party of Jews arrived in the city of Susa from Jerusalem. Some years previously another ruler had allowed a large company of captive Jews to return from Babylon to Jerusalem. Under the direction of Ezra they had repaired the Temple. Nehemiah had been happy to hear this and was hoping to learn that the rest of the city had been restored, including the walls and gates. It hurt him deeply to think of the city of God lying waste, with its enemies jeering at the inhabitants and also at the Lord Himself. Nehemiah had dreamed of the day when

---

*Ar-tax-erx-ees – emphasis on third syllable.

God would demonstrate His power through His people, and make Jerusalem safe and prosperous again. The wonders of the palace of Susa were nothing to him compared with the well-being of Jerusalem, where God had spoken so often to the human race. Imagine his sorrow when he learned from these visitors that Jerusalem was still in disgrace, with its burned-down walls lying in mounds of rubble. After the completion of the Temple, the Jewish workmen had lost their enthusiasm for the work, and had settled in their homes and farms. Now they were very poor, and suffered many indignities from local people, who hated them.

Sleepless nights! Describe Nehemiah's reaction to this news. Instead of shrugging off the information and thinking that it was just somewhere a very long way away, he was broken-hearted. He could neither eat nor sleep. He poured out his heart to God in prayer and pleaded for help (*Nehemiah 1.4-11*). Show to the class that this is a sign of a true believer in Jesus. A real Christian loves the Lord and puts His work far above all personal well-being. Christians want the Gospel to be told to all people. They are far more concerned about the success of God's work than about their own affairs. Even in practical things, they would rather paint and decorate the Lord's house than their own.

Explain that one of the first signs of God's Spirit beginning to work in our hearts is the feeling that we love our Sunday School and want to be there as often as possible. It is no longer a chore and duty, but something we look forward to more than anything else. Ask the class if anything like this has happened to them.

Earnest prayers! Compare Nehemiah's prayer with the cold, matter-of-fact prayers recited at many school assemblies. Show how he really meant what he prayed. His tears and fasting were very real signs of this. We can see that Nehemiah prayed about all his trials. When the king challenged him to explain why he looked so sad in his presence (regarded as a great insult to a king in those days, and likely to meet with heavy punishment), Nehemiah told the king about his concern for Jerusalem, and prayed silently to God for help.

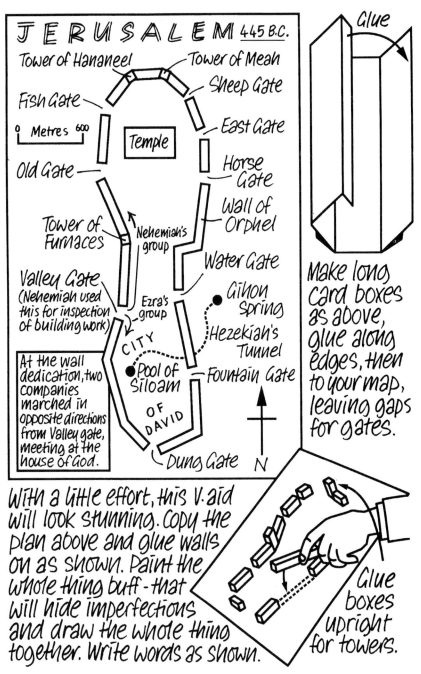

JERUSALEM 445 B.C.

Tower of Hananeel
Tower of Meah
Sheep Gate
Fish Gate
0 Metres 600
East Gate
Temple
Old Gate
Horse Gate
Wall of Orphel
Tower of Furnaces
Nehemiah's group
Water Gate
Valley Gate (Nehemiah used this for inspection of building work)
Ezra's group
Gihon Spring
Hezekiah's Tunnel
CITY
Pool of Siloam
Fountain Gate
OF DAVID
At the wall dedication, two companies marched in opposite directions from Valley gate, meeting at the house of God.
Dung Gate
N

Glue

Make long card boxes as above, glue along edges, then to your map, leaving gaps for gates.

With a little effort, this V. aid will look stunning. Copy the plan above and glue walls on as shown. Paint the whole thing buff - that will hide imperfections and draw the whole thing together. Write words as shown.

Glue boxes upright for towers.

VA 10 – Visual Aid for use with Lesson 164 – 'Unselfish Concern'.

The king granted Nehemiah leave to return to Jerusalem with much practical support. He gave a wonderful answer to Nehemiah, who knew that this was due to the Lord overruling the king's mind, and ascribed his gesture to *the good hand of my God upon me.* Tell the class that all Christians receive answers to their prayers, and are often overwhelmed at the way in which God influences all kinds of circumstances in their favour.

A huge task! Having reached Jerusalem armed with letters and materials, Nehemiah wasted no time before carefully surveying the ruins of the city wall (see VA 10, page 145). Then he called together the people and stirred them to urgent action (vv 17-18). Immediately after he had succeeded in convincing the inhabitants and leaders that they must begin work, the enemy began to protest. But the rebuilding proceeded and we are given (in chapter 3) a detailed account of how everyone, from priests to jewellers, and from rulers to perfumers, set their hands to the work.

Toil! Tell the class that often in the course of history God has stirred His people to great work. Men have worked longer hours and travelled more miles in unceasing labours for the Gospel than worldlings believe possible. Give examples of men like John Wesley, who on horseback visited practically every town in Britain. Or the extraordinary Dr Baedeker who, despite suffering from a diseased lung and severe curvature of the spine, travelled thousands of miles across Siberia at the end of the nineteenth century to preach the Gospel to Russian prisoners living in desperate poverty. One of the characteristics of true believers is that they want to please the Lord by serving Him in a vigorous way.

Conclusion. Give the class a hint of the drama of next week's lesson, when the enemies launch one attack after another in an effort to prevent the work proceeding. Revise the main points of this week's lesson, applying each to the heart of the individual.

(1) Nehemiah was different. Even in a rich, foreign court he stood out as a man who could be trusted. Though far away from God's house, he was faithful to the Lord. Has the Lord ever changed your character and converted you, so that you are faithful to Him – wherever you are? Are you able, with His help, to represent Him at home, at school, even if, like Nehemiah, the thought fills you with fear?

(2) Nehemiah's heart was for the Lord. Real Christians love the Lord because He first loved them and gave His life for them. They are much more concerned about His house and His work than about their own well-being. Do you feel this way? If not, ask the Lord to help you as Nehemiah asked the Lord to help him.

(3) Nehemiah really prayed. Have you learned to pray? Do you really mean what you say? Do you pray quick, casual and selfish prayers? Or, like Nehemiah, do you pray real and earnest prayers for important spiritual things – like the forgiveness of your sin, and the help of God for representing Him? Do you pray for parents and friends, that they may come to know the Lord?

Some lessons on prayer. With older classes, read Nehemiah's prayer and point out:

(a) How Nehemiah *prepared* to pray.

(b) That Nehemiah remembered that he was praying to a great and mighty God Who hates and punishes sin. But he also remembered that the Lord is kind and merciful, ready to forgive all who are truly sorry for their sin, and who give their lives to Him. Remind the class that they should always remember what God is like when they speak to Him – great and holy, yet loving and merciful.

(c) How Nehemiah repented of his sin; he told the Lord how it grieved him and how its consequences hurt him. When we pray we must also show real sorrow for our sin, and the damage it has done.

(d) That Nehemiah pleaded God's kind promises in His Word (spoken to Moses) that when His people returned to Him and repented, He would again bless and help them. God's promise to forgive us is fulfilled in the form of a Person – the Lord Jesus Christ, Who came to die for our sin. We can be sure that if we come pleading the name of Christ, God will hear, and answer our prayers for His sake.

(e) Nehemiah went to the Lord for help. He knew that only

God Himself could influence the actions of mighty Artaxerxes, and he simply and briefly explained his great need, trusting that the Lord would act. Encourage your class to go to the Lord for help when they need courage to bear a testimony before those who may threaten or scorn them. Assure the children that if they pray in this spirit, then the Lord, Who *is able to do exceeding abundantly above all that we ask or think,* will answer their prayers as He did Nehemiah's.

Visual Aid

Show Susa and Jerusalem on a map. Make a model or draw a diagram of Jerusalem with its gates and towers (see VA 10 on page 145). Point out the route which Nehemiah followed on his night survey *(Nehemiah 2.12-15).*

Determination and Courage (165)
Nehemiah Works On, Despite the Enemy's Schemes

Nehemiah 4 – 7

Aim: To show that Satan's methods have not changed, and to make the children fully aware of his intention to have and to hurt their souls.

Lesson Outline

Remind the class how Nehemiah had arrived in Jerusalem with timber and other materials needed for rebuilding the devastated walls and gates. Describe how he called together the city leaders, and unveiled his plan for rebuilding *(Nehemiah 2.17-18).* However, no sooner had they agreed to begin the work, than their enemies began to pour scorn on their efforts and to do their utmost to demoralise them. These enemies did not want to see Jerusalem strong and secure, and they used all their cunning and strength to devise means by which they could stop the work of God.

Our lesson will show the many different schemes they had for frustrating Nehemiah's plans. Tell the class that Satan, with his workers, is always determined to destroy God's work, and his techniques are repeated from one generation to another. By following the plans made by Sanballat, Tobiah and Geshem, we can prepare ourselves for the kinds of attack which the devil will make on any child or adult who tries to find and follow the Lord in this day and age.

Record time. Despite all the enemy's craftiness and brutality, the rebuilding of the walls took place in record time. Why? Because Nehemiah trusted in the power of the Lord, and prayed for help. Whenever the enemy attacked, he turned to God, and he refused to be frightened, tricked or flattered by them. Any suggestion which came from them was rejected immediately. The New Testament tells us – *Resist the devil, and he will flee from you (James 4.7).* Having excited the children's imagination along these lines, proceed to list in detail the crafty intrigues which Sanballat, Tobiah and Geshem employed.

(a) Ridicule *(Nehemiah 4.1-5).* First, the enemy ridiculed the workers and hurled derision upon their efforts. Could these Jews build a city wall from the heaps of charred rubble? Why, their efforts would be so feeble that even a fox could break it down! So they taunted, and Satan does the same to us. When we first begin to take the things of God seriously, he causes others to laugh at us and mock us, suggesting that our interest is just a joke. 'Why,' he says, 'how weak and pathetic to be a Christian!' If we are to withstand these taunts we must ask the Lord's help as Nehemiah did.

(b) Attack *(4.6-15).* Second, when the enemies saw the work proceeding, they became enraged, and planned an all-out offensive, but Nehemiah was ready, and his men worked with a sword (for defence) in one hand and a trowel (for building) in the other. The builders were ready to become soldiers at a moment's notice, and as such formed a formidable army. They were prepared *from the rising of the morning till the stars appeared* to confront any aggressor. Sanballat and Tobiah realised they were no match for such a force, and angrily turned away.

Similarly Satan is furious when he sees a boy or girl turning to the Lord, and does all he can to hurt and damage their faith, and turn them away from the Lord. He whispers doubts into our minds – that there is no God. He puts us off by making us think that life will be miserable and unhappy if we leave the world's side to follow the Lord. Only by using the Lord's armour will we be able to withstand his attacks, which are described by Paul as *fiery darts* fired into our thinking.

(c) Craft *(6.1-4)*. Having failed to make war, the next plan was one of deceit. Sanballat and Geshem adopted a friendly manner and asked Nehemiah to meet them for a talk. Nehemiah would not be tempted to leave his work and was therefore protected from their murderous plans. Warn the class that Satan can appear as an *angel of light*. If he realises that we will not surrender to his attacks, he tries another method. He becomes very reasonable, and suggests that we give consideration to his wise advice. He tries to lure us away from the Lord with other attractions, and makes all kinds of tantalising suggestions to us. (Give examples appropriate for the age of your class.)

(d) Fearful threats *(6.5-9)*. Describe briefly but dramatically the fourth scheme hatched by these men: to frighten Nehemiah by making an elaborate threat to arouse the hostility of King Artaxerxes. Again the plot failed and Nehemiah asked God to strengthen his hands. Tell the class that often young believers find that attempts are made to play dirty tricks on them. Perhaps lies are told about them, or they feel frightened at the consequences of taking a stand for the Lord. Sometimes parents become very angry when their children become Christians.

In such trials we turn to our Saviour in prayer and He always helps us. Sometimes He overthrows the 'plot' or soothes down the anger against us. At other times He draws close and encourages us to stand up to troubles. Sometimes the trouble turns out not to be too bad, and we are reminded of how Christian in *Pilgrim's Progress* discovered that the lions which he feared were chained up!

(e) Foul play *(6.10-14)*. The wall was nearing completion and Nehemiah's enemies began to panic. They had one last trick up their sleeves. This time their plan was really devious. They decided to bribe some Jerusalem prophets, whom they were sure Nehemiah would trust. Shemaiah was paid to be a traitor. It was arranged that he would frighten Nehemiah, and urge him to hide from trouble in the Temple. Once there,

Sanballat and his friends planned to expose Nehemiah's cowardice to his followers and have him laughed out of town.

But again his steadfast trust in God led him to see through this plot. He knew that the Lord could well protect His servants without their having to run like frightened rabbits into the Temple precincts. Shemaiah's prophecy did not make sense, and although it was uttered by a prophet whom Nehemiah hoped he could trust, he soon realised that this man had been bribed by Sanballat.

Explain to your class that Satan is never fair. He uses all kinds of evil devices to lead children away from the Lord. He often uses lying propaganda, making sweeping assertions which have never been proved. (The theory of evolution, so constantly referred to by the media as though it were a proven fact, is one such example.) Satan may tempt us to doubt that we are real Christians, just when we feel sad or depressed for some reason. Just as muggers pick on old ladies, so Satan often assaults us with doubts when we are ill or tired. We must be like Nehemiah and trust God's Word and His promises, and then we will be saved from Satan's snares.

Completion on time! Remind the class that so many building projects that take place today are finished late. Very large construction schemes sometimes fall years behind their target date. But the wall of Jerusalem was completed in fifty-two days, with voluntary workers! Amazing things have often been accomplished when God's people have been moved to do His work, and He has helped them. Ask the children if they are among the Lord's servants. Contrary to what Satan may have told them, a Christian enjoys the most thrilling and exhilarating life possible.

Urge the class to see how Satan plans to dupe us all and keep us under his control. How tragic it is that so many people do not know that there is a great battle going on in this life – a battle for the soul of each person! Do we realise we have an enemy – Satan? Help them to see through his methods and to turn to the Lord Who loves sinful people and came to die to obtain forgiveness for them. Suggest that they should set off with the same determination as Nehemiah to seek the Lord, and ask Him to set up His rule in their lives.

Visual Aid

Provide a box or tin marked: 'Schemes to stop the wall being built.' As the lesson proceeds draw out of this cards marked with the headings (a) – (e). As the enemies' schemes fail, tear up the card and take out another.

Kindness (166)
The Wall of Jerusalem Completed

Nehemiah 8 – 12; especially 8, 9, 12.27-43; see also 5.14-19

Aim: To describe the joy often experienced by God's people. Also, to continue our character study of Nehemiah, and to compare his devotion to Jerusalem with the lovingkindness of the Lord.

Lesson Outline

Remind the class that, despite the threats and opposition we heard about last week, the walls of Jerusalem and its gates were rebuilt within fifty-two days *(Nehemiah 6.15)*! Many of the workers were not professional builders, but because of their desire to please the Lord, inspired by Nehemiah, they *had a mind* [or heart] *to work (Nehemiah 4.6)*. They worked hard and long and amidst opposition until the work was complete. Their enemies were silenced and forced to admit that God had helped His people in this great project.

Dedication of their hearts. Show the class a diagram or model of the city walls and gates (see VA 10, page 145). Describe the scene when the people gathered at the Water Gate to listen to Ezra reading from God's Word. Outline briefly their varying moods: (1) sorrow for sin *(8.9)*; (2) joy in the Lord *(8.12-18)*; (3) appreciation of the Lord's past dealings with their nation (chapter 9); (4) willingness to reform their ways, ie: return to Sabbath-keeping, tithing and purity (chapter 10).

Having repented of their sins, confessing and forsaking them, they were ready to dedicate their newly restored city to the Lord. Explain to the class that it is never right to give anything to the Lord while there is sin in our lives of which we have not repented. Sometimes people try to 'bribe' God with good works and donations, but He will not accept these feeble gestures when hearts are unclean *(Amos 5.21-22)*.

Dedication of the wall. Help the class to enter into the joyful nature of this occasion. Perhaps teachers could compare it with a recent event in the life of the church or Sunday School when there was rejoicing on the completion of a special project. It is one thing to attend an opening ceremony of some kind, but the atmosphere is altogether better when those who have done the work are the chief participants. The younger classes will appreciate how proud the children must have felt to walk across the section of the walls built by their own fathers.

Using the diagram, outline the route of the two sections of the procession *(12.31-40)*, which culminated in a great service of praise in the Temple. The shouts of joy from men, women and children throughout Jerusalem could be heard *even afar off* (v 43). Explain to the class that there are no people more happy and amazed than the Lord's people, when they think of their great blessings. Surrounded as we are today by those who scorn God's Word and scoff at His laws, it is still possible for us to experience the Lord's mighty blessing as we set out to serve Him. There will be times of great rejoicing as we experience victory over our enemies – eg: (a) *the sins* that the Lord enables us to overcome; (b) *the fear* of telling our school friends that we belong to the Lord, when He gives us the courage to do so; (c) *the difficulty* of making the Gospel known to all those who live around us (when the television, the newspapers, even the schools seem so antagonistic to Christian values), as the Lord answers our prayers and enables us to win over the hearts of many who once were hostile.

Nehemiah's devotion. At this point it will be appropriate to assess Nehemiah's part in this great achievement.

(a) He left the court of Susa. Had it not been for his heartfelt concern the wall would never have been begun. His willingness to give up his position of highest comfort, honour and authority in the royal court of the emperor, led him to go to rescue a ruined city.

(b) He toiled against great opposition, against many enemies. Once there, he had to convince the people living in and around

Jerusalem that he had a feasible and practical proposition, and this itself entailed long work and preparation. Remind the class of all the threats of the enemy which would have terrified anyone who was not wholly dedicated to this grand project.

(c) He worked at his own expense. Explain that Nehemiah, as governor of Jerusalem under King Artaxerxes, was entitled to claim expenses and to impose extra taxes upon the people for his own benefit. But he felt sorry for the people who already bore heavy burdens. So he worked unpaid, and gave liberal hospitality to others (5.14-19).

(d) He experienced great joy as he saw the walls built up, the gates replaced, and the people of Jerusalem made happy and secure in the Lord.

The love of the Lord for us. Make a Gospel application by comparing the devotion of Nehemiah with the love of the Lord Jesus Christ for us. (This is not to suggest that Nehemiah is an 'official' type of Christ, but as one who was commissioned to restore Zion, there are obvious parallels between his work and that of the Saviour.)

(a) As Nehemiah left the comfort of Susa, so Christ left the courts of Heaven. Tell the class that Jesus lived in glory with angels to serve Him. Yet when He saw us, fallen, and exploited by our enemy, Satan, He chose to leave the glories above, and come to our poor world, in order to rescue and restore a people for Himself.

(b) Like Nehemiah, the Lord toiled against Satan's opposition, but on a far greater scale. His task was a lonely one, and His enemy, Satan, inspired evil men against Him. In the end He allowed Himself to be crucified on the cross, where He bore the punishment of sin for us.

(c) As Nehemiah paid for his work himself, so Christ paid a vastly greater price, the price of sin, for us. The Saviour was determined to save us, and was willing to pay. He took the pain and suffering due to sinners, and so set us free. Now He claims the hearts of those who are His own. Press the point home. In a world where even young people are exploited and manipulated for gain (eg: by producers of immoral teen magazines), it is hard to conceive the selfless kindness of the Lord in redeeming sinners.

(d) Just as Nehemiah was happy to see Jerusalem restored, so Christ rejoices to see sinners restored, all over the world, and in every age. He rejoices to see His kingdom grow in the hearts of all who receive Him. Urge the class not to ignore such wonderful kindness but to turn to the Lord and make Him King and Governor of their lives. Then they too will become citizens of the heavenly city – safe and secure for ever. Assure young believers that all those who are truly saved and converted by the Lord will indeed be protected by Him for ever. Satan may threaten, and sins may take them temporarily off the track, but they can be sure that they will be held secure by the Saviour Who so loves them.

Visual Aid

Use VA 10 (page 145) as directed in the lesson.

Fickleness (167)
The People of Jerusalem Go Back on their Vows

Nehemiah 13.4-31

Aim: To warn the children against the fickle behaviour pictured in *Nehemiah 13*. To describe the genuine and lasting nature of true conversion.

Lesson Outline

Disappointment. If the Bible had been written by an uninspired person, it would have closed at *Nehemiah 12*. But as God's Word is always faithful and true, it records the bad as well as the good. Help the class to feel the disappointment experienced by Nehemiah when he returned from a visit to King Artaxerxes.

(1) The enemy invited in. He could hardly believe that, of all people, Tobiah had been given a spacious suite of rooms in the Temple! Anxious to please his family, Eliashib, a priest who was related to Tobiah, had allowed the chief enemy of the Lord's work to take up residence within the Temple court. Not only was it lunacy to invite him in, but it was an insult to the Lord, as well as to His servant Nehemiah, who had built the city wall at so much cost to himself. Nehemiah was rightly grieved and angry, and immediately ordered Tobiah's removal *(Nehemiah 13.4-9)*. In this way the city was narrowly saved from a take-over by the enemy within her gates.

(2) God's work neglected. Next Nehemiah wondered why there were so few priests on duty in the Temple, and discovered they had not been paid. He summoned the people, and remind-ed them of their promise to tithe their goods and possessions.

(3) The Sabbath neglected. The next problem arose when Nehemiah woke up on the Sabbath to hear the clatter of horses' hooves, and the buzz of stalls and merchants. Instead of keeping the Lord's Sabbath, the people were busy setting up the market-place, and all kinds of merchants were displaying their produce for sale. Dare Nehemiah face the unpopularity and bitter hostility certain to erupt if he banned this wrong trade? People with vested interests no doubt put great pressure on Nehemiah to overlook the matter. But he believed that Jerusalem was the Lord's city. How could he allow God's commandments to be flouted openly? He therefore put into effect strong measures to outlaw this practice. The gates were to be closed and locked on the Sabbath-eve, and kept shut until the Sabbath was over *(13.19)*.

(4) Marriage with unbelievers. The final disappointment for Nehemiah was to hear foreign languages spoken in Jerusa-lem. This told him that the people had gone back on their promise not to marry heathen women. These women wor-shipped idols and taught their families to do likewise. There would have been nothing wrong in the Jews marrying people of other races if those people had renounced their false gods and served the true God. But these marriages broke God's law, defied Him, and turned Jerusalem into a heathen city. So Nehemiah set about putting the matter right *(13.23-31)*.

Setting our lives in order. These four points give teachers an opportunity to make corresponding pastoral applications to young believers and seekers in their classes. (The applications could be integrated with the unfolding of the four points just described, but generally it will be best to deal with them as a separate, subsequent portion of the lesson.)

For young believers: (1) Never invite Satan in. Warn all the children to be on their guard for the devil and his lying propaganda. He is determined to invite himself into our lives and rule over us, but he does not have our well-being at heart, only his own power and position. He aims to take over our desires, and inflame our sins. How tragic it is that so many young people believe his lying promises, and hand over the keys of their hearts to him, only to be taken captive for a life of godlessness and ultimate loss.

Warn all new Christians to avoid the enemy, and never to let him back into their lives, not even in the smallest way. Encourage them to occupy their minds with the Lord's work and Word, and not with worldly entertainment and activities. Recommend Christian reading, such as biographies of great servants of the Lord whose example they can follow, along with other books which will do them good, make them wise and enable them to answer the devil when he next attempts to get back into their lives.

(2) Remember the Lord's work. Encourage believers to put aside (voluntarily) some portion of their time, energy and pocket-money for the service of the Lord Who has saved them.

(3) Remember the Sabbath. Our Sabbath has changed to the Lord's Day, and it is kept in a rather different way. On this day we worship, and study the things of God, and serve Him. We do not work for personal gain, or do things we need not do on this day. It is the Lord's Day! It belongs to Him, and as Christians we know this.

(4) Think carefully about friendships. Explain that Christians find all their help, their guidance and their pleasures with the Lord and His people. Naturally they still relate to unconverted friends and are concerned about their spiritual state. Believers are known for kindness and care towards everyone among whom they live. But their closest friends and advisers will be members of the Lord's family. They never need to turn back to worldly literature, or parties, or counsellors to see them through. When older, they should not think of marrying someone who is not a Christian. It would be an impossible mix, because each would have a totally different outlook, with different aims, loyalties and interests. One would serve the Lord, and the other would serve the world.

Urge young Christians to serve the Lord with all their hearts and to be separate from the ways of the world. Suggest they make this their prayer:

> Take my heart – it is Thine own;
> It shall be Thy royal throne . . .
> Take myself, and I will be
> Ever, only, all for Thee.

A Gospel challenge. Alternatively, teachers could present an evangelistic challenge by returning to the topic of character, emphasising the fickleness of the citizens of Jerusalem at the time of Nehemiah. Remind the class of the enthusiasm shown by the Jews at the dedication of the wall. Then describe how they forgot their vows and promises as soon as Nehemiah's back was turned. He had to leave for a visit to King Artaxerxes, and, while he was away, they slipped into their old sins. All the progress they had made was put at risk and their security threatened. Their opportunity to regain special blessing as the Lord's favoured nation was cast off for the sake of short-term gains, such as making money, worldly friendships, and sinful pleasures.

Hot or cold? Show the class how fickle we can all be. One day we want to be the Lord's, the next we join up with those who have no time for Him and boast of their sinful ways! The Lord God says He would rather that we were either hot *or* cold. But to be lukewarm is no better than being cold, and yet it makes us feel good and deceives us *(Revelation 3.15-16)*. Remind them of Felix who, hearing the Gospel from the apostle Paul, trembled *(Acts 24.25)*, but still he delayed making a serious response to the message, and was lost for ever.

Inside or outside? Urge your children to seek the Lord with all their hearts, to take it very seriously and to realise that becoming a Christian means being deeply changed by God, and for ever. Unlike joining a club which they may leave later, it is more like being adopted into a new family. Explain that once a person has *truly* applied to the Lord Jesus for forgiveness of sin and experienced His Holy Spirit's work in his heart, he will never want to return to his previous life.

Yes or no? Challenge them with the question set by the Saviour, Who spoke of two brothers, each asked by his father to go and work in his vineyard. The first refused but eventually went. The other agreed to go, but never did *(Matthew 21.28-31)*. Ask the class which one pleased his father. Compare the second with those people in Jerusalem in the days of Nehemiah – changeable and fickle. Urge the children to consider carefully if they have taken Christ's invitation lightly. Explain that, as a Sunday School teacher, you would rather have a child who is at first unmoved by the Gospel, but who goes home and thinks about it earnestly, than one who immediately puts his hand up and volunteers to follow Christ, but who soon forgets the matter, and goes back to his old way of life.

Nehemiah's closing prayer. Close the lesson with the final words from the *Book of Nehemiah – Remember me, O my God, for good.* Nehemiah must have wondered how long Jerusalem would maintain the rules he had put in place. He knew that laws and regulations could never by themselves make people godly. Nehemiah knew, however, that God answers the prayers of individuals who believe in Him, however sinful and rebellious the society around them. Express your great desire that there will be those in your own class who will, like Nehemiah, know the Lord in a personal way, and belong to Him.

Visual Aid

For the Gospel challenge, provide a long piece of card with an arrowhead on both ends. On one end write, 'Hot?', on the other, 'Cold?' Two similar cards should be marked, 'Inside?', 'Outside?' and 'Yes?', 'No?'

Revision (168)

Aim: To encourage the children to consider the important but neglected subject of human character and the factors which shape it. To emphasise the difference between those whose lives belong to the Lord, and those who reject Him.

Lesson Outline

Suggest to the class that the study of human character is a fascinating one. Demonstrate that it is largely overlooked and ignored in our society. People measure themselves in terms of material and intellectual success rather than by the kind of people they are. 'How rich, how clever, how good-looking, how popular, how happy am I?' are the questions asked. Seldom do we hear, 'How kind, how honest, how helpful, how good, how pleasing to God am I?'

Help the children to stop and see how silly this can be. What use is it living in a world which is advanced in technology, full of computers, and capable of supersonic flight, if the majority of its people are overwhelmed by depression, unhappiness, fear, frustration, poverty and war? A glance at any newspaper will prove that our world is full of people who are expert scientists, successful sportsmen, wealthy businessmen, powerful politicians, famous entertainers, whose personal lives are unhappy and often engulfed by tragedy. So many people do not seem to be able to manage themselves. Ordinary families also find their lives blighted by violence, broken relationships and frustrated hopes. They have built their lives without the foundation of God's Word, and cannot cope with the storms of life.

The Bible pays great attention to the building of character. We have seen some wonderful examples of *really* successful lives in this series of lessons. Ask the class to name examples. We have also heard about those whose success was ruined by fatal flaws of character.

Teachers with older classes may like to give the lesson a visual aspect by presenting the outline of a human head. Divide it into five separate compartments, but leave a circle in the centre. Label the five sections:

(a) good looks – leading to friendships, admiration, popularity;

(b) intelligence – leading to exam success, good jobs, advantage over others;

(c) physical skills – leading to success in sports, physical endurance, long life;

(d) personality – leading to management ability, attractive character, control of others, popularity;

(e) giftedness in music, languages, humour, etc.

On the centre circle write the words, 'character needed to control and harness', with arrows pointing outwards. Over this, place another circle marked, 'the missing factor'. Explain that people could have all (or some of) the gifts or advantages of the outer circle, but could still make a disaster of life without the missing factor which enables them to keep these gifts under control.

Suggest that character includes values such as loyalty, faithfulness, concern for others, determination, courage and kindness. It also includes honesty, cheerfulness and gentleness. Ask how these unseen characteristics can be obtained. Show how only those whose hearts have been remade by the Lord can overcome the opposite traits of selfishness, pride, contempt for God and others, and changeability. Read (from *Galatians 5.22-23*) the features of the fruit of the Spirit in a person's life. Ask the class to test themselves by these standards. Remind those children who are proud of their Bible knowledge and Christian families that these are the characteristics which God desires. Do we have unselfish love, joy which springs from a grateful heart, peace amidst the storms of life, goodness even when tempted, etc? Having awakened an interest and provoked awareness of these great issues, refer briefly to the events in the lives of Daniel and Nehemiah which highlight so many interesting and helpful aspects of human character.

(1) Daniel's loyalty and courage – separated from his family as a youth, what prevented him from being lured into a sinful, wasted life in Babylon? How did he find courage to stand firm on the principles he had learned as a child, refusing the king's food and wine? What was the result? Did he lose out? Do we have the same standards and courage as Daniel? Do we know his God?

(2) Nebuchadnezzar's pride – he was a great king with a world empire. The hanging gardens of Babylon were one of the wonders of the ancient world. What was it in his character that brought him to humiliation, even after Daniel's warnings? Are we in danger of losing everything that is good because we are too proud to submit to God?

(3) Daniel's friends remained calm and unmoved even when they were thrown into a great furnace. How can we account for this? Who promises to be with all His people when they suffer for Him? How can we find the Lord for ourselves?

(4) Belshazzar was celebrating his own greatness whilst the Medes and Persians were invading his city. What was he doing at the feast which brought down God's judgement? What does it tell us about his attitude to the God of Heaven? Do we behave in such a way that we shall bring down God's judgement?

(5) Daniel's enemies planned to have him eaten by lions! Why did they so dislike him? Is there any cure for jealous, envious hearts? What does this lesson teach us about Daniel? Can anyone expect God to rescue them in situations of extreme danger, by quickly offering up a prayer?

(6) Nehemiah was a humble man, confessing his sins and the sins of his people to the Lord. Why does believing in God and knowing Him make such a difference? How did the Lord answer Nehemiah's prayer through King Artaxerxes?

(7) The enemies of Jerusalem used many schemes and plots to prevent the city walls being rebuilt. Why were they unsuccessful? How can young Christians resist Satan's attempts to ruin their future?

(8) The Lord Jesus Christ and His love were foreshadowed by the life of Nehemiah. Nehemiah left the king's palace to protect God's people. What did the Lord Jesus leave behind in order to save us? Nehemiah gave himself day and night to the work of rebuilding the wall. How did the Lord Jesus Christ give Himself to secure our future? Nehemiah paid many expenses from his own pocket. What did the Lord Jesus pay in order to redeem us? Christians are those who want to be 'altogether like the Lord'. Have you found this desire in your heart – as Nehemiah did?

Visual Aid

Make an outline of a human head and use it as suggested in the lesson.

Series 20
Exodus 20
THE TEN COMMANDMENTS

169 – An Introduction to the Ten Commandments
Why study these ten laws of God? Why learn about rules first written down nearly 4,000 years ago? What benefit would knowing and keeping these commands have for the future of today's young people? One day, at the end of life, we must all be confronted by this list of our Maker's requirements. Far better to consider them now, than leave it until it is too late to find a Saviour.

170 – Thou Shalt Have No Other Gods Before Me;
Thou Shalt Not Make Unto Thee Any Graven Image
What kinds of 'god' do people have in their lives as an alternative to the true God? What are *our* 'gods'? Why is it wrong to attempt to depict God in statues or pictures?

171 – Thou Shalt Not Take the Name of the Lord
Thy God in Vain
What is so important about a name? Our use of the Lord's name shows what we think about Him. Do we hold our Maker, our Keeper and our Judge in contempt? Or do we know how to approach Him in the right way?

172 – Remember the Sabbath Day to Keep it Holy
Why devote a whole day to God, His worship and His service? Our Creator commands us to set this day aside each

week, not only for our own physical and emotional well-being, but, more significantly, to hear His Word and to consider the most important matters of life.

173 – Honour Thy Father and Thy Mother

Is this just outdated advice for children? Why should they honour their parents? This commandment instructs everyone – all of society – to treat seniors and leaders with respect. It is the secret of a stable society. What happens to 'big-heads' who refuse advice? The Lord loves and blesses all who are humble before Him.

174 – Thou Shalt Not Kill

There is much more to this command than the forbidding of murder. This lesson explains the many acts and attitudes which are part of the 'murder' family of sins, such as jealousy, hatred and scorn of others. It also teaches about the uniqueness of life, which is in the Lord's hands.

175 – Thou Shalt Not Commit Adultery

This commandment which provides the family, and protects it with love and loyalty, must be proclaimed with greater clarity than ever before in the present climate of unfaithfulness. The Lord's provision of the family gives each one a special place of honour, love and care from the moment of birth to death. This lesson traces God's remarkable plan.

176 – Thou Shalt Not Steal

Stealing can be disguised in many shapes and forms, but we cannot deceive the Lord. He is the great Giver, but we are base thieves. How can we be forgiven? How can we then repay the debt of love we owe the Lord, and become kind and generous people?

177 – Thou Shalt Not Bear False Witness

What is wrong with a lie if it can help us out of trouble? This lesson tells the truth about lying – showing how it is arrogant and insulting to others, and how it perverts our own minds. What are the consequences? Is there anyone we can completely trust? Why does God ban all liars from Heaven? Is it possible for us to be made really honest and truthful?

178 – Thou Shalt Not Covet

When Paul picked out a commandment which deeply convicted him (when he was unsaved) it was this one. How opposite the Lord's standard is from the natural bent of every human heart! And how vital it is to define covetous desire to children, and to show them their need of salvation!

179 – Revision

So much depends on these great laws given by Almighty God. Are we listening to their message?

Teachers' Introduction to the Series

When the State took over responsibility for the education of children from Christian organisations in 1870, Bible teaching was included in the curriculum. Until comparatively recent years, children were taught at least the ten commandments in their secular day-schools. Our society acknowledged this set of moral absolutes as the best foundation for a stable and fair society. Such days are now behind us, and it is left to a remnant of Sunday School teachers to instruct the rising generation in this all-important subject. We need to absorb the spirit of *Psalm 119* as we take on this awesome responsibility and privilege.

The ten commandments are so vital and relevant to the life of each child that teachers, who at first may be apprehensive, may soon find that this series (carefully illustrated with narratives and bright graphics) is one of their favourites. The fact that the commandments are challenged and rejected constantly by present-day society makes the subject highly topical.

A word of warning for newer, younger teachers. The commandments deal with some sensitive topics (in sexual matters particularly). Therefore follow the outline closely, or consult a leader before making any radical alteration to a lesson. We have heard of disastrous lessons given in the course of youth work by those who take it upon themselves to deal with sexual conduct in an explicit manner.

Teachers' aims for the series. As teachers prepare these lessons the following questions will prove helpful.

(1) Have I helped the children to respect and admire these great laws, *and* their Giver, avoiding a trite and over-simple approach?

(2) Have I enabled them to appreciate the profound wisdom of each law, despite its plainness and brevity?

(3) Have I demonstrated that each command is very broad in its scope, generally naming the head of a family of sins?

(4) Have I given practical help to the young as to *how* they can avoid being dragged down to a lifestyle which shows disregard for God's ways, and ignores His rules?

(5) Have I been able to give a heartfelt warning of the dangers to their personal happiness of breaking these laws?

(6) Have I been able to show them their need of a Saviour?

Narratives. Often a narrative (rightly valued by the infants' teacher) is suggested to illustrate points, or as an introduction to the lesson. Look out for these and make full use of them. For example, teachers are advised to begin the lesson on the fourth commandment by describing a typical Sabbath Day in the Israelite camp in the wilderness. The way in which the people of that time prepared for and spent this special day will provide an intriguing and helpful means of introducing the subject of the Lord's Day.

Department memory work. It would be particularly appropriate for leaders of the various departments to plan a weekly session of memory work so that the whole department can recite together the ten commandments. Ideally, all children should be given the commandments printed out on a sheet to take home and learn.

Visual Aids

This series focuses on concepts and commands rather than events and narratives. It is therefore particularly important for teachers to provide lively and helpful visual aids. VA 11 (on page 167) gives suggestions for use throughout the series. These large, colourful shapes will provide a focal point for each lesson and fix the key points in the children's minds and memories.

Teachers of the very young should take full advantage of the visual aids suggested, embellishing these with pictures if the class cannot yet read. When dealing with 'non-narrative' sections of the lessons these will be particularly useful for keeping attention. For example, during the lesson on the seventh

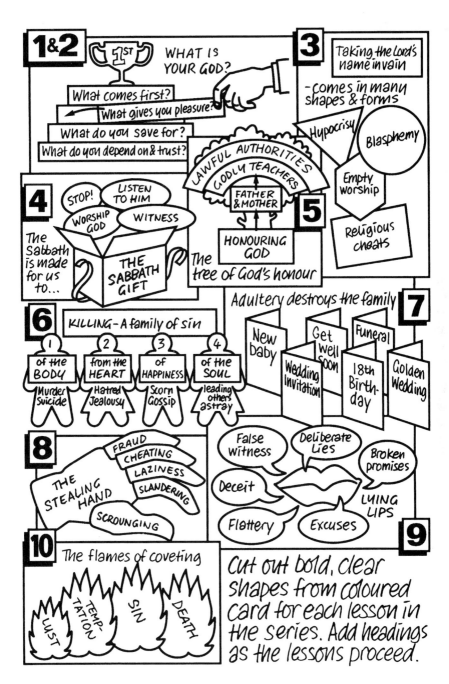

VA 11 – Visual Aid for use with lessons on 'The Ten Commandments'.

commandment, teachers are advised to have a set of greetings cards which will provide a novel means of illustrating the Lord's wonderful provision of the family unit to care for each individual from the cradle to the grave.

An Introduction to the Ten Commandments (169)

Exodus 19 – 20 (also Romans 3 – 7)

Lesson Outline

Illustrate modern contempt for the ten commandments by showing and quoting a selection of newspaper cuttings which give up-to-date examples of how much they are despised and ignored. Then suggest a number of atheistic reactions to the commandments, such as, 'Why should I be interested in God's laws, I don't even believe in God?' Or 'Don't I have the right to decide what I do, after all it's *my* life and *my* body?'

Ask the class about their own attitude to the commandments. Are they tempted to think of them as negative 'thou-shalt-nots'? Do they realise (as Moses pointed out in *Deuteronomy 30.15-20*) that they are a matter of life or death? The Lord Jesus Christ described them in His famous parable as a vital foundation for living, without which the storms of life will create havoc (*Matthew 7.24-27*). They are more relevant and vital than any other subject. Newspapers give much evidence of today's rejection of the ten commandments; they also record the pain and suffering experienced as a result. Point out to older classes that the world's most stable and successful societies have been those based on the principles of God's moral law.

Describe the awe-inspiring events at the time that the Lord delivered the ten commandments to Moses. Summarise the events of *Exodus 19*: (1) the solemn questions and promises (vv 3-8); (2) the thick cloud which shrouded Sinai (v 9); (3) the cordoning off of the mountain (vv 12-13); (4) the personal preparation – washing and abstinence (vv 14-15); (5) the thunders, lightnings and trumpet voice (v 16); (6) the smoke, the fire, the quaking of the mountain and the sound of a trumpet getting louder and louder as Moses was called up to the top of the mountain to receive the two great tablets of stone on which the commandments were inscribed (vv 18-20).

These two tablets of stone were written by nothing less than *the finger of God*. What priceless treasures these divinely autographed tablets would have been, had they not been destroyed so soon after their giving! Explain that the original stones are gone, but the commandments were re-dictated by the Lord to Moses. They remain and will remain unchanged and unchanging *(Matthew 5.18)*. They are the laws by which human beings should live, and by which, after they die, they will be judged. Using symbols from the Highway Code to catch the children's attention (see VA 12, page 229), invite the class to examine with you some of the great features of the ten commandments. Illustrate the points with descriptions and illustrations from children's everyday lives. They are:

(1) Ten aspects of God's character. Suggest that just as school rules give an indication of what a school is like, so the ten commandments provide a glimpse of God Himself. Parents anxious to send their children to a school where importance is attached to appearance and smartness will be glad to read that the school rules insist on the wearing of school uniform. Rules which ban smoking will indicate that the school is concerned for its pupils' health, etc.

Show the class how each commandment, in a similar way, teaches us something about the nature of God. The ninth commandment, for example – *Thou shalt not bear false witness* – teaches us that God is the Truth. He never lies. The eighth commandment, *Thou shalt not steal*, teaches us that God is the opposite of a thief! He is the great Giver of all good things. He is benevolent and generous. The seventh commandment, *Thou shalt not commit adultery*, teaches us that God is absolutely pure and trustworthy, for He outlaws impurity and unfaithfulness. The sixth commandment, *Thou shalt not kill*, teaches us that God is love, because He bans all hatred, malice and violence in His creatures. What a wonderful God we have! He not only gives us His laws, but He upholds them all Himself and sets us a perfect example.

(2) Ten instructions from our Maker. Remind the class that any machine or technical device is accompanied by a manual from the maker. It is very important to read this carefully before operating the machine, or there could be costly, dangerous and even fatal consequences. Mention the kind of accidents the children may have heard about, involving appliances, bicycles and cars, where maker's or safety instructions have been ignored.

Then point out to the class that the ten commandments can be seen as ten rules prescribed by the Lord Who made us, for safe and successful living. They warn against the misuse of the most complex, beautifully designed 'machine' in the universe – the human body. The rules deserve the greatest respect. If our Maker forbids sex outside marriage then we may be sure that such conduct will do great damage to us emotionally, mentally and physically.

Use as an illustration the case of a young motor mechanic who, while his boss was away, drove off in an expensive, high-powered sports car which he was meant to be servicing. Once on the road he could not resist the temptation to drive the car at high speeds, even round winding bends. Before long there was a terrible crash, leaving the sports car a tangled heap of metal, and killing the driver of another car. Show how this could be a picture of the way we abuse the bodies which God has loaned to us.

Viewed positively, the ten commandments offer clear guidance for the journey of life. They protect from sin and its deceit; give light and understanding for times of difficulty; give certainty in times of change and danger, and provide understanding and wisdom about human nature. No wonder that God's servants attach so much importance to them!

(3) Ten rules to protect Heaven. Introduce this topic by describing the scene above the clouds. Some children will already have flown in an aeroplane. Others will be interested to hear what it is like to rise above the clouds and discover a vast dome of blue, and beneath them, a carpet of pure white, fluffy clouds, with no dirt, filth or rubbish of any kind in sight. Go on to describe Heaven as a place where everything is pure, clean, happy and endlessly satisfying for all who live there. No pain or sin can exist there. There is no death in Heaven, for God dwells there. Pose the question – How can it stay that way?

Explain that the ten commandments are God's way of protecting Heaven from the sin and disobedience which has so disfigured and ruined the Earth since men and women rejected Him and His commands. Sin has been allowed a reign on Earth before the Lord restores it to righteousness. But He will never allow sin to approach Heaven. No liar, thief, adulterer, murderer, idolater or any other kind of sinner will be able to live there (see *1 Corinthians 6.9-10; Revelation 21.27*). Explain to younger children that even a single lie, like an unseen germ, would spoil Heaven. Therefore *all* sin is banned. Who then can ever hope to go to Heaven, for we are all sinners? The ten commandments are designed to show us our condition before God; our unreadiness to go and live with Him as we are. By them, the Lord alarms us as we see ourselves as we are, so that we can be jolted into seeking the only Saviour Who can wash away our sins.

(4) Ten laws by which we shall all be judged. Alert the class to the danger of becoming complacent about sin. Point out that it is all too easy to imagine that, because we can get away with wrongdoing on Earth (especially in present-day society), we will get away with it in the sight of God. The Lord Jesus Christ warned of a day when our secrets will be revealed to all.

We shall be judged according to the ten commandments, which are clearly presented and explained in detail in the Bible, and which are also written in our consciences. We will not be able to plead ignorance. All people who have not during their lifetime come to Christ for pardon, will be judged by these.

It is as if they will all be asked the same ten great questions – Have you worshipped other gods, have you stolen, have you lied, etc? There will be no favouritism from the Lord; no lenient treatment for a favoured few *(Acts 10.34)*. All will be proved beyond any doubt to be sinners and to have come short of the glory of God. All will be without excuse. The fact that people complain so bitterly about the misconduct of others will be proof that they knew the standards. The verdict for all will be: guilty. The sentence will be: eternal banishment from God's kingdom (see *Romans 1 – 2*). How glad and relieved we should be, then, that the ten commandments can also be viewed as . . .

(5) Ten encouragements to seek the Saviour. Explain that the commandments, though seeming to be hard and condemning, have a kind and merciful purpose. Use an illustration suited to your class, along the following lines. Having some kinds of X-ray investigations may involve unpleasant procedures (such as taking a barium meal), but if they show up a condition which needs treatment, and will end the pain, they are to be welcomed. It was God's plan that through the giving of His law, we guilty sinners would become conscious of our many failings, and so be driven to the Saviour Who alone can forgive and renew us. God knew that the law itself would never make us good, or even improve us enough to deserve Heaven. It was designed chiefly as a schoolmaster to lead us to Christ *(Galatians 3.24)*.

Ask the children to consider the pain which the Saviour had to bear in order to save us. In this series of lessons they will sometimes be surprised to realise that they have broken each commandment in some way, and deserve the punishment which is due. As we have seen, God is determined to exterminate and banish every transgression, putting an end to all sorrow, pain, disease, war and death (the bitter consequences of sin). In order to be forgiven, we must appreciate that the Lord Jesus Christ took the punishment which we should have borne, and suffered it Himself, concentrated into the space of a few hours, on the cross of Calvary. He Who is the Truth bore the pain of our every lie. He bore the punishment of our every selfish, hostile or unclean thought. What greater proof could we have of His immense love for sinners? Once the commandments of God shine into our conscience, they lead us to the Saviour Who is willing to wash away our every sin. And when we come to Christ for pardon, He gives us a new life, and from that moment we are so changed, and so grateful, that we *want* to keep His commandments. Not only does He deliver us from the guilt of sin, but also from its power *(Romans 6.14)*!

Visual Aid

See VA 12 on page 229.

Thou Shalt Have No Other Gods Before Me; Thou Shalt Not Make Unto Thee Any Graven Image (170)

Exodus 20.1-6; Psalm 115.1-9; Acts 17.22-31

And God spake all these words, saying, I am the Lord thy God, which have brought thee out of the land of Egypt, out of the house of bondage. Thou shalt have no other gods before me. Thou shalt not make unto thee any graven image, or any likeness of any thing that is in heaven above, or that is in the earth beneath, or that is in the water under the earth: thou shalt not bow down thyself to them, nor serve them: for I the Lord thy God am a jealous God, visiting the iniquity of the fathers upon the children unto the third and fourth generation of them that hate me; and shewing mercy unto thousands of them that love me, and keep my commandments (Exodus 20.1-6).

Lesson Outline

Introduce the first and second commandments by slowly reading the first three verses of *Exodus 20*. Some children may be unaware of these first commands, being familiar only with the later commands, which relate to stealing, killing, lying, etc. Others (perhaps like the rich, young ruler) may be aware of their existence but may never have grasped their real meaning.

Key commands. Tell the children that these two commandments are in some ways the most important. They are the key to unlocking all the other commands. If we were to keep these two, there is a sense in which we should not need the others. If the Lord were our God totally, we should have no desire to steal or lie or hate, etc.

Explain to older classes that the key question for today is – 'Can you be good without God?' (ie: can there be a morally structured society without religion?) People today want an end to violence, fraud, dishonesty, killings, etc, but they do not want to believe in or worship God. Ask if this is possible. The answer is – No! God states clearly in these commands that it is of first importance that we acknowledge Him, and Him alone, to be our God. To replace Him is to remove the foundation on which all the commandments stand.

Your God. *I am the Lord thy God, which have brought thee out of the land of Egypt, out of the house of bondage* [slavery]. Lest this command should seem hard and unreasonable, especially to young people from irreligious backgrounds and homes, point out that the Lord God introduced these commands in a very kindly and positive manner. He reminded the Israelites gathered around Mount Sinai that they were the 'family' or nation chosen to be His special people, and that it was He Who had rescued them from the cruel slavery of Pharaoh.

The Lord God also reminds us all that He is our Maker and Creator. He is also willing to be our Saviour. Use an illustration along these lines: ask the children to imagine a boy (or girl) who has grown to the age of ten without having ever seen or heard from his father. Let us suppose the father was kidnapped by terrorists when on a long journey overseas and has long been presumed dead. Life has been a struggle for his family, the mother doing her best to manage and provide. Then, one day, there is a knock at the door and the child sees a stranger standing there. He is the boy's (or girl's) long-lost father, who has at last been released and has come home. He throws his arms around his child, assuring him that he has never for one moment forgotten about him, that he loves him, and will now look after the family.

Show that many children grow up unaware of their heavenly Father, but not because He has disappeared! In our case it is because we are so foolish that we do not think about Him. In giving His laws He reminds us that He is *our* God. He gave us life in the first place. He provides the world with materials for food, clothing and shelter every day of our lives. He has wonderful plans and purposes for His people, and also lays down clear commands of discipline, and rules, for their benefit. The first condition is simply that we recognise and serve Him as our God, and never turn our best affection and trust to any other.

Who is your God? – some tests. Give the children some questions which will provoke their thought and help them to understand what we mean by God. Using the suggested visual aid (see VA 11, page 167 to which teachers can add pictures), ask: What comes first in your life? Who or what gives you pleasure and happiness? What do you save your money for? Where are your hopes and dreams centred? Who or what do you most trust and depend upon? Who or what do you most love and enjoy? Explain that the answers to these questions will help them to see who or what is the God (or 'god') of their lives. The Lord is the One on Whom we must depend, in Whom we must trust, Who we must love and obey most.

Other gods. Tell the class that ever since Adam and Eve disobeyed the true God, men and women, and even children, have been inventing and creating other 'gods' (lifeless things) to fill the aching void caused by being away from the Lord. List some, emphasising and illustrating points most familiar to your class (see visual aid suggestion). These will help to keep the lesson moving and hold attention.

(1) Handmade gods. The children will be familiar with, for example, the Baal gods of the Old Testament. Made from wood, stone, gold or silver, these gods were pathetic. Often they were animals, such as cats, or even giant beetles. They were gods made by men to replace the God Who made men. They could not see or hear or speak or help.

Of course, people thought that invisible gods would adopt these idols, and be pleased with the foolish worship of the people, and their burnt offerings. But these gods could not communicate with the people, nor the people with them. Superstitious people thought these gods caused all their misfortunes, and gave them benefits, and so they worshipped the idol statues in the vain hope that the unseen gods would take note of it.

Make the children see how degrading it was for intelligent human beings to bow down and worship such things. How insulting and hurtful to the true God Who made the heavens and the Earth, with all their magnificent systems and designs, that men and women should prefer to worship 'stocks and stones' (Jeremiah 2.27).

Describe the fear and superstition which led people to offer sacrifices to these handmade gods in the hope that they would protect them from famines, storms and other disasters, and that they would make their crops succeed. They assumed these gods were like themselves – ill-tempered and vindictive and needing to be won over by means of offerings or bribes. One great attraction (to sinful human hearts) in worshipping such lifeless gods, was that they could neither see, nor hear, nor notice sin. People could therefore live as they pleased. Their shrines were often temples of immorality. Remind the class that there are still millions of people whose lives are dominated by such idols. Show the children pictures of Buddhas, Hindu deities and statues of the Virgin Mary which are still idolised around the world today.

(2) **The 'made-to-please' god.** Remind the class that there are many people who claim to believe in God but who seldom, if ever, attend a church. They have a god of their own making, who is tailor-made to suit them. This god is easy-going, and overlooks all their sins. Even if they fail to lead a good life he will still welcome them into Heaven. If they do go to church, they like to worship him in a way which gives them enjoyment. These people may think that their god is the Christian God, but He is very different.

(3) **The 'pick and mix' god.** Another version of this 'made-to-please' god may be called the 'pick and mix' god. He consists of a mixture of bits taken from various religions. Children are often encouraged to make up such a god today, and schools sometimes celebrate the special festivals of each religion in turn. The infant school classroom may be decorated for the Chinese New Year, the Feast of Ramadan, Christmas, and so on, in turn. The idea (so often) is that children should pick the aspects they like best from each religion. Secondary school children also study the different religions and discuss the 'merits' of each. With such a wide variety of teachings, they may think it is possible to assemble a god who is to their liking. But if only one of these religions is true, then the people who have created their own god will be worshipping a fiction.

(4) **Playing god ourselves.** Before the children begin to feel contempt for primitive religions and contemporary false

religions, help them see that to believe in no God at all is just as bad. Instead of recognising a Person and power above and beyond them, atheists depend upon themselves. They live to please and enjoy themselves and so they become their own gods, deciding what is right and wrong for themselves.

(5) The god of money and all it can buy. It will be unnecessary to dwell at length on this theme (as some Sunday School teachers are prone to do), but it cannot be overlooked altogether. Remind the class of the enormous effort that the acquisition of wealth usually involves, such as long hours at work, loss of family life (and values), and so on. The promise of wealth and possessions is for many like worship. Remind them how insecure and failing are the goods which money buys *(Matthew 6.19)*. The Lord God promises that those who invest their lives in His service can be certain that they will be rewarded with heavenly treasure which never rusts and cannot be stolen.

(6) The god of fun. Many people who do not worship the true God can only get by in life by making *pleasure* their god. The true God gives us very many opportunities for pleasure, but to love pleasure instead of God is to make it our god. Even good activities, such as sports, may be turned into a god. How tragic that many live only for non-stop television, nights out at various entertainments, and places of lust and drug experience, because they cannot live without them! Their 'god' now rules them, and sooner or later they will become utterly dissatisfied and miserable.

No other gods; no images. Returning to idols and other religions, remind the class that these are forbidden by the one, true God. Why? To answer this question ask the children to remember the occasion when the apostle Paul visited the city of Athens. (This will provide a narrative aspect for younger classes.) Then base your answer upon the apostle's. He argued that to worship other gods is wrong because . . .

(1) Any god we make is fictitious. The one almighty and true God Who made Heaven and Earth is far too great to be investigated by the minds of mere mortals. He must therefore describe or 'declare' Himself to us, and He does so in the Bible. The apostle Paul told the proud people of Athens that he must describe or announce God to them *(Acts 17.23)*. Any attempt by humans to guess what He is like, using their imaginations, is bound to be a failure and false. The Bible is the only book which credibly bears the marks of His authorship (as we have seen in Series 17).

(2) There is only one God for the entire human race. He made *of one blood all nations of men for to dwell on all the face of the earth.* 'National' religions contradict this truth, and mixing a little bit of one religion with a little bit of another will take us even further away from Him. How could there be one God for one country or continent, and a different God for others? If the God described in the Bible is true, there is no possible room for another.

(3) Other gods divert attention from the God on Whom we all depend for life and everything – *in him we live, and move, and have our being.* How insulting and hurtful to attribute His works to other (non-existent) gods! How cruel to millions of needy people to divert their attention from the only God Who can really help them!

(4) The true God has appointed a day when He will judge all people according to their obedience, dependence upon Him, and love for Him. To lure people to fictitious gods is a terrible cruelty, because then they will be distracted from preparing themselves to face the true God and Judge. Just as Paul urged the Athenians to turn away from their superstitious, belittling ways, urge your class to clear their minds and hearts of *all* the many gods considered in the course of this lesson, and seek the one true God.

A jealous God. Close the lesson by drawing attention to verses 5 and 6 of *Exodus 20*. Explain that the Lord God so loves the people He has created that He is jealous (in the right sense) for them. He hates to see us giving our love and devotion to other gods. Often in the Old Testament the Lord pictures unfaithfulness to Him as causing the same pain as adultery. Show the children that their disloyalty to their Maker is very hurtful and offensive to Him, and He will severely punish those who choose not to believe He exists, so that they can ignore His commandments. He also promises to wonderfully forgive and bless those who return to Him in love and repentance.

Visual Aid

VA 11 (page 167) suggests an outline trophy on which to place lesson headings. In addition, prepare a set of pictures to represent the different gods worshipped in the place of the Lord: (1) Handmade gods – pictures of Baal gods and other idols; (2) the 'made-to-please' god – a picture of a family passing a church to visit a garden centre or shopping arcade on a Sunday; (3) the 'pick and mix' god – a globe with symbols of the different religions; (4) playing god ourselves – a picture showing the evolution of a monkey to a man; (5) the god of money – glossy advertisements for big houses, luxury holidays, lottery tickets and highly paid jobs; (6) the god of fun – pictures of video games, sports events, pop concerts, alcohol advertisements. (Pictures of Athens will also be useful.)

Thou Shalt Not Take the Name of the Lord Thy God in Vain (171)

Exodus 20.7

Thou shalt not take the name of the Lord thy God in vain; for the Lord will not hold him guiltless that taketh his name in vain (Exodus 20.7).

Lesson Outline

The importance of a name. Catch the children's attention by asking – What is the first thing people need to know when they meet a stranger? It is – that person's name. Remind them that before a baby is born the most pressing topic for parents is what the child will be called. Help the class to work out why names are so important. Explain that names identify. They are the means by which we distinguish one person from another. Our name is our lifelong identity.

The greater importance of God's name. Then tell the class that this is even more so with God, Who cannot be seen with human eyes. We cannot begin to picture Him or imagine how He looks. One means by which we can identify and appreciate Him and His character is by His names. There is one main name in the Bible, and a number of other names which help us to appreciate the many aspects of His wonderful character.

Respect for God's name. This commandment says that God's name must not be spoken 'in vain', which means carelessly or thoughtlessly. Why is this such a crime in God's sight? Why does God condemn the wrong use of His name, even before the condemnation of killing and stealing? Why does the commandment announce so solemnly that He will not hold us guiltless (or leave us unpunished) if we break it? Because insolent or careless use of God's name betrays our attitude to God Himself. Instead of showing respect for Him it indicates that we think nothing of Him. (Children often nickname teachers for whom they have no respect.)

The meaning of God's name. Ask the class to consider the meaning of the name 'Lord':

(1) The Lord – Who is life. 'The Lord' is a translation of the Hebrew name 'Jehovah', which comes from the verb 'to exist', or 'to be'. This name means that God is the self-existent One. He alone needs no help from outside Himself. He *is* life, and He is the source of life. We must be *given* life, and we can easily lose it. But God always has existed and always will. He has no beginning and no end. *In the beginning God . . . (Genesis 1.1).* In the beginning was God *(John 1.1).* He is Alpha and Omega, 'A' to 'Z'. He is the only God, a glorious Trinity – Father, Son and Holy Spirit – acting together in perfect harmony. Just as no other form of energy could exist without the sun, so no other form of life or being could exist without God. The first meaning, therefore, of 'Lord' is that God is eternally alive.

(2) The Lord – our Maker and Provider. It follows that we are dependent for everything on this great Being, *for in him we live, and move, and have our being* (see *Acts 17.23-28).* He is the only source of all good, the fountain-head for all our needs. We continue to depend on Him daily for life and breath, strength and health, and every other good gift. How we should use His name with awe! As boys and girls, and adults who fail and disappoint our Maker, we particularly depend on Him to find a way to forgive us, rescue us from sin, and elevate us to Heaven and eternal life. The second meaning, therefore, of 'Lord' is that God is the sole source of all good, including salvation.

(3) The Lord – our ruler. It also follows that if God is the only source of life and good, so that we are created and sustained by Him, then He is the only legitimate ruler of the universe, and Lord of our lives. The third meaning, therefore, of 'Lord' is that God is the supreme ruler to be obeyed.

The importance of praise for God's name. No wonder the Israelites trembled as they pronounced the Lord's name. No wonder they sang:

The Lord is my strength and song, and he is become my salvation . . .
Who is like unto thee, O Lord, among the gods?
Who is like thee, glorious in holiness, fearful in praises, doing wonders?
(Exodus 15.2, 11.)

Far from misusing the name of the Lord we too should use all our powers of mind and thought and heart to give Him praise. Prayers and praises, we must remember, will be acceptable to God only when we sincerely believe in the God Who is described by His names. Remember that 'Lord' means – (1) God is eternally alive; (2) God is the sole source of all good, including salvation; (3) God is the supreme ruler to be obeyed.

How the commandment is broken –

(1) Blasphemy. First, there is an obvious, vile form of blasphemy, which is when people insult God by using His name as a swear-word. When people do this, they use God's name to express their greatest disgust, hatred and revulsion, as though there was no better word to describe the worst things in life than the name of God! In this, they show how much they loathe the idea of God, and how little they respect or fear Him. Blasphemy is the opposite of worship. Every swear-word is a shout of hatred toward Heaven. Warn the children never to do this. Sympathise with any who live in surroundings where such use of God's name is everyday language, and give encouragement to those who are determined not to swear. Warn others in the class who do not have such expressions in their normal vocabulary, that they will be particularly guilty if they resort to their use.

Illustrate the point by using a comparison which is meaningful to the children. Would they insult the bank manager from whom they desperately needed a loan? Would they hurl abuse at the surgeon on whom their lives would soon depend? Would they curse the teacher who would be writing their report or reference on the next day? How then can they misuse the name of God, on Whom they and their souls depend for all life and health and happiness?

(2) Thoughtless worship. Surprise the class by explaining that this command is most often broken in church! Explain that when people use God's name in hymns and prayers without thinking about the meaning, they take His name in vain. To sing hymns only for the enjoyment of the tune and the singing, when all the time the mind is not consciously thanking God, is offensive and insulting to Him. To pray without any realisation of Who God is, also insults Him. Urge your class to remember that when we sing and pray and hear God's Word, we do so in the presence of a mighty and holy God, and we should do so thoughtfully. Remind the children that the Lord ordered Moses to remove his shoes when he set foot on holy ground *(Exodus 3.5)*, and although we do not show our reverence in this particular way, nevertheless we should be sincere and thoughtful in the Sunday School hour.

At this point, especially with older classes, point out that hypocritical worship, and pretending to be Christians when we are not, is another breach of this command.

(3) Blatant hypocrisy. Comment on the fact that there have always been evil people who have used God's name to get a livelihood, or to get fame and fortune, and that this is a particularly arrogant and reprehensible example of taking the Lord's name in vain. Those who present themselves as God's spokesmen and use their position to gain personal power and large sums of money donated by those who are fooled into believing it is for the work of the Lord, will one day suffer the severe judgement of God. Tell the children that should they come across such wolves in sheep's clothing, they should remember that such men were exposed and harshly condemned by the Saviour when He was on Earth. He would have nothing to do with them – nor should we. Certainly we should not let them shake our faith in the true God Who is faithful and good. (Teachers may wish to give examples known to their class, especially if such are in the news currently.)

A Gospel application. Suggest to the class that before the lesson they might well have thought that words were of little importance, and that mere language would be unlikely to condemn them to hell. Now that they realise the importance of God's name, and what it says about Him, they will understand why the breaking of this commandment will be treated so seriously on the day of judgement. Explain that to insult a judge (contempt of court) is a very serious matter. So is indifference to God's name.

As the children recognise their failure to keep this third command, easy as it might at first appear, they may appreciate their need of the Saviour in a way they have not done before. Help the children see the love of the Saviour Who, at the very time that men and women were insulting and cursing Him, hung on the cross bearing their sin and its punishment (see *Galatians 3.13*). Show the class that we are no better than those present at the crucifixion who hurled their abuse at the Lord Jesus. So often it becomes clear that we treat Him little better, and give Him no more reverence. Urge them to examine their hearts *and their language,* and seek God's mercy and forgiveness.

Encourage the class to look at this commandment in a new way, and let it reshape their thinking and attitude to God. (Suggest that if young believers were to concentrate on keeping this law, then they would find it a great help in keeping every other.) Use James' description of the power of the tongue – comparing it with a small rudder steering a large ship, or a little flame setting light to a huge forest *(James 3.4-9).*

Finally, show the children how they can learn the way to worship and appreciate God by pondering the meaning of His many wonderful names given to us in the Bible. Remind the class that the Lord Jesus and the Holy Spirit are equally God with the Father. Many names are given to the Father: Creator,

Everlasting God, Lord God Almighty, Holy One, King of Glory, Rock, Redeemer, Shepherd, the Righteous Lord, and God of love and peace. Many are given to the Lord Jesus, including: Saviour, Prince of Peace, Emmanuel, Sun of Righteousness, Truth, Life, and Friend of Sinners. These names provide us with many ways of thinking of the love and power and the ways of God, especially in His dealings with those who love Him.

Visual Aid

VA 11 (page 167) suggests outline shapes on which to place lesson headings describing the various shapes of blasphemy. In addition, provide (a) pictures or items connected with the giving of names (eg: a book of Christian names for a new-born baby, a class register, a picture of a ship-launching ceremony, a list of local electors); and (b) cards with the names of God referred to in the lesson, printed clearly.

Remember the Sabbath Day, to Keep it Holy (172)

Exodus 20.8-11

Remember the sabbath day, to keep it holy. Six days shalt thou labour, and do all thy work: but the seventh day is the sabbath of the Lord thy God: in it thou shalt not do any work, thou, nor thy son, nor thy daughter, thy manservant, nor thy maidservant, nor thy cattle, nor thy stranger that is within thy gates (Exodus 20.8-10).

Lesson Outline

An example. Show the children a picture of a nomad's large tent, probably made from animal skins, which served as home to a big family of Israelites as they journeyed through the wilderness. Describe how the tent would have housed several generations of a family (from great-grandparents down to the latest baby), together with their servants, and perhaps their guests. Explain the work and toil involved in keeping such a large family fed and cared for in those days. (Modern children are unaware of the amount of labour which was involved before the arrival of electricity and the gadgets this brought.)

Manna had to be collected in the mornings. Water had to be

fetched, meals cooked on fires and the tent kept clean and hygienic. Often the whole camp moved on, so that tents had to be dismantled, transported and then re-erected. Even young children helped in the labour to survive.

Then picture the surprising change which came about on the seventh day, after the final exertion of the sixth afternoon gave way to the quiet and stillness of the Sabbath. Of course, there was the sound of congregational singing as the Israelites gathered to praise their God.

Explain that this was all done in obedience to the Lord's fourth commandment – *Remember the sabbath day, to keep it holy.* Then remind the class that this great law of God applies to all mankind, not just the Jews of old. Right from the beginning of time the Lord wrote this principle of rest into the blueprint of His creation, setting an example Himself on the seventh day *(Genesis 2.2).* Read verses 9-11 from *Exodus 20.*

'Remember!' Tell the children what happened to the Israelite who 'forgot' (whether wilfully or carelessly) to collect a double portion of manna on the eve of the Sabbath. He went without! *(Exodus 16.27.)* This teaches us that we also must remember and make a conscious effort to arrange our lives so that there will be time for the Lord on His day. Just as they had to collect twice as much manna the day before, and in later years to organise their farming timetable to allow for a day of rest, so we need to plan our time with Sunday in view. Children, for example, must make a real effort to do homework at other times. Christians successful in sport have made a brave stand for the Lord by refusing to participate in Sunday games, a stand which has often threatened their success.

Encourage the children to honour and respect this commandment by showing them its wisdom. It may be humbling, but it is true that human beings cannot function properly without rest and sleep at regular intervals. How foolish to defy this God-given natural law! But above all, this commandment is for the health of the soul – the spiritual life.

'To keep'. This word *keep* means to guard or protect. We must be firm about guarding this time for the Lord or else it will soon become neglected. The keeping of this day (and the regular habit of attending Sunday School) establishes God's rule at the centre of our weekly programme. Many children today have been taught to regard such a Sunday as old-fashioned. Remind them that *all* our lives belong to God our Creator and Lord. Therefore we ought not to steal from Him or begrudge this one day in seven which He reserves for Himself.

'**Holy**'. Explain that this word means set apart, and kept different from other days. (Perhaps the children have a cherished book or item of clothing which they keep in a special place for a special purpose.) The Sabbath was a day to be kept special. Explain that it was not merely a holiday, a day of rest, but a day positively dedicated to the Lord. It was to be reserved for matters more precious and more important than those which occupy people during the other days of the week.

In case the people of Israel might think that God was being unreasonable in demanding their time, they were reminded that:

(a) God had made them His *peculiar treasure . . . above all people (Exodus 19.5)*. He had set them aside for His special blessing before asking them to set time aside for Him. But this really applies to all people, who are created not as beasts but as intelligent human beings – made in the image of God, and given rational minds and everlasting souls.

(b) God had saved them from the slavery of Egypt. Christians remember how the Lord Jesus Christ has redeemed them with His precious blood and set them free from the slavery of sin.

(c) God is a holy God, and it is His desire that His people should be holy too. Unless believers give time to learning about God and His ways, they will easily be dragged back into the wrong and harmful lifestyle of the world which occupies so much of their time. A day for worship and spiritual feeding is therefore vital.

'**In it thou shalt not do any work**'. Help the children see that it is part of God's kindness that we should all be granted the opportunity to have this rest, break and change from the drudgery of life. (In expressing this, teachers should be sensitive to the fact that some parents of their class-members may be unemployed or forced into Sunday employment reluctantly.)

At a time when there is so much stress on the advantages of healthy diets and lifestyles, we can tell them that the Bible was centuries ahead of society in general in providing a day of relief, to strengthen physical, mental and spiritual health.

Point out that adults who prefer to trade, shop, go to sporting events, and so on, rather than worship and learn about spiritual matters, are heading for trouble. Many people become dissatisfied, depressed and dependent on entertainment, drink and drugs to dull the emptiness of godless lives. Nothing can replace the deep-seated human need to worship and love our great God, and to understand His plans and ways. Serving the gods of money, possessions, or human achievement, cannot replace the Lord. Urge the children to value their Sunday School hour and not to drop the habit lightly. Express your appreciation of their attendance and remind them how much this observance pleases the Lord.

'Thou, nor thy son, daughter, manservant, maidservant, cattle, stranger'. Explain the beauty of this command in its recognition of all people before God. Describe how, in olden times, the vast majority of people carried out hard and lowly work, including the children. Foreigners particularly would be taken as servants and slaves. But on the Sabbath Day they were all borne in mind and granted a break from work. In God's sight, all are equal. This reminds us that people from all nationalities, all age groups, and all 'classes' may be blessed by God, and may seek and find the Saviour.

What should be done on Sunday? Using the gift box suggested as a visual aid, comment on the following headings, applying them appropriately to your particular age-group.

(1) Stop! and consider high and holy things. Tell the class about the famous epitaph that was inscribed on a man's gravestone many years ago: 'Born a man, died a grocer.' Describe how the keeper of a small shop might be tempted to spend his entire life working in and around his shop. He might never go on holiday or take a day off. It might have been that he was mean or grasping, and this made him unable to put aside his business for a second. What a pointless life! The man who was given that epitaph had almost ceased to be a person! Yet in

some ways we are all like that person if we ignore the principle of the Sabbath.

Show the children that they are more than flesh and blood. The Lord has made them with living souls. His provision of a day apart provides them with an opportunity to stop and consider the *big* questions of life. Where do I come from? What is life? What will happen to me and those I love when we die? How can I find God and know Him? What is He like? What are His plans for the world and for the future?

The Lord Jesus Christ taught that there were questions to be asked of far greater importance than, 'What will I eat, what shall I drink, what shall I wear?' (see *Matthew 6.25.*)

(2) Worship God. Assure the children that the Sabbath (now renamed 'the Lord's Day' and observed on the first day of the week because the Saviour rose from the dead on that day) was intended to be a happy and joyful occasion when everyone could join together to praise and consider their great Creator. It is our chief purpose as created people to love and enjoy Him for ever. What a vast subject! What an uplifting exercise!

(3) Hear His message of forgiveness. Best of all, by attending the Lord's house we have the opportunity of hearing of God's saving love. Compare those who refuse to come, with a prisoner who claims to be too busy to read the letter announcing his pardon. Remind the class of the wonder of the Gospel message – that the Lord has provided a way for sinful people to be forgiven and restored, by coming Himself to bear the punishment of their sin. Remind them also that this message is unique to the Bible. No other religion announces *grace* – the favour of God given freely to those who humbly acknowledge that they do not deserve it, and cannot earn it.

Describe the Sabbath Day when the Lord Jesus went to the synagogue in Nazareth and, having read the Scripture passage from *Isaiah 61*, He said that it had been fulfilled. Tell the class that the Saviour was following the normal Sabbath practice in reading the Bible and then expounding and applying it to the people gathered. Christians followed His example from the earliest days of the Church *(Acts 20.7; 1 Corinthians 16.2),* and we must do the same! We must read the Bible for ourselves, but we must also hear it presented and taught to us by pastors and teachers. The Lord's Day provides us with a regular opportunity to do so.

(4) Witness to others. Tell the children of the deep impression made on neighbouring peoples by the Israelites, as weekday activities gave way to the peace and quiet of the Sabbath Day. The observance of this day marked them out as the Lord's people. Similarly, Christians today offer a challenge to the world around as they withdraw from trade, shopping, entertainment and sporting activities in order to meet with God, and worship. Christian boys and girls also have this opportunity to show their relatives and friends, by their desire to attend Sunday School and church, that they stand for the Lord. Courage will frequently be needed to represent the Lord, and His day is a time to experience His help and strengthening, and to associate with His people.

Visual Aid

VA 11 (page 167) suggests a gift box in which to place the lesson headings. In addition, provide a picture of an Israelite encampment (see VA 6 on pages 100-101 of *Lessons for Life 2*).

Honour Thy Father and Thy Mother (173)

Exodus 20.12; Colossians 3.20; Ephesians 6.1-3

Honour thy father and thy mother: that thy days may be long upon the land which the Lord thy God giveth thee (Exodus 20.12). That thy days may be prolonged, and that it may go well with thee (Deuteronomy 5.16).

Lesson Outline

Begin the lesson by making four simple but interesting comments to whet the children's appetites for a deeper understanding of this commandment:

(a) Its relevance to children. Emphasise that while this command applies to all, it is obviously particularly relevant for children. While the present age shows so little interest in, or understanding of, the young, we remember that the Lord has an important place for them in His plans. He never overlooks the rising generation, and places great importance on their education and training.

(b) Its positive presentation. Most of the ten commandments tell us what we should not do. Here we are told, positively, what we should do.

(c) Its included promise. The people of Israel, gathered at the foot of Mount Sinai, were assured that if they obeyed this commandment it would lead them to a prosperous and lengthy life in the land to which they were going. We must point out that this promise was made to the people *as a whole*. It meant that if the younger generation learned well from their parents, caused no rebellion, and kept up the well-tried customs, then the nation would survive in security and stability in the land which the Lord would give them.

Teachers can point out that this formula still holds true *(Ephesians 6.1-3)*. Societies which respect the parental or previous generation (representing the well-proven knowledge and wisdom of the past) will survive and succeed far better than those where a proud, new generation has thoughtlessly experimented with new and untried lifestyles. To ignore and scorn the advice of history and of experience is generally disastrous. We live in a time when long-honoured principles of morality and family order are being thrown away, and replaced by untested ideas. The result, already, is pain and disorder. The very breakdown of society is taking place before our eyes. (Teachers should give examples of the changes in only the last thirty years.) The children could at this point be shown a picture of an arrogant young person with his nose in the air, just about to step over the edge of a steep cliff, with the words coming from his mouth, 'Don't tell me where to go!'

(d) Its far-reaching nature. Tell the children that the terms 'father and mother' in Bible days referred to much more than just literal parents. 'Father', for example, included the fathers of the nation (rulers), forefathers (previous generations), and fathers of the church (spiritual leaders). Develop these comments using the following categories of 'parent'.

(1) Lawful authorities. Ask the children again to picture the large encampment of Israelites at the foot of Mount Sinai (VA 6, pages 100-101 of *Lessons for Life 2*). How could the two-million-plus Israelites have survived their time in the wilderness, or conquered the promised land, or continued happily in it if everyone had made up their own rules? Suppose everyone had done just as they liked! Instead of buying, many would have stolen. Instead of reporting a crime to the rightful judge or magistrate, many would have retaliated with violence. Soon their nation would have disintegrated.

In order to make life fair and just, peaceful and safe for everyone, it was important that each generation respected the laws and rules laid down by their society in accordance with God's commands. (The older generation had experienced the pain and poverty of slavery and had learned much from their time in Egypt which they could hand down.)

In other words, the 'father and mother' of this command-ment represent respect for God's rules for law and order. God says to all, 'You must honour and promote good order, and co-operate humbly, readily and promptly with the rules and laws of your society' – eg: nation, home, school.

To honour father and mother means first that we respect and follow the traditional (and biblical) way of life which our seniors have come to see is right. It means also that we acknowl-edge that we are inexperienced, and that we have to learn. The Lord Jesus instructed His disciples, telling them that they should obey the lawful authorities and pay their taxes *(Matthew 22.21)*. The apostle Peter warned the early Christians against wrongdoing and law-breaking, and instructed them to pray for their rulers, who were granted by God the power to punish evil-doers *(1 Peter 2.14)*. Only when governments urge citizens to break God's law are they to be defied *(Acts 4.19)*. Apply this principle to the children in your class. Christians, for example, should not be amongst those who play truant from school. They should be amongst those who work hard and behave kindly and honestly wherever they are.

(2) Godly teachers. Israelite children were taught many practical skills by their parents, teachers and elders. These included cooking, tent-making, hygiene (most important in their huge desert encampment), and as time went on, farming and various trades. The younger generation would have been at a great disadvantage if they had not appreciated and learned these lessons. Their future success or failure depended on how well they listened and learned. Their pastors and parents also instructed them in spiritual matters, teaching them God's commands, and His kindness to them as a nation.

Honour thy father and thy mother means that we also should appreciate and remember the things we are taught, whether at home, school or elsewhere. Gratitude keeps us humble. Food, clothing, love, pleasures, education – perhaps to university level – all these things have been given by the parental generation in our society. Soon we will have to take their place. Unless we honour (appreciate and respond to) those who teach us, we shall have little to hand down to the next generation.

'Honour' includes learning. Big-heads will not listen. Rebels will not listen. Fools will not listen. God says, 'Listen to the wisdom that existed before you.'

Today many people sneer at the Bible and its standards. They experiment with a new way of life (having rewritten moral values), and as fast as they try it, it plunges them into trouble. 'Listen!' says God. 'You are not so brilliant that you can ignore advice from others' experience and invent a new lifestyle.'

Many generations of people (from the best and happiest times in history) have listened to the teachers of old whose experiences of the Lord are recorded in the Bible. If we refuse to listen and follow their advice we shall be like a person throwing out a painting from his attic because it was old, only to discover later that it was worth millions of pounds!

(3) Parents. No doubt the young Israelite children were proud to belong to their nation with its special history, rules and customs. But at the close of the day it meant even more to them to return to their own family tent, where they would receive a warm meal, a bed to sleep in and, best of all, the love and care of their parents. The family is one of God's greatest gifts to mankind.

As children the Lord commands us to obey our *parents in the Lord: for this is right (Ephesians 6.1)*. They deserve our respect because of all they do for us and because they should represent the important values and principles which hold society together as cement holds the walls of a house together. Parents, and grandparents, urge their children to behave well, study hard, be honest, and show kindness and courtesy. They urge them to grow up to work in a job or career, to seek a happy, stable marriage, to care for their children and to be loyal to their families. They warn their children to avoid company which could lead them into promiscuity, drug-taking, drunkenness, crime and so on. The Bible urges us to take their wise advice.

We live in days when many fathers and mothers have not followed the instruction of their fathers and mothers. Some have lived to regret it, and now they urge us to learn from their bitter experience. The commandment does not tell us to imitate the ways of adults who have left the right path. It assumes that most parents have learned to appreciate that a stable family and a law-abiding life is best for their children.

Urge the children to treat their parents or guardians with the love and honour they deserve. Cheek and rudeness are never fitting. Even when parents behave badly (as most do at least sometimes) we still owe them respect. Assure the class that parents are also under instruction from the Lord *(Colossians 3.21; Ephesians 6.4)*. Remind them that Jesus Christ, when He was a boy, even though He was the Lord, honoured and subjected Himself to His parents *(Luke 2.51)*.

A disastrous experiment. Tell the class that the Bible predicts that when people turn away from belief in God, they will become, among other things, *proud, boasters . . . disobedient to parents (Romans 1.30)*. Remind the class that we live in an atheistic world where people despise God and His laws – particularly this fifth commandment. Children and young people today are often encouraged to ignore and dismiss the advice of those in authority, and to say, 'What do *I* want to do, what will please *me*?' They are encouraged by the behaviour of fictional television characters to brush aside the warnings and advice of parents and teachers.

Ask the class if this social experiment has been successful. Warn them that it has not only brought disaster, tragedy and untold misery to many lives, but it will also bring down God's condemnation on the day in which He will judge all people, and bring them to account for their wilful trampling over His clear, distinct commands. (If necessary, sympathise with children who may report that their schoolteachers are in the vanguard of the present godless regime. Urge them to accord personal courtesy to all such, but to treat their views with profound caution, if they contradict the clear teaching of God's Word.)

God's mysterious rules. Close the lesson by reminding the class that God's ways are higher than our ways *(Isaiah 55.9).* We, in this world, think that we have to fight for *our* rights, look after ourselves, put our needs first, or we shall get nowhere. Success depends on asserting ourselves. With God it is quite the opposite way around.

(1) He highly exalted the Lord Jesus Christ because He was willing to humble Himself, becoming obedient unto death – even the death of the cross *(Philippians 2.5-11).*

(2) Mary, the mother of Jesus, praised God because He had *put down the mighty from their seats, and exalted them of low degree (Luke 1.52).*

(3) The Lord Jesus promised that in His kingdom the *least among you all, the same shall be great (Luke 9.48).* He also said that, *The meek . . . shall inherit the earth (Matthew 5.5).*

(4) Peter wrote, *Humble yourselves therefore under the mighty hand of God, that he may exalt you in due time (1 Peter 5.6).*

Urge your class to value the fifth commandment because, if they repent of their sin and give themselves to Christ, it will help to make them humble, careful and wise people, and this will lead to their being truly valuable throughout life.

Visual Aid

VA 11 (page 167) suggests an outline tree on which to show the various groups that we are taught to honour. In addition, provide a picture of a young person walking towards a cliff edge (suggested in point c). Also, pictures of children learning from their parents on the farm and around the family tent in Old Testament days, and pictures of children receiving education today at school or college. Newspaper headlines relating to modern tragedies can be used to illustrate the disaster of ignoring this law of God.

Thou Shalt Not Kill (174)

Exodus 20.13; see also Matthew 5.21-22; Galatians 5.19-21; Ephesians 4.31-32

Lesson Outline

Comment on: (1) The simplicity and plainness of God's laws, compared with the complexities of man-made rules and regulations. This commandment can be immediately under-stood by all, including the youngest. (2) The fact that, of all the commandments, this is the one most people accept as right, partly because they value their own lives, and no doubt also because most are unlikely to break it (or so they think). How self-righteous humans are! When they find a law they have kept, they proudly announce that they agree with it. When the law condemns them as law-breakers, they protest against it.

Innocent? Ask your class if they feel able to congratulate themselves on having kept this law of God. Then show there is more to it than at first appears.

The gift of life. Show the class two objects, one man-made (eg: a watch or an ornament) and one God-made, living item (eg: a flower or a fruit). Then ask what is the main difference. They may soon realise that the flower has life, while the man-made article (though ingenious and attractive) is lifeless or dead. Point out that God alone can bestow the gift of life. Scientists, though skilled at unravelling the workings of living creatures, have never been able to *make* life. They become increasingly excited when they discover a long-hidden aspect of life, such as the DNA code, and they begin to behave as if *they* had invented it! The truth is that they have only discovered some of the highly complex 'secrets' of life which God has operated since the world began. If God alone can give the sacred gift of life, ought we not to respect and obey the law He gives to protect human life?

Different forms. Point out to the children that murder is a sin which may be committed in four ways. First, it may be committed literally, by killing a person.

Secondly, it may be committed in the heart. Turn the class to the teaching of the Lord Jesus on the subject of this sixth great commandment. He shows that hatred in the heart is seen by God as a form of murder. *Ye have heard that it was said by them of old time, Thou shalt not kill; and whosoever shall kill shall be in danger of the judgment: but I say unto you, That whosoever is angry with his brother without a cause shall be in danger of the judgment (Matthew 5.21-22).*

Thirdly, it may be committed by 'murdering' or taking away an essential part of another person's life, such as their liberty, or their happiness, or their reputation. Kidnapping was condemned by Moses as a form of murder *(Deuteronomy 24.7)*, and punished in the same way. A person's liberty had been murdered.

Fourthly, it may be committed by taking away from another person the prospect of eternal life – the well-being of their soul.

Teachers should use the visual aid, depicting murder as the chief sin, and the other forms as sins of the same 'family'.

(1) Murder of the body. We as human beings have a privileged place as the highest form of life in God's creation, made in God's image. Because of this, God reserves to Himself alone the right to take life, with only a few exceptions (such as self-defence, fighting a just war, and as the punishment for certain very serious crimes). The giving and taking of human life is something we should stand in awe of, and we must accept God's rules with total respect. The birth of a baby should fill us with wonder, and cause us to appreciate that life is a gift beyond our power to give. We should guard life, and value it, recognising that the Giver alone has the right to withdraw it when He sees fit. Those who tamper with God's laws (in, for example, abortion or euthanasia) do so in absolute opposition to God, and in defiance of His law.

God's law forbidding murder includes the taking of one's own life. Young people in particular should be urged never even to contemplate the possibility of suicide. If God forbids them taking their own lives, it is certain that He will give them courage and hope in the darkest hour, if only they will turn to Him. The lives of many young people in recent years might have been saved if in their time of terrible depression or trial they had looked to the Lord for help.

(2) Murder in the heart. (a) Hatred! If we allow bitter feelings to build up towards a person (once a friend perhaps), and we fan these feelings into hatred, then in God's view we murder that person in our hearts. Hatred wishes the person was not there. Hatred wants a person to be hurt, and wants that person out of the way. Hatred would like to take away that person's happiness and success. It is like murder; it is in the same 'family'. (The example of Joseph's brothers, whose jealousy for their young brother led to their attempted murder of him, is a helpful illustration. Remember how they schemed together to get rid of him. The fact that they did not literally kill him, but sold him, so that he lost his family, his country and his friends, demonstrates that they were guilty of murder in their hearts even though their first plan was not literally fulfilled.)

(b) Jealousy. This provides a clear example of the rottenness of the human heart. Jealousy is usually unreasonable and unfair to its victim. Because someone cannot have what he wants (or because his ambitions are thwarted), he fuels his dislike for someone who does have those desired things. Give suitable examples. (A boy, perhaps, wants to get into the football team, but because another is selected, he hates him, and wants to hurt him in some way.) Jealousy is very common. It despises others. It wants their hurt. It is a form of murder in the heart.

(3) Murder of happiness. (a) Scorn. A common form of murder of a vital part of someone's life is scorn. It is seen in the school playground, and everywhere else. Children can be very unkind, spiteful and heartless towards other children, particularly if they are disadvantaged in some way. Scorn and derision, instead of help and sympathy, are often heaped on those with physical, emotional or cultural handicaps. The children will agree that this kind of treatment can crush a person's spirit and happiness, and hurt them cruelly. Scorn is murder because it does away with the happiness of another person, as well as their access to friends.

(b) Shame. People who cursed their parents in the days of Moses were to be punished as severely as a murderer *(Exodus*

21.17). Parents can be deeply wounded when we shame and hurt them, 'murdering' their dignity and happiness.

(c) Gossip. Like scorn, another form of murder familiar to children is murder with the tongue. Wicked insinuations and spiteful gossip can inflict great damage. These are a form of murder because another person's reputation or character is killed. (The children may have heard the term 'character assassination'.) Children can be particularly guilty in this matter. Cliques form, and those who are unwanted become the victims of lies and exaggeration aimed against them.

(d) Violence. The children will now see that these heart sins can quite easily get out of hand and erupt as violent acts in a matter of moments. Little children sometimes display fits of rage and bad temper. (Those who watch endless hours of violent films and videos harden themselves to the horror of such acts and some actually boast of their ability to inflict pain on others.) Remind them that God records each thought and act, and one day we must all appear before His judgement seat. God will want an account of how we used our lives, and how we treated others. He will certainly outlaw from Heaven those whose record shows callous acts for which they have never sought forgiveness.

(4) Murder of the soul. The Lord Jesus Christ warned that anyone who offended a child (put them off believing in God) could expect the most severe punishment *(Matthew 18.6).* People who scoff at the Bible, casting doubts into the minds of the young and leading them into godless ways (eg: militantly atheistic television producers, magazine editors, etc), are guilty of murder because they murder everlasting souls.

Warn the class that inviting friends to some activity which prevents them from attending Sunday School (for example) might seem trivial to them, but if it endangers their friends' eternal souls, it is a serious breach of God's commandment. Warn older children that they could be guilty of murdering the souls of their brothers and sisters. Our own unbelief could be a destructive example to others, and one day we shall have to answer for the influence we exerted.

Murderers all! Point out to the class that we are all guilty of some form of this sin. All have behaved as murderers. All have hearts that produce hate, scorn, and so on. Perhaps some have thought that it was an exaggeration to call them sinners. But when we look into the mirror of God's Word, we see the truth about ourselves. Even in the case of this extreme sin of murder, we are guilty, and we should feel ashamed, and alarmed about the consequences.

Not only are our hearts desperately wicked, but they are also *deceitful above all things,* fooling us into thinking what nice, kind people we are, when we may be nothing of the sort. How much we need a Saviour! It is surely amazing that God's perfect Son should come to suffer and die for such guilty people! Urge the children to see themselves as they are seen by God. Only then will they be ready and willing to seek the Saviour and ask forgiveness for all their sin. Only then will they long for a new nature.

The Saviour alone can remove the hard, stony heart and replace it with a kind and unselfish heart which is capable of showing concern for others.

Conclude the lesson by reading Paul's words to the Ephesians: *Let all bitterness, and wrath, and anger, and clamour, and evil speaking, be put away from you, with all malice: and be ye kind one to another, tenderhearted, forgiving one another, even as God for Christ's sake hath forgiven you (Ephesians 4.31-32).*

Suggested outline for very young children. Teachers with very young classes could base their lesson on the behaviour of Joseph's brothers – which illustrates murder in its various forms. They knew it was wrong to kill, yet: (1) They allowed *jealousy* to develop into bitter hatred. (2) They *gossiped* to their father and *scorned* Joseph as he relayed his dreams. (3) When the opportunity arose they planned how to *kill* him literally. Later they refrained from the actual deed but the consequences of their actions were still terrible for Joseph. (4) His *happiness* was murdered as he experienced being cut off from his family, his country and his family career. (5) Had it not been for the Lord, his *soul* could well have been destroyed in Egypt, a land of idolatry.

Remind the children of Joseph's love in forgiving such

murderers, and then tell them of the Lord Jesus Who gave His life so that we who are guilty too might be forgiven.

Visual Aid

VA 11 (page 167) suggests an outline family-chain to represent the various member-sins in the family of murder listed in the lesson. Pictures of the first part of Joseph's life will be valuable for the youngest classes.

Thou Shalt Not Commit Adultery (175)

Exodus 20.14; Matthew 5.27-32; 1 Corinthians 6.9-11; Jude 23-25

Teachers' Introduction

This commandment, understood in the light of Christ's teaching that it involves sins of the heart and imagination, as well as the physical act, is particularly necessary for children and young people today. Following the pattern of the previous commandment, our aim will be to include the whole family of sins named in the commandment by its chief manifestation.

Young people in our society are threatened as never before by an avalanche of immoral entertainment and propaganda, even in their own homes. At the same time they receive less instruction and protection than previous generations. It is often the case that the instruction they do receive is of an anti-moral character! Secular schools now shrink from laying down guidelines, and even churches seem fearful of addressing the subject clearly. A Sunday School or Bible Class teacher cannot avoid being in the front line of the battle, for the young desperately need plain, practical and positive instruction.

This commandment lays a firm foundation which will support young people through the sexual perils of life. It provides us with an opportunity to extol the beauty and desirability of God's great gifts to mankind – marriage and the family. We begin with these two positive themes. As the children begin to appreciate and respect the Lord's wonderful provision of the family unit, they will more easily learn to view with disgust the damage it sustains from the various deviations.

The application of this commandment will vary with the age and background of the class. Some children in our classes may come from broken families. Some may scarcely know their fathers, and many will be well aware of the fact that the adults around them have no respect for this commandment. (We need to be sensitive in what we say, and yet not cowardly, for it is often children from the most unnatural backgrounds who most appreciate light on these matters.) Teachers (especially young teachers) should be careful not to say more than is necessary when dealing with personal matters. Despite the godless propaganda around them – which appears to harden them – children still have tender consciences in these matters, and are instinctively offended by vivid descriptions and explicit details in God's house.

Lesson Outline

God's character. Announce at the start that this commandment tells us about God, for it reflects His tastes and desires. It particularly highlights two wonderful aspects of God's character:

(1) That He is absolutely faithful and true. He is loyal. He never breaks His promises, or goes back on His word (as the adulterer does).

(2) That He is absolutely pure and holy. (Explain, or demonstrate, that the word adulterate means to debase by mixing – eg: milk can be adulterated by mixing in some water or ink.) The adulterer (and fornicator) takes God's pure and special gift (the physical relationship of husband and wife) and mixes it with things which are unclean and polluting.

The Lord, by contrast, is wholly pure and genuine. He never mixes virtue with sin. He never mixes kindness and unkindness. He never mixes truth and falsehood in His Word. It is because His character is perfect that He hates adultery. How we should appreciate Him and love Him for His perfection.

The family. Ask the class a question. (This will avert any embarrassment aroused by this subject and provoke serious thought.) Given this world with its teeming millions, how is it possible to ensure that every individual person is loved, appreciated and provided for? Suggest that if governments had created mankind we would probably all arrive in the world on a huge conveyor belt with only a number plate to distinguish us one from another! Announce God's answer – the family. Then using a visual aid (we suggest a series of greetings cards featuring the chief events of life – birth, birthdays, marriage, silver weddings, retirement, death, etc), quickly demonstrate how the family unit provides for all these needs from the cradle to the grave:

(a) New members of the human race are delivered into a home which welcomes their arrival and provides all that is needed by a helpless baby.

(b) Children are protected and guided in a secure and happy family atmosphere.

(c) Young people may mature and assume adult roles gradually rather than suddenly, the family supporting them until the process is complete.

(d) Young adults have the support and example of relatives as they fall in love and marry their future life-long partner.

(e) Older adults share the ups and downs of life with a committed spouse and share the pleasure and responsibility of bringing up their family.

(f) The elderly benefit from the fruits of their labour, and when sickness, old age and death approach, know the love and care of children and grandchildren.

In case older classes begin to think that Christians are naive, seeing family life through rose-tinted spectacles, assure them that the Bible teaches more clearly than any human philosophy about the ravages of sin inflicted on the family ever since Adam and Eve disobeyed the Lord. Nevertheless, even in this fallen world, the family unit bears the marks of its loving Creator, and provides the chief source of security and happiness for the vast majority of people world-wide.

Marriage. Pose the question – what then is marriage? What is the importance of a wedding? Explain that Christians go to church to be married *before* they live together because it is only God Who can truly join them together as husband and wife. It is before Him that they must make their promises to one another. Ask the class if they know what promises are made by the couple before the wedding rings are given.

Explain that the man and woman make solemn promises to love, honour, care and provide for one another, whatever may happen to them – 'for better, for worse; for richer, for poorer; in sickness and in health'. (Perhaps you may wish to give examples of couples known to you who have encountered great difficulties, such as tragedy, ill-health or unemployment, yet have remained loyal and supportive to each other.)

Then move to the all-important promise, that neither husband nor wife will give themselves to another person but will be totally loyal to their spouse – so long as they both shall live. Children will readily accept that if people truly love one another it will be with their whole heart, and will naturally exclude disloyalty. (Even after the death of a parent, children find it difficult to accept a new partner for their remaining parent. Although their qualms may not be well founded, they are clear evidence of an ingrained concept of the exclusivity of marriage.)

Tell them that after the solemn vows have been made, the couple are pronounced to be married. They are no longer two entirely separate individuals, but one unit. Often there is a time of happy rejoicing amongst friends and family, and then the couple set off on their new life together. If sincere in their prayers, they will have God's blessing, and will share together and grow ever closer to each other. It is into such a loving, secure setting that God provides for a new life to be born. What care He takes!

Defiled! Having drawn this ideal picture and helped the children to appreciate the arrangement our heavenly Father has designed, remind the class that, sadly, God's gift of marriage is frequently misused and perverted by people who refuse God's way. Often the beautiful union of loving, giving and sharing is barely recognisable. Ask the children to imagine that a girl made or bought an exquisite gift for her friend, perhaps an intricate piece of embroidery. Years later she visits the friend and discovers that her expensive or time-consuming gift, instead of being appreciated and used with respect, is being used to clean the drains!

Show the class that this, sadly, is a picture of how God's gift of marital love is so often used. As they look at the newsagent's shelves, turn on the television, watch videos, etc, they see it cheapened and disfigured totally beyond recognition. Depending on the age of the class, mention how:

(1) Boys and girls lose their respect and awe for marriage by listening to rude and silly talk and exchanging dirty jokes. They harm themselves and pollute their minds by watching and reading things which they know to be wrong and which change their values.

(2) Young people, instead of keeping themselves and God's special gift reserved for the one person they should love with all their hearts throughout life, experiment with the opposite sex just for kicks.

(3) Couples start living together without serious, lifelong commitment, and soon discover that in these circumstances it is difficult to trust one another and to work towards a real and lasting union.

(4) Adults who are married (including people committed to live together) break their promises by having an affair with another person of the opposite sex. They then walk out of their relationship and into another, causing much hurt and suffering. The parent left behind to cope has a hard and lonely struggle to provide for the children.

God hates this sin. The Lord Jesus Christ pointed out that it is not just the people who violate their marriage by sleeping with another person who are adulterers, but also those who toy with these sins in their hearts. To feast one's emotions and senses on experiences which should be reserved for marriage is adultery. The Bible warns that people who commit these sins will not be allowed into God's kingdom, to spoil and pollute it *(1 Corinthians 6.9)*.

Outlawed. By God's great mercy and kindness, people may repent of their sin (which includes leaving their old ways) and ask for His forgiveness. The apostle Paul said to the Christians at Corinth that no fornicators or adulterers would inherit Heaven, and then he added – *and such were some of you: but ye are washed, but ye are sanctified.*

How could this be? Tell them how the Saviour, when He died on the cross of Calvary, took upon Himself all our sinful thoughts, words and deeds, including, most amazingly, our unclean thoughts and acts. He bore the punishment of sin for all who would believe on Him.

Help the class appreciate the love of Christ involved in bearing all the vile and unfaithful deeds and imaginings of sinful people. Help them try to comprehend the weight of agony as He bore the punishment of all these crimes. Show them the wonderful results – 'The vilest offender who truly believes, that moment from Jesus a pardon receives.'

Assure them that the Saviour is willing to forgive them if they throw themselves on His mercy and plead His atoning death. But they must truly regret their sins and repent. He is also able to keep in purity of mind and actions those who repent and give their lives to Him *(Jude 24)*. Give some practical advice to young believers and others:

(1) **Do not play with fire!** Only proud fools think they can put their hand in the flame and not get burnt. The Bible warns (in modern language) – 'Bad company corrupts good morals' *(1 Corinthians 15.33)*. Explain that this means that those who desire to serve and obey the Saviour must, with His help, make determined efforts not to play with evil. Sympathise with them as they face temptations unknown to previous generations. Warn them against the flood of magazines and literature targeted at young people. These pretend to give helpful advice for the new generation, but they promote sexual promiscuity and experimentation at a very early age. (Sunday School teachers need to make themselves aware of the literature now circulated for younger teenagers. They will be astonished at the explicit and arousing character of the new wave of magazines.)

Encourage young people to choose their closest friends carefully, avoiding those who are obviously godless. Urge them to keep clear of parties and places where drink and sexual arousal are the aim. Discuss ways in which they can avoid obscene films and programmes viewed by other members of their family.

(2) **Fear the consequences!** Anticipate the objection which will be raised in some minds: 'But what will my friends say? How can I explain that I don't want to join their activities?' Read to the class the words of the Lord in *Matthew 5.27-30*, and ask them to work out His meaning. Show that we should fear

the damage likely to be done in our lives, and the eternal consequences of sinful behaviour, much more than a few scornful words from some friends.

Offer a word of encouragement too, by telling young believers that their refusal to associate with wrong will actually earn secret admiration from others. They may be surprised to find that some who scoff and ridicule at first will later come to them for advice and help.

(3) Love the Lord! Assure young Christians that there is nothing to compare with the joy of knowing the Lord. As the children's chorus puts it:

> *Turn your eyes upon Jesus,*
>   *Look full in His wonderful face,*
> *And the things of Earth will grow strangely dim*
>   *In the light of His glory and grace.*

Remind them that their Saviour is the mighty God Who made Heaven and Earth. His Word and the experiences of the Christian life are enough to excite the mind throughout life. Daily audiences with Him are the believer's high privilege. A direct part in the plans and purposes of God is the greatest role possible for any person.

(4) 'Whatsoever things are pure . . . think on these things' *(Philippians 4.8).* Encourage your class to cultivate positive virtues – self-control, honesty, kindness, unselfishness. These will stand them in good stead in days of temptation and provide for real power and accomplishments. Instead of living stunted, selfish lives, they will be used by the Lord to bring great benefit and grace to many others.

Visual Aid

VA 11 (page 167) suggests a set of greetings cards which will be particularly helpful in presenting this important subject. Teachers can also provide two cloths (one clean and embroidered, the other a dirty rag) to illustrate ways in which God's gift is misused. Pictures of weddings, wedding rings and new homes may also be appropriate, but avoid those which are too showy.

Thou Shalt Not Steal (176)

Exodus 20.15; see also other texts quoted in the lesson

Lesson Outline

How this law may convict the conscience. Remind the class that God's supreme purpose in giving His laws was not to reform us (for we are hopeless sinners) but to show us our great need of a Saviour. As an example tell how the Lord used this particular commandment to bring an awareness of sin to the bright young shoemaker, William Carey (later to be used by God to set the missionary vision alight in the eighteenth century). Describe how his Christian friend, John Warr, made many efforts to convince him of his need of personal conversion. They talked much over the work-bench. William nearly always won any argument, not because he was right, but because he was the more clever of the two. He was certain that his life was good enough, and that there was no need for him to repent and ask God's forgiveness. The only effect of the discussions was to make him attend church more regularly, and give up some of his lying and bad language. But he mainly did this so that he could proudly insist that he was a 'good Christian' without conversion. He still resisted all appeals to seek a Saviour. Then the Lord used this eighth commandment to open his eyes to his real standing in His holy sight.

The shame and fear he felt when his master discovered that he had stolen a shilling (by exchanging a counterfeit coin) caused him to acknowledge that he was not only a thief, but a sinner in many other ways. He was forced to abandon his self-righteousness and boasting, fearing he would be put to shame before the whole village, and possibly removed from his livelihood. Above all he was made to think about the eternal punishment of sin.

The relief he felt when his master forgave him and allowed him to remain at his work did not deliver him from the painful insight he had experienced. It was only as he called to mind John Warr's Saviour, Who through wonderful grace and mercy was willing to pardon and forgive, that he felt there was any

LESSONS FOR LIFE

hope for him. Soon he was to admit to his colleague that he, above all, needed the love of that Saviour, and he found the Lord himself. He then began worshipping with John and his despised nonconformist friends and family.

Suggest to the class that should they ever find themselves convicted by a law of God, as Carey did, they also should allow conscience to lead them to the Saviour Who forgives all sin. Urge them never to harden their hearts and suppress their consciences.

Stealing is unnecessary. Individuals are promised by the Lord Jesus that if they give priority to seeking His kingdom and its righteousness, then their essential needs will be provided. He reminded His disciples that the God Who so marvellously clothes the flowers and birds will provide much more grandly for His people *(Matthew 6.25-33)*. The apostle Paul, speaking from personal experience, promised the Philippians – *My God shall supply all your need (Philippians 4.19)*. Stealing is not necessary. It is usually done to get more than the person really needs, or to avoid work. So God forbids us to steal. Instead we should be grateful to Him for His bountiful care.

Stealing is arrogant and selfish. Help the class to see what lies behind the acts of theft, which God so hates. Show how arrogant stealing is. It does not care about other people. The thief says, 'I need something, and I will get it,' not caring about the pain, the fear, the anxiety and the poverty he inflicts on his victim.

The first theft. Remind the class of how this sin first manifested itself when Eve stole the fruit which was not hers. Think of all the Lord had provided for our first parents in that beautiful garden which we call Paradise. Yet Eve took the one thing the Lord had said they should not have. No wonder that she and Adam were filled with shame when their sin was uncovered! No wonder they wanted to hide from God's presence!

Theft continues. Describe how stealing, so hated by the Lord, has continued in many forms ever since that first theft, proving that, had we been in Adam and Eve's place, we should have done exactly as they did. We are all thieves in some way.

List the various forms of stealing which continue to this day. Interest the children by first describing how stealing manifested itself in:

(1) **Old Testament times.** (a) Theft of goods and people (in days of slavery – *Deuteronomy 24.7*) and theft from parents *(Proverbs 28.24)*.

(b) False balances. Describe how traders weighted their scales so as to take advantage of their customers *(Proverbs 11.1; Amos 8.5)*.

(c) Oppression of the poor. High interest rates – confiscation of basic necessities *(Exodus 22.25-27; Proverbs 28.8; Ezekiel 22.29; Jeremiah 5.25-29)*.

(d) Absalom stole the hearts of his father's people *(2 Samuel 15.6)*. It is a particularly nasty form of theft, when by flattery and bribery someone's loyalty is stolen. Children are often guilty of stealing friendships from one another.

(2) **New Testament times.** (a) Organised violent theft. The robbers who stole from the Jew in Jesus' parable of the Good Samaritan *(Luke 10.30)*.

(b) Extortion by tax-gatherers, eg: Zacchæus *(Luke 19.8)*.

(c) Extortion by Temple authorities. They had made the Temple into a den of thieves *(Mark 11.15-17)*.

(d) A 'take-over' by a work-force, pictured in Christ's parable of the vineyard *(Mark 12.7)*.

(e) Purloining by servants (employees) *(Titus 2.10)*.

The many fingers of stealing. Lest children assume that Sunday School teachers think that only common thieves steal, outline some of the wide-scale forms of fraud and corruption which are perpetrated in modern society by:

(i) The 'authorities'. Even governments steal by printing banknotes, which promptly lose value (inflation). Big businesses collude to fix and keep prices high. Corruption in high places often robs ordinary citizens. However, all this big stealing does not excuse children who steal, even though the value of what they take may be small.

(ii) Citizens. Many ordinary people steal by falsifying tax returns, expense accounts, benefit claims, insurance claims, and by running up huge rent arrears as well as other debts. Then there is stealing in the form of fare dodging and credit card fraud.

(iii) Children. Even little children snatch one another's toys, sweets and belongings. Some even steal from their parents. Older children steal when they cheat in exams, or copy work from friends. It is possible to steal a person's good reputation by wrongly blaming him or her for trouble, or by untrue gossip. Laziness is another form of theft, when, for example, children do not bother to work hard at school and benefit from the costly education which is provided for them.

(iv) Young people steal when they accept their daily needs from their parents without feeling any obligation to help with household jobs; others steal by not bothering to work sufficiently hard to obtain a job within their reach, 'scrounging' off others instead. Even young believers in a church may steal by expecting everything to be organised for them, instead of contributing to the Lord's work by their own efforts. How good it is to hear of children and young people who express and show gratitude for what is done for them!

The consequences of stealing. Point out that stealing is a very foolish sin for many reasons. Not only does it make us guilty sinners in the sight of God, and bar us from Heaven, it also ruins our peace of mind. Thieves are often jumpy, wondering if their crime will come to light. Even if they are never discovered, they will have a bad conscience. Stealing often backfires. The thief or cheat will be copied. Soon no one can be trusted and everyone is at risk.

Stealing from God. Worst of all, we steal from God (Malachi 3.8). He made us and loves us and is entitled by right to our gratitude and obedience. If we withhold these, we are keeping back something to which God is entitled. We steal our lives from God, for we belong to Him by right, and not to ourselves. Like someone who steals a car for pleasure, we drive off *in our lives*, and live for our own personal pleasure. We enjoy God's creation, indulge ourselves, and do not stop to acknowledge His existence, or thank Him, or serve Him. One day He will claim back our life. Ask the class if they will be caught out as thieves on that day.

What should we do? Urge your class, if they have recognised themselves in some of these descriptions, to 'own up' to the Lord, and 'return what they owe' to Him. This is a helpful and practical picture of repentance. Tell them about the Saviour Who was willing to be punished and humiliated for all our sins (including those of stealing) as He hung between two thieves at Calvary. What shame He endured in order that the price of our sin could be paid!

How can Christians avoid breaking this commandment? Encourage young believers to remember constantly what the Saviour has done for them and to see Him and His life as their model. Though He was rich, yet for *our sakes He became poor, that we through His poverty might be rich (2 Corinthians 8.9)*. Explain that Christians are people who have been radically changed, so that instead of always *taking,* they become like their Lord Who *gave* Himself for others *(Galatians 2.20)*. Believers give out to others. This new attitude is summarised by the apostle Paul – *Let him that stole steal no more: but rather let him labour, working with his hands . . . that he may have to give to him that needeth (Ephesians 4.28)*.

Ask the class to consider some of the kindnesses commanded in the Bible, particularly kindness shown to strangers *(Leviticus 19.34)*; to neighbours *(Deuteronomy 22.1)*; to the poor *(Matthew 25.35-40)*; to your enemies *(Luke 6.27-35)*; to the weak *(Acts 20.35; Romans 15.1)*; to the sad *(Romans 12.15)*; and to one another *(Ephesians 4.32)*.

Suggest a test for the believer's behaviour – *whatsoever ye would that men should do to you, do ye even so to them (Matthew 7.12)*, or as children may more easily remember – 'Do as you would be done by.' This is virtually the opposite of stealing.

Ask older classes to consider this key verse – *Godliness with contentment is great gain (1 Timothy 6.6)*. At the bottom of stealing is a mind always on the lookout for something more; always ready to be jealous of what someone else has; always open to temptation. The Christian should be content with what he has. This is *real* strength. And it is easy to be content when we remember all the spiritual blessings which we have received through being converted.

Visual Aid

VA 11 (page 167) suggests a large hand on which the different forms of stealing can be placed. Teachers who use the experience of William Carey to open the lesson could provide pictures of him and his work as a shoemaker. Illustrations of other thieves listed in the lesson will be helpful.

Thou Shalt Not Bear False Witness (177)

Exodus 20.16

Lesson Outline

Make it clear from the start that this commandment has to do with lying. The Bible tells us that – *Lying lips are abomination to the Lord (Proverbs 12.22)*. God hates every form of lying because He is the Truth. Lying is nearly always at someone else's expense. Conscience tells us that lying is a particularly hateful sin. Many people have been haunted by the memory of their first deliberate lie. Strange as it may seem, even hardened criminals and habitual liars become indignant when they are called liars. In our parliament the very word is considered so offensive that it is ruled out of order.

A 'gateway' sin. Lying opens the gate to many other sins. If people never lied, they would be protected, for example, from stealing and adultery. Help the class to think for a moment how difficult it would be to break the other commandments without using lies first to prepare the way, then afterwards to cover up the crime. This is why it is particularly important for children to pay attention to this commandment. Older children might like to consider that when they become parents, one of the greatest obligations they will have to their children will be to plant in them a hatred of lying.

The history of lying. Remind the children of how lying first entered the world in the Garden of Eden. The devil cruelly deceived Adam and Eve by telling lies. He lied when he told them that they would not die. He lied when he told them that they would be much better off by taking the fruit, implying that God was withholding things from them. They soon discovered the bitter truth, when they were cast out of the Garden to experience a world of sin and shame, sorrow and death. Since then the world has been full of lies. Many children grow up without knowing the truth about themselves and God.

The father of lies *(John 8.44)*. Satan is the father of lies and he sees to it that the world is filled with many different lies intended to keep men and women from the Lord. Satan even dared to confront the Saviour with his lies, promising Him *all the kingdoms of the world, and the glory of them,* if He would fall down and worship him *(Matthew 4.8-9)* – a promise he had no power to keep. Since his defeat by the Lord Jesus at the cross of Calvary, he has continued to flood the world with his lying propaganda (eg: that there is no God; that the world has come into existence by chance; that the way to Heaven is by good works or by religious observances; that sin is no longer sin; and that God is in us all, so there is no need to seek Him). The Bible warns people not to be fooled by Satan's biggest lie – that God does not exist, and need not be feared.

Many faces of lying. Tell the class that lying appears in many forms.

(1) False witness – eg: when the Jews falsely accused the Lord Jesus of making Himself an earthly king who would oppose Caesar *(John 19.12)*. People tell lies which get others into serious trouble, blaming them for their own misdemeanours. This is a horrible sin, but one frequently committed by children.

(2) Deliberate lies – eg: when Joseph's brothers told their father that he had been killed by wild beasts, when in fact they had sold him to the Ishmaelites *(Genesis 37.29-35)*. Blatant lying, like all sin, may be forgotten by the liar, but it is indelibly preserved in God's record, and the guilty will one day be judged. Only the forgiveness of God can take that record away.

(3) Deceit. Jacob deceived his blind father *(Genesis 27.6-29)*. Herod tried to deceive the wise men into thinking he also wanted to worship the new-born King *(Matthew 2.8)*.

The class may remember how Jacob was tricked by his uncle Laban, and given Leah instead of Rachel to be his wife *(Genesis*

29.21-25). Though this incident took place at the beginning of history, this type of lie has been repeated frequently. (How up-to-date the Bible is in its description of human sin!) How often children, among themselves, sell or swap things using similar deception.

The Bible warns that we can also deceive *ourselves* – because our own hearts are deceitful *(Jeremiah 17.9).* People convince themselves that their sinful acts are justified and excusable, and so deceive their own hearts, and shrug off their guilt.

(4) Excuses. Adam sinned against his kind Creator, deliberately disobeying His command, but he blamed Eve (and the Lord Who gave her; *Genesis 3.12).* How easily we blame our friends, our family, our circumstances for the wrong we do! This is just another way of meddling with the truth, and we do this because we will not face up to our sinfulness.

(5) Hypocrisy. The Pharisees pretended to themselves and others that they were godly, upright, religious people, while beneath the surface there lurked pride, hatred, self-righteousness *(Luke 18.11-12).* How easily we see faults in others while imagining that we are faultless!

(6) Flattery. *Proverbs 7.21* speaks of the woman who tempted a young man with *much fair speech* and *flattering of her lips,* using these to lure him into sin. Warn the children not to believe the flatterers around today, nor to use this nasty lying device to get their own way.

(7) Broken promises. The Lord Jesus condemned the son who agreed to work in his father's vineyard, but failed to do so *(Matthew 21.30-31).* Remind the class of the disappointment, heartbreak and distress which can be brought about by those who go back on their promises (from politicians downwards). Are they guilty too of giving their word when they have little or no intention of keeping it?

(8) Duplicity. King David complained bitterly of people whose words *were smoother than butter* and *softer than oil,* but whose hearts were full of war and drawn swords *(Psalm 55.21; see also Jeremiah 9.8).* Children can be guilty of this form of lying quite frequently as they change their loyalty from one friend to another. At one moment they can be full of sweetness to a person's face, and within days or even hours they are full of spite and making harsh accusations. They are 'two faced', but only one position can be truthful.

The consequences of lying. Children may be tempted to think that lies are of little importance, because they cannot be seen. Many young people convince themselves that it does little harm to tell a lie here or there. Point out that lies do great damage in several ways:

(a) Each lie twists our character. An honest person is described as straightforward, but liars become bent and crooked *(Proverbs 2.14-15; 8.8)*. People who get into the habit of lying come to the point when they themselves can barely distinguish truth from lies. They lie so much that they begin to believe themselves. Having lost all sense of reality, Satan is easily able to convince them that eternal values are of no importance, and the result is they do not want the Lord.

(b) Lies steal our credibility. Lies offer us only short-term gain. One lie may get us out of trouble for a moment, but once others discover we have lied they never trust us again. Illustrate this point. It may be appropriate to refer to Hillaire Belloc's Matilda who was burnt to death, because firemen refused to answer her call for help. She had called them out previously on a false alarm. Then a real fire broke out, but

> *Every time she shouted, 'Fire',*
> *They only answered, 'Little liar'.*

Politicians who lie blatantly live to regret it. Often they have to resign, having lost their credibility, or the electorate refuses to vote for them. Businessmen who go back on their word, break their delivery dates, or cut the quality of their goods, find that their dishonesty catches up with them sooner or later and they lose their trade.

(c) Lies take us to hell. The *Book of Revelation* graphically depicts the end of *whosoever loveth and maketh a lie.* Liars take their place alongside murderers and adulterers in the – *lake which burneth with fire and brimstone: which is the second death (Revelation 21.8).*

What must we do to be saved? Turn the class's attention away from lies to the Lord Jesus Christ Who said of Himself – *I am . . . the truth (John 14.6)*. Those who lived closest to Him were able to write that He *did no sin, neither was guile found in his mouth (1 Peter 2.22)*. He was *full of grace and truth (John 1.14)*. Of no other human being could this be said. Why then did He come into this world so full of lies and deceit? He came into the world so that we might know the Truth, and the Truth would make us free *(John 8.32)*. He came to bear the pain and punishment for every lie we have ever told, so that (if we believe in Him as Saviour) we shall not be punished with eternal death.

Ask your class if they have seen through the lies that Satan has planted in the minds of men and women – lies saying that God is unkind and unfair; that there is no life beyond the grave; that sin will not be punished, and so on. Ask them to place their trust in the Lord Who never lies. When He says He will forgive all who come to Him, He means it. Becoming a Christian means that we abandon all lying ways and return to our true and faithful Father, repenting that we ever ignored Him and ready to serve Him in the future.

How can young believers stop lying? Make helpful suggestions:

(a) Bind truth about your neck, write it upon the table of your heart *(Proverbs 3.3)*. Remind the children that if a mother wants to be certain that a small child will not lose a vital item (eg: a door key) she ties it round his neck where it cannot get lost, forgotten or stolen. The Lord God directs that this is how we should treat the truth. We must value it very highly, and take every precaution not to tarnish it. Young Christians will examine themselves day by day and ask – Have I been honest and truthful today? They will ask the Lord's forgiveness as they admit their failings in this matter. They will ask their Saviour to protect them from this disfiguring sin.

(b) Control the tongue. James compares the tongue to a fire *(James 3.5)*. If we pray for the Lord's help and make a real effort to control the tongue while we are young, then we shall be protected from great weakness and loss of honesty in the years ahead. Learn to hate lying with all its consequences. Avoid it 'like the plague'.

(c) **Open your lips** to speak God's praise *(Psalm 51.15)*. Christians are those who turn away from lies and wasted, flippant talk, and use their lips to say positive, valuable things, and to witness to others. They give comfort to those who are cast down, and speak about good and useful subjects.

Conclusion. Close the lesson by emphasising the Lord God's high regard for, and willingness to bless, those who are truthful – *Surely they are my people, children that will not lie: so he was their Saviour (Isaiah 63.8).*

Visual Aid

VA 11 (page 167) suggests a large pair of lips with 'speech bubbles' on which to place lesson headings. A large gate, opening the way to other sins, would also be useful. Pictures of various Bible characters used as illustrations throughout the lesson will help younger children follow closely.

Thou Shalt Not Covet (178)

Exodus 20.17; 1 Timothy 6.6-11; Matthew 6.19-34

Thou shalt not covet thy neighbour's house, thou shalt not covet thy neighbour's wife, nor his manservant, nor his maidservant, nor his ox, nor his ass, nor any thing that is thy neighbour's (Exodus 20.17).

Lesson Outline

What is coveting? Coveting is a heart sin. It is a desire, rather than an act. (We covet something before we take steps to get it.) It means wanting, desiring, dreaming of or demanding things which belong to others. These may be things we do not really need. We want these things simply for the sake of having more, or because they bring us status and admiration. Men, women and children who do not know the Lord can never find true satisfaction in life, and they try to fill the aching void within them with possessions. The world panders to this human greed, and dangles before people all kinds of tempting wares.

Such values as kindness, concern for others, and unselfishness are trampled down in the rush for personal gratification. Give as an example the attitude of many children towards Christmas and birthday presents. Their chief thoughts are –

What will I get? What do I want? How can I persuade people to
give me what I want? So often there is little time given to
asking – What shall I give?

The history of coveting. Remind the class that the first
example of coveting is seen in the Garden of Eden. When Eve
listened to the serpent, he offered her superior status or power
(the knowledge of good and evil) and suggested she could be
like the gods. Remember that God had built the universe with
Adam and Eve in mind. They had everything they could
possibly desire. But they became discontented and desired even
greater powers. They were not satisfied with what they had.

Children may also remember the case of Lot, who had
experienced immense benefits with his uncle Abraham, but
who threw away his peace and happiness when he coveted the
riches and power of that evil city Sodom.

The folly of coveting. Explain to the class that apart from
being sinful, covetousness is very foolish. Living only to desire
and get possessions is senseless for the following reasons:

(1) Possessions cannot be taken with us. The apostle Paul
said – *We brought nothing into this world, and it is certain we can
carry nothing out (1 Timothy 6.7).* He taught that the right way is
to learn how to be content. This is real strength. Young people
often see through the covetousness of adults. They see them
rushing through life, getting exhausted, anxious and distressed
in the endless pursuit of bigger and better possessions, holidays,
and so on, and they wonder if it is worthwhile. Why struggle,
toil and worry in order to acquire wealth and status if, when
death arrives, they must leave life just as they entered it, taking
none of these things with them? How much better to be content
with the reasonable things of life, and to walk with the Lord so
that they are ready for the next life!

(2) Riches are deceitful. The Lord Jesus spoke of the deceit-
fulness of riches, which choke the Word *(Matthew 13.22).* Warn
the children that possessions cannot give real and lasting
happiness (whether they are sought by the rich, who can never
have enough, or the poor, who worry and pine for them). Tell
them about rich, professional men who have no time to enjoy

their money, and about people who live behind oppressive security gates in order to feel safe and secure. Tell them about the multi-millionaire lottery winners whose lives are wrecked and ruined by their winnings. Tell them that many families have sacrificed their happiness together in order to become richer and have many possessions. These things *seem* wonderful, but they cannot make us better or give a truly happy life.

(3) Riches trap us. The Lord Jesus also warned that it was very hard for people who trust in riches to enter the kingdom of God *(Mark 10.24)*. Help the children understand why this is so, from *Proverbs 30.8-9*. Although possessions and riches cannot make people truly happy, they become so important to people that they have no time for God. They 'play' endlessly with their 'toys', dream of bigger and better things, boast about and gloat over things. Meanwhile poor people (when covetous) are tempted to cheat or steal to get what they want. So, because of covetousness, rich and poor alike do not want to seek the Lord.

Surprise the children with the information that in comparison with most children of past ages, they are all very rich. Even princes of olden times did not expect instant hot water, fast cars fitted with CD players, and strawberries in winter! We have so many gadgets and possessions today. Is this why many children today see no need of a Saviour?

(4) Covetousness is one of the worst sins. Tell the class that, along with fornicators, adulterers, thieves and drunkards, the Bible shuts the covetous out of God's kingdom *(1 Corinthians 6.9-10; Ephesians 5.5)*. No wonder Jesus called the rich farmer who had his earthly barns stacked full, but his heavenly account empty, a fool. Urge the children not to make the same mistake and find themselves turned away from the eternal kingdom.

The results of covetousness –

(1) It gives birth to other sins. Children may wonder why something is so wrong when it is a desire rather than an act. Explain that lust conceives and brings forth sin. Show them how – *Man is tempted, when he is drawn away of his own lust, and enticed. Then when lust hath conceived, it bringeth forth sin: and sin, when it is finished, bringeth forth death (James 1.14-15).*

Use illustrations to show how covetousness develops. One example with which the children are familiar is the sin of David with Bathsheba. David, instead of fighting his covetous lust, sent for Bathsheba, and soon adultery, deception, and murder resulted from his desire.

(2) It leads to much suffering. Show how covetousness and greed are the cause of so much oppression and pain in this world. The strong take advantage of the weak to feed their unquenchable thirst for more and more *(Micah 2.2)*. Nations go to war to gain territory and possessions by force. Even children often behave in a spiteful and violent way to get what they want. Unbelievers like to blame God for wars and suffering, but if only they would keep this commandment not to covet, wars would be banished.

(3) It insults the Lord. Explain that, above all, covetousness is offensive to the Lord our Maker. He links it with idolatry *(Ephesians 5.5)*. To give our hearts and affections to earthly things is very hurtful to our heavenly Father. It is as if we say we would prefer anything to Him. It is saying that possessions and riches on Earth are, in our opinion, far better than knowing God.

The cure of covetousness. Covetous desire is so deeply rooted in the heart that it cannot be eradicated by human effort. We need the new heart that God gives when He converts us. We need a new nature and a new outlook, and only God can give this to us. Without this, we shall remain selfish, and interested in what we have and what we can get in life.

At this point of the lesson the children should be reminded of how Christ died to take the punishment of our sin, including all our covetous desires (if we believe in Him). They should also be urged to see their covetousness, to own up to it in prayer to the Lord, and to ask for the new nature, so that they can be victorious over it.

Antidotes to covetousness. Let us suppose there are children who have been converted; how can they protect themselves from the covetous thoughts which Satan continues to pop into their minds? Give suggestions:

(1) Lay up treasure in Heaven, where neither moth nor rust can corrupt and where no thief can break through and steal *(Matthew 6.20)*. Instead of dreaming of and coveting possessions, Christians use their minds and energies to think about and work at much more important things. They realise they are on the Lord's side in a great battle or campaign to win souls. They witness to unsaved friends and family. They learn the great plan of God. They follow the news of the work of God's kingdom, and support it *(Matthew 6.21-22)*. The cause of Christ is more important to them than mere empty show.

> Saviour, if of Zion's city,
>   I through grace a member am,
> Let the world deride or pity,
>   I will glory in Thy name:
> Fading is the worldling's pleasure,
>   All his boasted pomp and show!
> Solid joys and lasting treasure,
>   None but Zion's children know.
>   John Newton

(2) Weigh the benefits. Tell the class how Moses weighed this matter carefully as a young man. He realised that even rejection and disgrace for the sake of Christ would lead to far greater riches than all the treasures in Egypt *(Hebrews 11.26)*. Charles Wesley expressed this same conclusion:

> Thou, O Christ, art all I want,
> More than all in Thee I find.

Here is an opportunity to describe to the class how much the Saviour means to you, and to all others who have tasted His power and love.

(3) Give away riches. Explain to the class how Christians look at riches and possessions. They regard them as gifts from God on loan to them, to be used wisely in God's service, and for the benefit of others. Christians should never think – this is *my* house, *my* car, *my* exam success. Give examples of those who gave themselves and their assets to the Lord. People born rich like William Wilberforce, Lord Shaftesbury and Lord Radstock became believers and died poor, having given themselves and their possessions to the Saviour's work and to benefit others. God's servants like Luther, Whitefield, Spurgeon and Carey all devoted their earthly gains to His work, and by doing this they kept themselves away from the temptations for gain which could so easily have diverted them.

What must I do to be saved? Close the lesson by speaking again to all who sense their need of forgiveness over the matter of coveting. The parable of the Prodigal Son provides the perfect picture. We, like him, have sinned grievously – telling our kind and heavenly Father that we are no longer satisfied with Him, but want to find our happiness and pleasure far away. We have wasted away our heavenly blessings. What can we do? The answer is to return to our heavenly Father, admit our sin, and give ourselves to Him, trusting only in what Christ did on Calvary's cross to purchase our forgiveness.

Visual Aid

VA 11 (page 167) suggests four large (card) flames (red, yellow, orange and black) on which to attach headings.

Revision (179)

Aim: To fix the ten commandments firmly and meaningfully into the minds and consciences of the children. To point them, once again, to the Lord Jesus Christ, Who came to rescue all those who recognise themselves as law-breakers in need of a Saviour.

Teachers' Introduction

If, as teachers, we succeed in nothing more than teaching our classes the chief words of the ten commandments, we shall have handed them a privilege beyond estimation. A grasp of God's law in early years will not only protect them from many dangers, but will also equip their consciences for the spiritual issues of life.

Lesson Outline

The exact form of this lesson will vary with the character of the class and the School. The following suggestions can be adapted and moulded to suit each need. Some Sunday Schools may wish to give two weeks to the revision process, one to help children learn and revise; the second to test and learn from mistakes.

(A) A test (either written or oral). This would be particularly appropriate for groups made up of children mainly from Christian homes. They should be expected to know the commandments precisely. Some kind of acknowledgement prize would be fitting for those who have made the effort to learn the work to a high standard. However, a reminder should be given that *learning* the commandments is quite a different matter from *keeping* them. Questions which test the children's understanding as well as their memory will be helpful. We do not want our lessons to produce Pharisees, but young people who recognise themselves as sinners.

(B) Older classes may find it helpful to revise the material under the headings of the introductory lesson. This will have the advantage of revising the *application* of the commandments. (Teachers should have the VA 12 'signs' to hand.)

(1) What have we learned about the character of God from the ten commandments?

(2) What wise instructions have we received from our Maker for happy and healthy living?

(3) Can we list the types of sin which God has said will shut people out of His kingdom?

(C) Younger classes and those needing a more evangelistic presentation. This novel but simple graphic representation will help children remember the commandments and see their spiritual lessons.

To prepare. (a) Print out on ten strips of card the chief words of the ten commandments, eg: 'THOU SHALT HAVE NO OTHER GODS', or a summary, 'NO OTHER GODS'. (b) Cut out from stiff card ten outline figures of children all walking in the same direction (a mixture of boys and girls of different ages and from different racial groups). (c) Place these ten figures on a background of contrasting colour, all facing in the direction of Heaven, marked by a signpost. (d) Cut out a large outline cross for use at the end of the lesson.

Application. Suggest that these children are all confidently marching (so they think) to Heaven. Then, sadly, explain that one must be turned round and sent to hell (marked on signpost). Why? Because he or she has broken the first commandment. Ask the class to recite commandment one, and attach the written card to this 'child'. Then explain (by way of revision) *how* the child is guilty. Now only nine are marching to Heaven, but . . .

Explain, regretfully, that the second child must also be turned around, for he or she has broken commandment two. Again ask the children to recite the command and give examples of how it may be broken, in terms appropriate for the class. Now only eight are marching to Heaven, but . . .

By this means review all ten commandments until all the children in the visual aid are shown to be disqualified from Heaven, and heading instead to hell. Then show the class that this group represents not ten separate children breaking ten separate commands, but one child or adult who is guilty of breaking all of God's commands. How can such a person be rescued from hell? Tell them about the Saviour and all He was willing to do for every child who believes in Him and who is truly sorry for his sin. Remind the class that in order for us to be forgiven, the Saviour had to take each sin and suffer its punishment on the cross of Calvary. Take the ten commandment card-strips and place them one by one on the outline cross. Only by this means was our guilt removed and our journey back to the heavenly city made possible.

The commandments 'in a nutshell'. Conclude the series by teaching the children the summary of God's laws so beautifully expressed in the words of Moses, and quoted by the Saviour:

Thou shalt love the Lord thy God with all thy heart, and with all thy soul, and with all thy mind, and with all thy strength, and, Thou shalt love thy neighbour as thyself (Mark 12.30-31).

Series 21
Romans and Other Epistles
HOW GOD FITS US FOR HEAVEN

180 – God's Purpose Despite a Great Fall
Sinking down for ever! This is the terrible fate of men, women and children who, created in the image of God, have fallen into every kind of degrading sin. But the Lord's will cannot be thwarted, and long ago the Father, Son and Holy Spirit conceived a plan so that countless people might be restored and conformed to the Son of God.

181 – Called
Like all great plans and schemes, there are many arrangements to be made, and steps to be taken. Firstly, those to be rescued are living far away from God in an alien land and must be awakened to the danger. God must call them, persuade them and incline their hearts to return to Him, so that they feel their great need of a Saviour and believe on the Lord Jesus with all their hearts. Who are these people? How does the Lord call them? How do they respond?

182 – Justified
In order to enter the heavenly realm, they must have a sound passport and credentials which can only be obtained for them by a perfect Saviour, Who must pay their debts by suffering the

just punishment for their sins in their place. Once declared fit and qualified on His merits, the gates of God's kingdom swing open to receive them, and they are safe for ever.

183 – Adopted (and Sanctified)

All who look to Christ as Saviour discover that they are the chosen and much-loved sons and daughters of God. Throughout the remainder of their earthly lives their heavenly Father not only hears their prayers and provides for them, but also kindly and firmly conforms them to the likeness of His Son, and restores them to His image.

184 – Glorified

Even more wonderful things are in store for those who die in Christ. For just as the Lord Jesus Christ was raised from the dead and highly exalted by His Father, so Christians will be raised to walk in newness of life. If they are to live with Christ for ever, how will their dead bodies be raised? The humble seed provides perfect answers to such questions.

Teachers' Introduction to the Series

In our atheistic day and age few young people have any framework of belief for facing life. This four-year survey of the Bible has, we trust, shown them God's view of world history from its start to its finish. As the syllabus concludes, we follow the pattern of the Scriptures by closing with a short, simple doctrinal series which provides a clear overview of the teaching of God's Word, especially God's plan of salvation for all who believe on Him. The lessons are based on the teaching of the epistles, especially *Romans*. Such information should be full of interest for today's young people, commanding their respect at a natural level and leading them to consider their own place in God's eternal purpose.

To make a series of more doctrinal, theoretical lessons attractive and enlightening to children, a key concept has been picked out of each lesson to give cohesion to each topic. This should also help teachers.

May this final series be used by the Lord to provide His First-born with many brethren *(Romans 8.29)*.

Visual Aids for the Series

VA 13 on page 229 is designed for use throughout the series. In addition, each lesson centres around a concept which can be presented visually to the class: lesson 180 centres on a coin; lesson 181 on an envelope containing invitations; lesson 182 on arrows which change direction; lesson 183 on a family, and especially a father; and lesson 184 on a seed and its produce.

God's Purpose Despite a Great Fall (180)
Fallen, Predestinated

Romans 1.16-32; 8.29; Genesis 1.24-27

Aim: To present the doctrine of the Fall, and the Lord's plan and purpose to restore lost sinners to the image of His Son, in a simple, memorable and evangelistic manner for children.

Lesson Outline

(1) **A bright image** *(Genesis 1.26-27)*. Attract the children's attention by showing them a valuable coin – shining and new with the image of the head of state embossed upon it. Point out that the image identifies the coin, and gives it value in the country to which it belongs. Our coins bear the image of the queen and indicate that we are in the United Kingdom. Surprise the class by explaining that we were made with the image of God, our Creator and King, stamped upon us! Just as a mirror reflects our image so we were made to reflect the likeness of our Maker. We were meant to be like Him – good and kind, pure and honest, just and faithful.

Pointing to the coin again, explain to the class the message of the Bible which tells how God made men and women not as animals, but in His likeness. He breathed into them a living spirit, an immortal soul, and then gave them dominion (or power) over the Earth and all its creatures *(Genesis 1.26)*. What a high privilege! What endless fulfilment and satisfaction would have been ours! Use a visual aid to represent mankind's privileged position at the top of a staircase (see VA 13, page 229).

Contrast this with the popular view that human beings are

nothing more than highly evolved animals. No wonder that many young people see little point and purpose in life, and live only to enjoy themselves whilst they can.

Returning to the Bible's view of the human race, explain how the Lord God not only bestowed upon us this privileged position in His world, but He also endowed us with all the necessary abilities to fulfil it. Unlike the animals, who have only physical instincts, we were given a sense of God's standards – a sense of right and wrong (a conscience). We were also given the ability to reason and think. In addition, we received an awareness or instinct that there is an eternal existence beyond this short life on Earth. Everything lay at our feet! What a wonderful place Earth would have been if things had remained as God created them – all being *very good*, as bright as the new coin. Ask the question – What happened then to spoil God's glorious intention for His highest creation? What has made life so miserable, so frustrating, so pointless? What has brought death and pain into the world and separated us from the Lord our Maker?

(2) Exchanging the image. Suggest that a little child, not knowing the value of money, might be tricked into exchanging the valuable coin for a cheap trinket. In the light of *Romans 1* teachers can explain the horrific nature of mankind's Fall, and its enormous folly. Illustrate the point made by the apostle – that we *changed the glory of the uncorruptible God* [the image stamped upon us] *into an image made like to corruptible man, and to birds, and fourfooted beasts, and creeping things.*

Tell the class how human beings, made in God's image and capable of adoring Him, the glorious Maker of Heaven and Earth, soon preferred to literally bow down and worship idols. Today, many people who consider themselves too civilised and sophisticated to bow down to idols, worship the concept of man as no more than an animal. Both have exchanged the truth of God for a lie. Both worship *the creature more than the Creator (Romans 1.25).*

Use some vivid illustrations to help the children see how foolish we are in dismissing God and His lofty role for us. What *have* we given away? Ask the children, for instance, how they

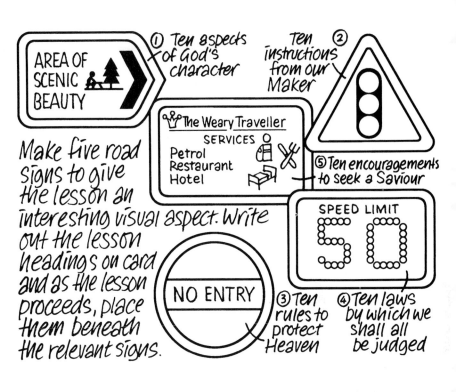

Make five road signs to give the lesson an interesting visual aspect. Write out the lesson headings on card and as the lesson proceeds, place them beneath the relevant signs.

AREA OF SCENIC BEAUTY

① Ten aspects of God's character

② Ten instructions from our Maker

The Weary Traveller
SERVICES
Petrol
Restaurant
Hotel

⑤ Ten encouragements to seek a Saviour

SPEED LIMIT 50

NO ENTRY

③ Ten rules to protect Heaven

④ Ten laws by which we shall all be judged

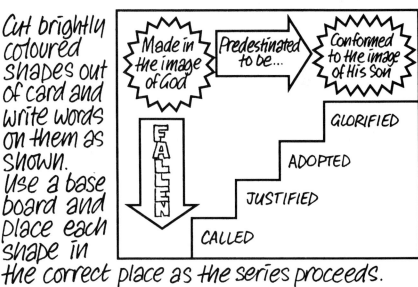

Cut brightly coloured shapes out of card and write words on them as shown. Use a base board and place each shape in the correct place as the series proceeds.

Made in the image of God

Predestinated to be...

Conformed to the image of His Son

FALLEN

GLORIFIED

ADOPTED

JUSTIFIED

CALLED

Top: VA 12 – For use with Lesson 169. Bottom: VA 13 – For use with Series 21.

would feel if they had swapped or sold something very valuable (a toy, brooch, video player, car – adapt the illustration to suit the age of the class) for something they later realised was absolutely worthless. Remind them of Esau who, due to inherit a large fortune and the honour of headship over a large and privileged family, exchanged his birthright for a bowl of soup!

Tell the class that it was a similar step, only far more disastrous, which Adam and Eve took when they ignored the warnings and commands of the Lord and played into the hands of Satan. No wonder we call this event – the Fall! (Show the fall to the bottom of the staircase on the visual aid.) They were cheated by the devil into exchanging all the glory God had granted them for the worthless promise of some fruit and dubious wisdom! What an unequal exchange!

Tell the class that Adam and Eve were the representatives of us all. They could equally be viewed as a 'test case'. Had we been in their place we should have done the same, because *all we like sheep have gone astray; we have turned EVERY ONE to his own way (Isaiah 53.6).* Day by day we act in the same manner – refusing God's ways and thinking we know better. Professing to be wise, human beings have made themselves into fools *(Romans 1.22).*

(3) A lost image. At this stage of the lesson show the class a coin which is old and bent, tarnished and coated with greasy dirt. Compare it with the first coin – what a difference! Show that a similar change has overtaken men and women as a result of the Fall. Instead of knowing the Lord God, walking with Him, and fulfilling His glorious plans, human beings degrade themselves and behave in unspeakably dirty, selfish, violent and disgusting ways. Instead of reflecting God's goodness, they sink to the horrible sins listed by the apostle in *Romans 1.29-31.* Make a selection of those offences known to your class, and hint at worse.

Is the image lost for ever? Suggest to the children that, if they were the owners, they would probably want to get rid of the dirty, tarnished coin. Did God's plan to create human beings in His image fail? Did He, in righteous anger, destroy our race? Remind the class that God, Who is absolutely holy, hates all sin. Because He is perfectly just, He must banish and punish those who have turned their back on Him so wickedly. We deserve the sentence of death *(Romans 1.32)*. Yet God's heart of love yearns to save us. He says, *How shall I give thee up . . . ? how shall I deliver thee* [ie: hand you over to punishment]? *(Hosea 11.8.)*

Like the woman in the parable of Christ, who lost her coin, the Lord God is determined to find and restore lost sinners. His will and purpose cannot fail. His plan, from before the world began, was to have a large family of men and women, boys and girls who would bear the image of His dear Son, and share the eternal ages with Him in Heaven. This plan cannot be thwarted. Despite *our* failure, the Lord God had this plan to save us already in His mind. He would take us, ruined as we are, and save us, and conform us to His glorious standard, by His mighty power. And He planned to do this for very many people.

(4) A restored image. Show the children how a badly tarnished item of silver, from which coins were once made, can be polished until the image or engraved pattern is once again clear and recognisable. (Most teachers will be able to locate or borrow a hand-mirror or teapot or serviette ring or something of real silver.) Though we have failed and fallen, and are utterly unable to earn or deserve a place in Heaven (by the covenant of works), yet in His wonderful love and mercy the Triune God has found a way to save and restore many people. Though we could never climb the stairs back up to God, He has come down to pick us up and carry us up to a place of privilege – membership of His family and household (use visual aid again). Next week we shall discover the steps He takes to do this.

Why did God allow the Fall? – children might ask. First of all point out that it is not for us to question God's wisdom. He is the potter, we are the clay. Would we expect a bag of flour to protest if we chose to make it into biscuits? However, we can see some reasons why God permitted this to happen, though there are no doubt many.

Tell the children that if the Fall of the human race had not taken place, we would never have known or realised the great lengths to which God was ready to go to secure our salvation.

We see the love of Christ for us in what He was willing to do to save us.

Older children may also grasp the importance of God allowing *full knowledge* and *liberty* to be received by the human race. He made the first people *free to disobey*. If He had not done so, then throughout eternity we would never know the dangers of total liberty to disobey. And we would never know that God is essential to our well-being. The Fall was a terrible event, but because it occurred, we will never again want freedom to disobey God, and we will never forget that all goodness and blessing comes from Him alone.

Picture the joy of Heaven described by the Lord Jesus over lost sinners – who were lost and then found. In Heaven the loudest praises will be to the Lord Jesus, the Lamb of God, Who gave His life so that we might be saved. Such is the power of Almighty God to work all things together for good that even the Fall of mankind, though tragic, has by His wisdom been used to display a dimension of His love and grace otherwise unknown. No wonder the apostle breaks into raptures and writes, *O the depth of the riches both of the wisdom and knowledge of God! how unsearchable are his judgments, and his ways past finding out! (Romans 11.33.)*

Visual Aid

Have ready a bright, shining coin and a grubby, bent coin. Provide also a piece of tarnished silver with a polishing cloth which will restore it to its original beauty.

Called (181)

Romans 8.28-30 and other verses listed in the lesson

Aim: To demonstrate God's great love and mercy in calling rebel sinners to return to Himself. Also, using Bible examples, to consider the manner, timing and objects of His general and effectual calls, in a simple way.

Lesson Outline

Show the children a large envelope (the kind in which they might receive an invitation, with the flap at the top, and preferably handmade so that it measures about 45 x 30 cm). Arouse their curiosity by telling them that this envelope contains some of the world's greatest invitations. They are from a King!

Putting the envelope to one side for a moment, remind them of last week's lesson. Do they remember how men and women, made to be sons and daughters of the King of Heaven, exchanged their royal image and fell from their high position into sin and shame? Having insulted the Lord and tarnished His image, they are now nothing more than guilty sinners deserving God's anger and judgement.

(1) An invitation to all. How amazing then to read these words from God's Book (take out of envelope): *If thou shalt confess with thy mouth the Lord Jesus, and shalt believe in thine heart that God hath raised him from the dead, thou shalt be saved (Romans 10.9)*. And (take out another 'invitation' or promise), *Whosoever shall call on the name of the Lord shall be saved (Acts 2.21)*. And then another, *Look unto me, and be ye saved, all the ends of the earth: for I am God, and there is none else (Isaiah 45.22)*.

Point out that these wonderful invitations are given to all people *(all the ends of the earth)*. Would the children not expect people to receive these calls of God with great relief and gladness? Tell them that sadly this is not their reaction. Describe, for example, the sorrow of the Lord Jesus as He looked over the city of Jerusalem which had rejected Him *(Matthew 23.37)*. Its people had become proud, self-righteous and foolish and before long they would crucify their Messiah. How like people today! They ignore God's message, they are not interested, they are cynical, they see no need of a Saviour, and they turn against Him.

(2) A call to come. Assure your class that there were some in Jerusalem who did see their need. These were touched in a special way by the call of Christ. In every age there are many people who hear the call of God very clearly. You can tell who these people are, because, as they hear God's call, it has a great effect upon their attitude, and they become . . .

(a) Those who are thirsty – those who sense they have a great

need of forgiveness and new life, and who are not satisfied with
the things of this world. The invitation of the Lord causes them
to long to come to Him, and to know His converting power.
The Lord says, *Ho, every one that thirsteth, come ye to the waters
(Isaiah 55.1)*.

(b) Those who are humble – those who realise they have no
goodness of their own to deserve God's favour. They want a
new heart and character to be given to them. They are glad to
hear that salvation is free. God says, *He that hath no money;
come ye, buy, and eat; yea come, buy wine and milk without
money and without price (Isaiah 55.1)*. Also, the Lord says, *The
GIFT of God is eternal life through Jesus Christ our Lord (Romans
6.23)*.

(c) Those who labour and are heavy laden. The Lord calls,
saying, *Come unto me . . . and I will give you rest (Matthew
11.28)*. These people realise that they cannot improve themselves to attain God's standard. It is so high that they despair.
They are tired of their sin and failure, and they are glad to hear
that Christ will earn Heaven for them, and help them to change.

(d) Those who long for this message to be true. The disciples
of John the Baptist may have been doubtful when he pointed
them to Jesus. Could He be the Messiah? Was He not, like them,
from Galilee? But they wanted it to be true. They asked Him
where He was staying, and He extended that wonderful invitation, *Come and see (John 1.39)*. Those who hear God's call
respond, like John's disciples, and want to hear more. They may
be attacked by doubts, but they long for this message to be true.
Friends may scoff and try to put them off, but they are
determined to find out for themselves. The Lord Himself
invites them to find out and search, and taste, and see. The
disciples were not disappointed, for soon they were telling
others, *We have found the Messias*.

(3) Why 'come'? The children can be reminded that they do
not say 'Come' to someone who is already with them. 'Come'
reminds us that we have wandered far away from God, and are
cut off from Him. We have to recognise that we are *not* His
children; we are *not* Christians; we are *not* in touch with
Him – until we have been converted. We have to be reconciled,

or brought in touch with the Lord. And this involves *repentance*, and leaving behind the old way of life. 'Come' tells us that conversion is coming to find and know the Lord – a totally new experience. When we really hear His call we long for this to be our experience, and we respond. Another Bible text puts the invitation in these words: *He is able also to save them to the uttermost that come unto God by him (Hebrews 7.25).*

The call of God – some examples. This part of the lesson enables teachers to survey many fascinating aspects of God's call. Feel free to adapt it to the particular age and knowledge of your class. Teachers with young classes may prefer to use just one favourite example, while those with older classes can take a brief and thought-provoking survey of several lives.

(1) To what does God call people? Abraham was called to leave his country and his family *(Genesis 12.1)* and go to a land that God would show him.

Peter, Andrew, James and John were called to leave their fishing nets so that the Lord could make them fishers of men *(Matthew 4.19-22).*

The rich young ruler was called to sell all he had and follow the Lord so that he might find treasure in Heaven *(Luke 18.22).*

The Lord comes to us and calls us to leave our ambitions, hopes and trust in this world, and to discover the wonderful purposes He has in store for us. As we learned last week, His purpose is to restore us to the image of His Son, so that He may be the First-born (elder Brother) of a large family in Heaven.

(2) For how long does He call? The Bible gives us many varied examples. Some people were called on the spot, quickly and suddenly. For example: (a) Zacchæus little thought, as he went out of curiosity to see Jesus, that before nightfall his life would be transformed *(Luke 19.1-10).* (b) The dying thief's conversion was necessarily very rapid! (c) The woman of Samaria set out to get a jar of water and returned home with *living water (John 4.5-30).*

When the Lord calls, we should never delay, but sometimes He shows great *patience* over a long period of time. Can the class think of some examples? (a) Jacob, who was shown a ladder up to Heaven on his first night away from home, but with whom the angel of the Lord wrestled on his return many years later *(Genesis 28.12; 32.24).* (b) Solomon, who set out with such high intentions, but who was turned aside by women and had to be restored in later years.

Ask the class – Has the Lord been touching your heart for some time? Have you heard His call? Remind them that it is a matter of great urgency – for who knows how long the Lord will wait? God is very patient and kind, but we should never assume that He will *keep* [hold] *his anger for ever (Psalm 103.9).*

Felix delayed, even though the Lord so convicted him that he trembled *(Acts 24.25),* and we assume he died still a great sinner, only to meet God in judgement.

(3) Who does He call? Mention two main groups who were called in God's great mercy and grace to demonstrate that He calls all kinds of people to Himself – the most wilful sinners and also the quiet and outwardly good. Despite extreme godlessness which would shock almost anyone, the Lord convicted and converted Manasseh who, with horrific sins behind him, had to be humiliated and imprisoned in a foreign land before he humbled himself and acknowledged God's call.

Onesimus is an example of someone who had heard the Gospel from a converted master, and who deliberately turned in the opposite direction, before the Lord laid hold on him. Could there be young people in the class fighting against God's call – rebelling in their hearts and going the wrong way? Maybe they will have to learn hard lessons also, before acknowledging the Lord.

At the other end of the spectrum, the Bible tells of those who did not have a dramatic conversion but whose lives confirm that God's call was very deep and real: (a) Isaac, who never strayed far from home and conformed to his father's wishes, however difficult *(Genesis 22.7-10; 24.61-67).* (b) Jeremiah, who, while feeling very young and inadequate, was sent by the Lord to deliver His messages *(Jeremiah 1.4-10)* and who obeyed, no matter how hard his circumstances.

We must especially mention that the Lord calls many who are young. The Lord had to be very firm with the disciples when He found them sending away young children. He insisted that they should be received saying, 'Let *them* come to me' *(Matthew 19.14)*. The King of kings and Lord of lords calls them to His kingdom. Never allow adults to suggest that you are too young to experience a real and lasting conversion.

(4) How does the Lord call? (a) Personally. Give the example of young Samuel, called by name in the night. God's call is a personal matter. Becoming a Christian is not a matter of accepting a theoretical point of view. People are not called as families, or as nations. Each individual has to hear God's call (not audibly of course), and experience the new birth for himself or herself *(1 Samuel 3.4)*. (b) By moving our hearts. Becoming a Christian involves our minds, and wills, and our hearts. The Lord God, when He calls, causes us to appreciate what Christ has done, to act (by repenting and asking for salvation) and to love Him. Remember Lydia, *whose heart the Lord opened.* (c) By showing us our sinfulness. The apostle Peter fell down at Jesus' feet saying, *Depart from me; for I am a sinful man, O Lord (Luke 5.8)*. When the Lord showed Paul (then Saul) how much he had kicked *against the pricks,* he cried out, *Lord, what wilt thou have me to do? (Acts 9.6.)*

(5) How must we answer? Summarise the work of God's Holy Spirit as He leads us to repentance and faith, causing us – (a) to deeply regret and turn away from sin and the old life, and (b) to believe and to put our trust in the Saviour and all He did for us on the cross of Calvary. Having called us, He teaches us *how* we are justified in God's holy sight (for our repenting and believing do not save us). The remarkable way in which the Lord saves and justifies us, turning guilty sinners into 'innocent saints', is the topic of next week's lesson. In the meantime, urge the children to give top priority to that most prestigious of all invitations – from the King of Heaven.

Visual Aid

Provide the large envelope described in the lesson from which cards printed with Gospel invitations can be drawn. Pictures of people whose response to God's call is featured in the lesson will be an added point of interest. Many of these appear on *Bible Learning Course* sheets.

Justified (182)

Romans 8.30

Aim: To describe and explain, by means of simple diagrams and pictures, the wonder of what was accomplished for our justification on the cross of Calvary, and to convince the children that their only hope lies there.

Lesson Outline

Fallen. Remind the class that the human race, made in the image of God, has fallen into sin and shame (represented in VA 13, page 229). Instead of reflecting our Maker's kindness, honesty, goodness, etc, we have rebelled, turned away from Him and become (like the coin in the illustration) disfigured and tarnished. What will God do with us? Will He be angry, cast us into hell, and punish our guilt for ever?

Should we be worried? This frightening state of affairs does not bother many people today. In ages gone by, many were worried and fearful (including young children), but now it troubles very few. Why? Because some are:

(a) Atheists or careless people. They do not believe God exists. Or they say, 'I am enjoying my life so do not trouble me with thoughts of death and judgement.' To such we have to say – 'Whether you believe in God or not, or just never think about Him, it makes no difference to the facts. He is there and He has warned that we must all appear before His judgement seat' *(2 Corinthians 5.10).* If an offender refuses to turn up at court, he will soon have the police knocking at his door with a warrant for his arrest! It would be no use saying, 'I do not believe in the courts and magistrates!' Trying to convince ourselves that there is no God (even though we are surrounded by evidence of His existence) makes no difference to the fact that He exists, and that He will deal with us.

(b) Self-righteous. Others say, 'I do not think I am a sinner. In any case, I believe I can do whatever is necessary to be acceptable to God. If I have fallen, I can climb back quite easily. God will overlook my few faults and be pleased with my efforts.' To these we have to say that they have never grasped God's high standards, nor glimpsed into Heaven and seen what a beautiful, perfect, holy, good and wonderful place it is. Even people who try hard would never be allowed into that home of God, for it would soon show up all their great shortcomings and loathsome sins.

Compare this kind of person with a boy (or girl) who boasts to family and friends that he is going to be a doctor, judge, international footballer, etc, but who goes very quiet when the exam results are announced or his name is not even included for the school B team! When we are examined by God's laws, we realise that we have all *come short of the glory of God (Romans 3.23)*. We shall never qualify for Heaven.

(c) Optimistic and superficial. Yet another group of people will say, 'I think that God is love, and that He will forget all our sins, and let bygones be bygones. He will let everyone into Heaven.' But these people think that their opinions are better than what God has told us Himself!

(1) God is just. Show how the Lord God, despite His love, cannot act in this casual manner. He is the everlasting God Who rules time and eternity in justice, not a mere mortal man. Just as travellers need to have the necessary documentation to justify their entry into another country, so He insists that all who enter His kingdom are perfectly good and righteous. Since we have no such qualifications, God Himself must 'justify' all those who desire entrance into His Heaven. However, our sin has created a great problem even for Almighty God, for –

(2) He loves righteousness. While God is willing, in great love, to make peace with those who in the past have spurned Him and rebelled against Him, yet He is also *righteous* and cannot lower His standards in order to allow us into Heaven. Teachers could illustrate this point by explaining it to the class along these lines. A headteacher may discover a child with, say, cigarettes in his pocket. Perhaps he feels sorry for this particular offender and would like to overlook the matter. But if he were to do so, the news would soon spread round the school and other children would assume there was nothing wrong or harmful in smoking. God upholds the universe with His holiness and He can never allow sin to be overlooked or go unpunished. God hates sin (and all its selfishness, violence, greed, dishonesty) and cannot overlook or forget it.

(3) He is Truth. While God is willing to show mercy, He is also *Truth*. Unlike people on Earth, He has integrity; He does not say one thing and do another. He does not make promises one year and break them the next. His Word must stand, and He has said the soul that sins must die *(Genesis 2.17; Ezekiel 18.4, 20)*. He cannot break His Word.

How then can God remain righteous and show us mercy? How can He extend mercy to sinners and still preserve His Truth? This seems to be an unsolvable problem even for the Lord God. Is there any hope for us?

God's wise solution. Give the children a moment to consider this dilemma, then outline the Lord's amazing solution, agreed to by the whole Godhead before the world was made. The cross of Calvary, and all that the Lord Jesus Christ did there for us, makes God:

(a) Just and the Justifier of all who believe *(Romans 3.26)*. Explain that by coming Himself into this world, and living a perfect life, the Lord Jesus (Who was God the Son) was able to take the punishment of our sin upon Himself – the Just for the unjust *(1 Peter 3.18)*. By paying for our sin, He met God's legal requirement on our behalf. And by His perfect offering of righteousness He obtained the necessary 'qualifications' to enable all His saved people to enter the kingdom of God. It was as if the judge himself paid the penalty or fine which he had sentenced the offender to pay, so that the law could be satisfied, and the offender pronounced 'Not guilty!'

(b) The God of righteousness and peace. On the cross of Calvary, the Saviour felt the pain of every one of our sins (eg: every lie, every greedy desire, every hateful thought, every proud dismissal of God), and bore the full punishment for each one, so that God's *righteousness* is satisfied. As a result, He is free to make *peace* with those who, having rebelled against Him and become condemned enemies, now trust in Christ and love Him. The Bible says that *righteousness and peace have kissed each other (Psalm 85.10)*.

(c) The God of truth and mercy. By giving Himself for us, God's *truth* (that He would condemn and punish sin) holds eternally firm and true. At the same time He is able to pour out His *mercy* on undeserving adults and boys and girls. *Mercy and truth are met together (Psalm 85.10)*. On the cross of Calvary the Lord God demonstrated for ever and for all His hatred of sin by not even sparing His own dear Son from its consequences. And the Lord Jesus took all our sins and paid the full price for them.

(Tell younger children how all the filthy rags of our sins were placed upon the Saviour as He hung on the cross, and He suffered terrible punishment there for us. At the same time all His beautiful robes of goodness were passed to His children so that they might stand before God's judgement seat – boldly and without any shame.)

Help children appreciate the vast wisdom of God in designing this amazing plan of salvation. Help them appreciate His wonderful love and grace in carrying it out. Even while we were still sinners, hating Him, fighting Him, scorning Him, etc, the Lord Jesus willingly came into this world and allowed Himself to be taken by wicked men and crucified, so that we might be pardoned, forgiven and restored. Human imagination could never have devised such a plan. Other religions tell us, 'Be good or we cannot help you.' The Bible alone tells us of the God of grace Who Himself suffered in our place. Ask the class – Could there be greater love than this? No wonder the Bible explains what real love is in these words: It is *not that we loved God, but that he loved us, and sent his Son to be the propitiation* [atoning sacrifice] *for our sins (1 John 4.10)*.

Is everyone forgiven? Lest the children heave a sigh of relief and take the view that all is now well, we must point out that this does not mean that God will forgive the entire world population, both believers and unbelievers alike. Use Paul's words – *the righteousness of God which is by faith of Jesus Christ* [is] *unto all and upon all them THAT BELIEVE (Romans 3.22)*. Also the words of the Lord – *Whosoever BELIEVETH in him should not* *perish, but have everlasting life (John 3.16).* Those who reject the Saviour must be judged for their unforgiven sin *(John 12.48).*

Why justification by faith – not works? Faith in the Lord Jesus is an admission of our own failure and hopelessness, and the means by which we place our trust and hope entirely in God's gift of grace. *For by grace are ye saved THROUGH FAITH (Ephesians 2.8).* Faith in the Lord Jesus is the way in which we come humbly to receive and depend on our Saviour's offering of righteousness on our behalf. Faith says, 'I am saved not by what I can do, but by what the Saviour has done for me; not by *my* works but *His* grace.' Faith says, 'I believe that when Jesus died on the cross, He did all that was necessary to save me for ever. Nothing more is needed.'

Salvation, says Paul, is – *Not of works, lest any man should boast (Ephesians 2.9).*

Being justified – how it happens. Describe the experience which comes to all those who stoop down and receive the Saviour's love, giving up any proud boast of climbing to Heaven in their own strength, and believing with all their hearts that the Lord came down to rescue them. At that moment they are forgiven by a decree from Heaven. They are declared clean – just as if they had never sinned. This is being 'justified'. At that moment the burden of sin falls from their back. At that moment they are reconciled to God and embraced by His love. From that moment He will give them the eternal benefits and rewards of people who have never sinned, and who have deserved Heaven. The condemnation of God is removed, and full acceptance with all its privileges bestowed upon them. That is justification *(Romans 5.1-3).*

At the same time, their hard stony hearts are removed, and they are given a great and genuine love for God. Now they desire to please and obey their Saviour, and the Holy Spirit begins His work of changing their character and behaviour.

Ask the class if they have ever had this happy experience. If not, urge them to think seriously about that great day when they must stand before the Lord. How tragic it would be if those who have heard about being justified should have to stand before Almighty God still clothed in their guilt, having refused to listen and take the subject seriously. Urge all those who claim to be seekers but who still doubt whether they have found the Lord, to look away from themselves and towards the Lord and His amazing love.

Encourage young believers by reminding them of their great privilege and peace in the Saviour. If they are justified by Christ, how can any sin ever be laid to their charge? Who can ever separate them from their Saviour's love? No, in all the hardships of life, and amidst all the opposition of Satan, they will be more than conquerors through Him Who loves them (summarise *Romans 8.31-39*).

Visual Aid

Cut out of stiff card four arrow shapes with a wide shaft. On each arrow print one of the following words on the front and back: RIGHTEOUSNESS, PEACE, TRUTH, MERCY.

Take the arrows marked righteousness and peace and point them away from each other. Do the same with the arrows marked mercy and truth. As you describe how Calvary made it possible for righteousness and peace to meet, reverse the arrows so that they now point towards each other. Similarly, point the arrows marked truth and mercy towards each other.

Adopted (and Sanctified) (183)

Romans 8.14-21; see also Hosea 2.23

Aim: To describe the wonderful attributes of God, appreciated by all those who are adopted into His family, so that unbelievers may see the great advantages of turning to Him, and so that young believers may appreciate the Lord's wisdom and ways in reshaping their lives.

Teachers' Introduction

The illustration of adoption is used in the Bible to describe the Christian's new status at conversion. Adoption has always been a wonderful provision for children without parents. However, given the condition of society today, it is better to keep this lesson firmly in the context of Bible times. Similarly, in describing the virtues of a father, we should keep to the conscientious father of that far-away rural society. This will avoid embarrassing or upsetting any member of the class who comes from a broken family with no father (and such children are numerous).

Lesson Outline

Returning to the visual aid for the series, remind the class that human beings made in the image of God fell from that lofty position into sin. Then remind them of the steps which God takes to restore a vast number of people in every age of time. He *calls* them, one by one (the special work of His Holy Spirit), and saves and *justifies* them (through the death of the Lord Jesus on the cross of Calvary). In this lesson we shall be learning how He *adopts* them into His heavenly family, and prepares them for the day when He will *glorify* them in that heavenly land.

Ask the class if they have seen television pictures of large numbers of children orphaned by war, being herded into refugee camps. Hopefully they will be fed and clothed, but their future is bleak without any parents to care for them. Only a fortunate few will be *adopted* into a natural family.

Earthly adoption. Having introduced the term, go on to ask the class to travel in their imagination to visit a family of Bible times. Paul mentions this term in writing to Romans, to whom adoption was a familiar practice. Imagine that a child of a servant family had become orphaned. He now faces a life of insecurity and deprivation. But this boy is to be adopted by a prosperous family, bound to them by a legal document, and chosen to be theirs. All the privileges of a free Roman family belong to that boy who previously came from servant parents. The boy can now run into his new parents' room, crying, 'Father'. He is no more a servant, but a son and heir. He will now grow up beside brothers and sisters who accept him as their own, and share all the advantages of education and training that are theirs. (The children will remember how Moses grew up as a prince in the house of Pharaoh – adopted by Pharaoh's daughter.)

Heavenly adoption. Tell the class how all Christians have a similar experience. As unbelievers they have no spiritual Father and must face life alone. They have no relationship with God – in fact He is their enemy. To them He seems a hard taskmaster Who will one day call them to account. They have no spiritual privileges, no future inheritance and no family. But then the Lord calls them out of this *crooked and perverse* world and becomes their Father, and they become His sons and daughters *(2 Corinthians 6.17-18)*. The Lord Jesus Christ (the eternal Son of God) becomes their elder Brother, and they take their place amongst many other members of the Lord's world-wide family.

Describe to your class the wonder of Christian conversion in these terms. Not only does the Lord forgive our sins, but He stamps the family likeness upon us, and grants us all the family privileges, and His special care and attention throughout the remainder of our days on Earth.

The father's role: (a) He was the decision-maker. Varying the illustrations and presentation for the age of your class, explain how the father of olden times had many characteristics which illustrate the attitude of our heavenly Father – if we are adopted into His family. A father wisely planned, and was responsible for the family policy – where they should live, what crops they should grow, what they would buy and when they must save. If he made a wrong decision, the whole family would suffer. There were no government welfare schemes to help people in those days. Remind the children of the disastrous decision of Lot to move his family close to Sodom. A wise father considered the welfare of the whole family, and made decisions which would benefit them all.

Help the class to see the enormous advantages bestowed on all those people who can call the Lord their Father. How 'wise a Counsellor and Guide' they have! What a privilege to receive His wisdom in all the affairs of life! We pray, and He answers, and guides.

(b) He was a tower of strength. In days before the invention of modern machinery, it fell to the men of the family to tackle jobs needing great physical strength. Trees had to be felled, family homes and sometimes tents erected, drainage channels dug, and so on. Land had to be levelled and de-stoned. Fences had to be put up. At harvest the corn had to be reaped and baled. In many regions, enemies had to be fought off. The father needed to be a tower of strength and endurance.

Remind the class that Christians have no less a Person than the Maker of the universe to give them strength. He never grows weary. He never fails or experiences weakness, and all His vast resources of power are available to His sons and daughters. Those who are protected by Him need not fear the storms of life or the devil's threats.

(c) He richly provided. Describe how it was the father's responsibility to provide food, clothing and shelter for the extended family. He was responsible for growing a successful crop, raising healthy herds, and mastering some craft or trade, which would enable him to earn sufficient to support his wife and children. Tell the children of hard days, when perhaps a cloud of locusts would descend and devour an entire crop in a few hours. It was the father who would have to put on his boots and walk for miles, in order to find other means of providing for the family in the months ahead. If he shirked this responsibility the whole family would starve. So the Lord provides everything spiritually for His children, now and eternally.

(d) He handed down his skills. The father in those days was never content until he had passed on his knowledge to his sons. They were taught the secrets of farming by him – when to sow, how to protect the crop from disease and insects, and how and when to harvest, process, and store.

Believers have as their Father the infinitely wise God. His textbook, the Bible, furnishes them with all they need to know, but most important of all it teaches how the soul can be saved and kept secure.

(e) He trained the young character. Agricultural knowledge, however, was not enough to ensure success. A wise father recognised that children needed *character* training if society was to be well regulated and happy. They needed to master *themselves*! So the wise father administered kind but firm discipline from an early age. Children would be punished if they were caught stealing, and they would be rewarded for overcoming bad temper. They would be taught that lying was harmful and wrong, and they would be shown how their actions affected others.

Explain to the class that in the same way the Lord chastens those He loves, and trains and enables them to put to death their sinful ways, and to manifest Christian virtues (such as the 'fruit of the Spirit'). He troubles their consciences when they do wrong, and helps them to get progressively better.

(f) He laid up for future generations. Remembering how self-seeking our own society is becoming, teachers can describe how fathers once considered it a goal of life to provide for their families. Often they spent very little on themselves to try to secure a better life for their children. Even today we see in developing countries parents going short of everything to send their children away for education.

How much more the Lord, the perfect heavenly Father, plans and provides for His children. The apostle Peter spoke of the inheritance which God has created for us – *an inheritance incorruptible, and undefiled, and that fadeth not away, reserved in heaven for you (1 Peter 1.4).* History teaches us that, in this world, the largest inheritances can be quickly lost, frittered away or stolen. But there is no such threat to the Christian's blessings stored in Heaven. They will be safe for ever. The class will have to wait until the next lesson to hear more of this.

Adopted sons and daughters of the living God. In the meantime ask the children if they have experienced adoption into the Lord's family, so that they have become sons and daughters of the living God. Remind them that there can be no greater privilege. Young people yearn to meet or catch a glimpse of some famous person here below, while all the time the Lord of Glory invites them to be privileged members of the royal family of Heaven.

(a) At great cost. Remind them of the enormous price which God had to pay in order to make our adoption possible. Almighty God *spared not his own Son, but delivered him up for us all (Romans 8.32).* What greater love could there be than this?

(b) In order to bring honour to the Father. Urge those who are 'the sons and daughters of God' to live *blameless and* *harmless* lives, shining as lights in this dark and godless world (see *Philippians 2.15*), which will bring credit to their heavenly Father. Encourage them to battle against those sins which bring disgrace to the Saviour and the Gospel, and to learn quickly and humbly from His chastenings. Remind them that none of us can begin to imagine the glories the Lord has in store, but in the few years left to us here on Earth let us grasp every opportunity to advance our Saviour's kingdom and share our Gospel light with all around us.

Visual Aid

Provide pictures of a Roman family featuring an older brother and an adopted son. Also show pictures of a father of Bible times – with scenes which can be used to describe his various tasks and responsibilities.

Glorified (184)

Romans 8.30; 1 Corinthians 15.35-44; Revelation 7.9-17

Aim: To open the children's eyes to a future world, and, using Paul's helpful illustration, to share with them the plans which God has in store for all who love Him.

Lesson Outline

Remind the class of the four steps already considered, by which the Lord God conforms those who love Him to the image of His Son. He calls them one by one and makes them His own. He justifies them as they come to believe in the Lord Jesus Christ and all that He did for them on the cross of Calvary. Then He changes their life and character (sanctifies them), as they learn day by day to please and obey their heavenly Father (Who adopts them).

But there are even better things to come, which will be seen when the believer is finally freed from this earthly realm, with all its hindrances. The best and final step of the Lord's plan is to glorify His people. God's plan will never be complete until we are entirely conformed to the perfect image of His dear Son.

The Lord Jesus Christ exalted. Explain to the class that while God the Father did not spare His Son the agony and pain of Calvary, which was necessary for our salvation, yet once that atonement was made, He soon 'rewarded' Him. On the third day the Saviour was raised from the grave by mighty power. After a short time during which He appeared to the disciples to encourage and instruct them, He ascended into Heaven, to be highly exalted and given a name which is above every name. The One Who so humbled Himself for our sakes, stooping to take a human body, and going to the extreme of an agonising death on the cross, became the object of Heaven's praise. Nor will it be long before every knee will bow to Him, both those who love and welcome Him, and those who sink terrified before Him as their Judge. Before long we must all acknowledge Him whether we do so with terror and alarm (as unbelievers), or as those who know Him as Saviour, and look forward to being glorified with Him.

What happens when we die? Remind the class that many people tell us not to think about death. They say death is the end of us, and we should concentrate on enjoying life while we can. But how do they know that? Can they be sure? Supposing they are wrong? After all we all have a strong instinct that there is more to us than mere flesh and bones. We have this inner awareness that our souls survive death, to live on elsewhere.

Glorified with Him. As if announcing a piece of definite good news, tell the class that Almighty God, Who alone knows what lies beyond death, assures us in His Word that this life is only a short, temporary existence. The *real* life is to come. All who believe in the Lord and belong to Him may look forward to the day when they will go to be with Him in His heavenly home, a place which is *far better* than this world. Death, for those who have had their sins washed away, is the gateway to everlasting life. At the moment they die their souls will be carried safely to be with the Saviour. Then, on a great coming day, they will be given their new bodies also, especially suited to the eternal home.

How are the dead raised? *The hour is coming,* said the Lord, *in the which all that are in the graves shall hear his voice* [the voice of the Son of God], *and shall come forth; they that have done good, unto the resurrection of life; and they that have done evil,*

unto the resurrection of damnation (John 5.28-29). The day of
resurrection (the end of the world) may take place long after we
have died, having left our bodies buried in the ground, and
gone either to Heaven (as souls only) or to hell (as souls only).
Then our bodies will be brought again to life and united with
our souls, so that we shall all stand before God. Those who are
unconverted, who have been waiting in hell, will be finally
judged and condemned. Those who belong to the Lord will
have the experience here described by Paul.

The apostle Paul could imagine someone asking the same
questions that the class might be asking: *How are the dead raised
up? and with what body do they come? (1 Corinthians 15.35.)* To
help us understand, he compared the experience with the plant-
ing of a seed or bulb, and its coming to life. He said the seed is:

(1) Sown in corruption, raised in incorruption. Show the
class a seed or bulb (a potato or onion could be used). It looks
as if it is a *dead* thing, shrivelled, lifeless, even rotting and
decaying. But if it is buried in soil it will suddenly send up a
shoot, spring to life and grow into a living, fruitful plant. Apply
this spiritually:

This world, since the coming of sin, is a world dominated by
corruption and death. Everything decays and grows old. Ask the
class to name some obvious examples – buildings, cars, clothing, our own bodies. Give the example of a brand-new work
book which a child may intend to keep neat and correct, but
which is so often grubby and dotted with mistakes within
weeks.

But on the great day of the resurrection, the bodies of
believers will be raised *(2 Corinthians 4.14)* and renewed, so that
they will resemble that of the Lord Jesus. No matter what state
of corruption the old body may be in (having been long
buried), it will be transformed into a new body, full of energy,
life and power. This new body will never get sick, or old, or
suffer pain. It will never die again.

In the new, heavenly world all our faculties will function in a
new way. In the new body, the memory will not fade, but
remain bright and vivid. Our minds will be capable of
absorbing more and more, and of exploring the never-ending
horizons of wonder and delight which lie before us in the

rejuvenated, new Heaven and Earth of the future. In *this* world, trying to do good (even as Christians) is so often like driving a car with the brakes on. There is always this body of sin, with all its appetites, pulling us back. But in the *next* world our new bodies will be a help not a hindrance.

(2) Sown in dishonour, raised in glory. Return to another aspect of the unplanted seed or bulb. It is *ugly*; a brown, scaly thing not worth looking at. It is kept in a box or packet, and then buried in the ground. But that is just the beginning of a new process. Soon, leaves and flowers appear, and all is changed. The plant quickly becomes an object of beauty, to be admired and perhaps even exhibited.

Describe how our earthly body comes to an ugly, unsightly end. Whether suddenly in an accident, or by violent attack, or slowly as a result of illness and old age, the death and disintegration of the body is obviously a 'dishonourable' event. Within days a 'finished-with' corpse is buried. It will not be used again in this life.

But the new body given to believers at the resurrection will be quite different. It will be adapted and suited to its new heavenly surroundings, able to enjoy and drink in all the spiritual values, and to achieve all the glorious things intended for it before sin entered. It will be a triumphant body. Best of all it will be made fit to approach the Lord God and join the triumphant hosts of Heaven in praising Him, and enjoying Him for ever.

(3) Sown in weakness, raised in power. Emphasise the fact that the seed or bulb, left alone, is a *weak*, useless, pathetic thing which can do nothing. But if it is buried in soil, it will suddenly spring to life and send up green shoots and grow into a healthy productive plant, able to produce a crop of beautiful scented flowers, or rich supplies of food, or life-saving medicines, or, in the case of a tree, valuable supplies of timber.

Draw parallels with the spiritual process. Earth is a place of weakness and frustration. Ever since the Fall men and women have been rendered powerless by sin to control and conquer its great forces. Families still live in poverty, conflict and oppression. And whenever a dead body is buried we see before us a scene of *weakness*. It is a body that will never achieve anything again. It is powerless.

But when (in the case of a believer) that body is raised, at the end of time, it will be powerful. No longer will it be vulnerable to sin and all the problems sin produces. It will be perfect for ever. It will be able to travel and participate in countless activities unaffected by fatigue or failure. It will be crowned with an intelligence which will enable it to understand and appreciate the wonders of God's new, eternal creation.

How wonderful it will be to find ourselves, through the redeeming love of our Saviour, in that better land to which all believers can now look forward and say:

> *Then shall I see, and hear, and know*
> *All I desired or wished below;*
> *And every power find sweet employ*
> *In that eternal world of joy.*
>   Isaac Watts

No wonder death (the gateway to new life) and the coming day of resurrection are no longer dreaded but looked forward to with eager anticipation by all true believers *(2 Timothy 4.8)*.

Conclude this short series (which has no revision lesson programmed) by pointing out the triumph of this situation (VA 13, page 229). Men and women, boys and girls will finally be conformed to the image of the Lord Jesus Christ, as Almighty God planned. All sin will have been eradicated, and all the glory will go to the Father and to the Son, Jesus Christ.

Urge your children to be certain that they will be numbered amongst that great crowd from every nation, race, language and century, which will spend eternity with the Saviour Who redeemed them at such great cost. Describe the glorious scene by reading directly from the Scripture itself – *Revelation 7.9-17.*

Lessons for Life Sunday School Aids

Lessons for Life users may wish to use the take-home leaflets to accompany the lessons each week. These are entitled: *Lessons for Life Bible Learning Course.* They feature an outline picture for colouring by children, questions and a hymn verse related to the lesson, and suggested passages for personal Bible reading for the ensuing week.

Sunday School hymn sheets, and chorus and verse sheets, for hanging or mounting are also available. (These can also be obtained on A4 sheets for those who wish to have their own enlarged copies made locally, or who wish to have overhead transparencies made.) Other helps, such as visual aid materials, are also in course of preparation. Enquiries concerning take-home leaflets, hymn sheets, and news of other materials should be made to:

Lessons for Life, Metropolitan Tabernacle,
Elephant & Castle, London SE1 6SD.

Lessons for Life, books 1-4

Lessons for Life 4 is the final volume in a series of four books of Sunday School lessons designed to cover a four-year syllabus. Each book follows the same format, consisting of lessons which have proved successful in Sunday Schools over many years, now revised by the author. The contents of each book are as follows:

Lessons for Life 1 (lessons 1-46)

Miracles Demonstrating Jesus' Power (Mark's Gospel – Part I)
The Lord's saving power seen in His power over nature, death, the devil, human need and illness (5 lessons)

In the Beginning (Genesis – Part I)
The truth about God, creation and the Fall, with the earliest salvation testimonies (6 lessons)

Opposition to Jesus (Mark's Gospel – Part II)
Examples of key sins – prejudice, pride, hardness, hate, etc – seen in the Lord's opponents, and to be repented of by all (6 lessons)

Highlights from the Conversion and Preaching Journeys of Paul (Acts – Part I)
Evangelistic lessons from the life (and converts) of the apostle (8 lessons)

God's Great Plans (Genesis – Part II)
Character studies from Abraham to Joseph showing the power and goodness of God towards His people (12 lessons)

The 'I AM' Sayings of the Lord Jesus (John's Gospel)
Exalting the Saviour through His own great metaphors – the Living Water, the Bread of Life, etc (9 lessons)

Lessons for Life 2 (lessons 47-92)

The Christian Pilgrimage – Salvation from Sin's Slavery (Exodus – Joshua – Part I)
The journey from Egypt to Sinai (8 lessons)

People Who Followed Jesus (Luke's Gospel – Part I)
Christian conversion and its chief characteristics (11 lessons)

The Christian Pilgrimage – Pictures of Salvation and Heaven (Exodus – Joshua – Part II)
The journey continues from Sinai to Jordan (6 lessons)

Gospel Appeals in the Saviour's Parables (Luke's Gospel – Part II)
Teaching the consequences of sin and the only way of escape (11 lessons)

Judgement and Deliverance (Joshua – 1 Samuel)
Examples and warnings for all, from Rahab to Saul (10 lessons)

Lessons for Life 3 (lessons 93-138)

Gains and Losses in Following Jesus (Mark's Gospel – Part III)
Repentance, faith and conversion, and their alternatives (8 lessons)

Great Differences (1 Samuel – 2 Chronicles)
Contrasts drawn from the lives of David and Solomon to illustrate conversion and the believer's privileges (12 lessons)

Early Reactions to the Apostles' Message (Acts – Part II)
Various categories of hearer and the Holy Spirit's work in their lives (6 lessons)

Sin and Its Cure (1 and 2 Kings – Elijah and Elisha)
The nature of sin and its punishment, with God's remedy graphically presented (8 lessons)

The Saviour Comes and Begins His Work (Matthew's Gospel – Part I)
A chronological account of the life and teaching of the Lord highlighting His attributes and saving purpose (12 lessons)

Lessons for Life 4 (lessons 139-184)

The Word of God (The Division of the Kingdom to the Exile)
The Bible authenticated in history and in transformed lives (11 lessons)

The Life, Death and Resurrection of the Lord Jesus Christ (Matthew's Gospel – Part II)
Continuing the chronological account of the life and teaching of the Lord (10 lessons)

Character Studies from Daniel and Nehemiah
The transforming work of grace and its dramatic results (9 lessons)

The Ten Commandments
The 'schoolmaster' to lead us to Christ and the way of safety and fulfilment (11 lessons)

How God Fits Us for Heaven
The steps of salvation explained from Romans and other epistles and applied to young people today (5 lessons)